AL QAEDA, THE ISLAMIC STATE, AND
THE GLOBAL JIHADIST MOVEMENT

WHAT EVERYONE NEEDS TO KNOW®

AL QAEDA, THE ISLAMIC STATE, AND THE GLOBAL JIHADIST MOVEMENT

WHAT EVERYONE NEEDS TO KNOW®

DANIEL BYMAN

OXFORD
UNIVERSITY PRESS

OXFORD
UNIVERSITY PRESS

Oxford University Press is a department of the University of
Oxford. It furthers the University's objective of excellence in research,
scholarship, and education by publishing worldwide.

Oxford   New York
Auckland   Cape Town   Dar es Salaam   Hong Kong   Karachi
Kuala Lumpur   Madrid   Melbourne   Mexico City   Nairobi
New Delhi   Shanghai   Taipei   Toronto

With offices in
Argentina   Austria   Brazil   Chile   Czech Republic   France   Greece
Guatemala   Hungary   Italy   Japan   Poland   Portugal   Singapore
South Korea   Switzerland   Thailand   Turkey   Ukraine   Vietnam

Published in the United States of America by
Oxford University Press
198 Madison Avenue, New York, NY 10016

© Oxford University Press 2015

Library of Congress Cataloging-in-Publication Data
Cataloging-in-Publication data is on file at the Library of Congress
ISBN 978-0-19-021725-9 (hbk.); 978-0-19-021726-6 (pbk.)

1 3 5 7 9 8 6 4 2
Printed in the United States of America
on acid-free paper

CONTENTS

ACKNOWLEDGMENTS

For a short book, my list of people to thank is long. A number of young researchers helped considerably in my research. They include Jessica Agostinelli, Sarah Collins, Jamie Geller, Johannah Lowin, and Lauren Mellinger. The biggest thanks go to Jennifer Williams. To say Jenn helped in the research is a bit like saying Obi Wan Kenobi gave Luke a hand: true, but a gross understatement. Her knowledge of all things terrorism-related is daunting for such a young scholar, and she is a witty and thorough editor. Each essay bears her mark, and the book is far better as a result.

My friends and colleagues read essays in this book, helping me avoid mistakes and making the analysis far stronger. Thanks go to Jonathan Brown, Mike Doran, C. Christine Fair, William McCants, Michael O'Hanlon, Kenneth Pollack, Benjamin Wittes, and Jeremy Shapiro. I stole from them all liberally.

I'd also like to thank the Security Studies Program and the School of Foreign Service at Georgetown University and the Center for Middle East Policy at Brookings. Bruce Hoffman, Joel Hellman, and James Reardon-Anderson make Georgetown a wonderful home for any scholar. At Brookings, Martin Indyk, Bruce Jones, and Michael O'Hanlon provide a vibrant intellectual environment where my ideas are tested and honed. Particular thanks go to Tamara Cofman Wittes for her wonderful job running the Middle East Center.

Writing a book, of course, is only one part of the process: someone has to be willing to publish it. David McBride of Oxford University Press has long been a supportive and kind editor, and my thanks also go to Sarah Rosenthal and Suvesh Subramanian for their assistance. And without my agent Larry Weissman my book might not be published anywhere.

Last in my thanks, but first in my heart, is my family: my sons Josh and Ben, and my wife Vikki. When I ask myself, "What do *I* need to know?" the answer always begins and ends with them.

AL QAEDA, THE ISLAMIC STATE, AND THE GLOBAL JIHADIST MOVEMENT

WHAT EVERYONE NEEDS TO KNOW®

INTRODUCTION

Al Qaeda became a household name on the morning of September 11, 2001. But the terrorist organization that shocked the world and unleashed a whirlwind of controversial counterterrorism measures and two major wars had been on the scene long before that bloody day. I did not predict the 9/11 attacks or anything near that magnitude—but perhaps I should have. For unlike most Americans, I had long studied and followed the activities of Al Qaeda and its jihadist fellow travelers.

Al Qaeda grew out of the anti-Soviet struggle in Afghanistan in the 1980s, but the broader jihadist movement was around well before that. I saw fragments of this movement everywhere in the 1990s. As a CIA analyst working on the Middle East at the beginning of the decade, I followed individuals who had fought in Afghanistan against the Soviets and who, upon returning home, became the nucleus of local jihadist groups. As an analyst with the RAND Corporation, a defense think tank, I followed the growth of jihadism in Saudi Arabia, the American counterterrorism response after Al Qaeda blew up two US embassies in 1998, and the metastasizing danger of the shadowy new government of Afghanistan—the Taliban.

The 9/11 attacks, however, transformed Al Qaeda from an issue of peripheral interest to a few analysts, scholars, and policymakers to the issue at the center of US foreign policy. Al Qaeda and the US response continued to fascinate me, and in my work for the 9/11 Commission, for the Brookings Institution, and at Georgetown University, I studied how Al Qaeda adapted to the ferocious US-led counterterrorism campaign yet often stumbled after overreaching or making foolish mistakes. The politics within the broader jihadist movement fascinated me in particular, and I watched how Al Qaeda, and later rival groups like the Islamic State, navigated them.

But my personal fascination alone does not justify a book. Nor am I in the habit of treading in the footsteps of other writers who have written so impressively on Al Qaeda, including several Pulitzer Prize winners. Yet I remained frustrated that well over a decade after the 9/11 attacks, so many basic questions about Al Qaeda remain unanswered in a straightforward, comprehensive book. And although authors before me have provided answers to many vital questions about Al Qaeda, over time the answers—and even the questions—have changed; many of the best books on the group are about the pre-9/11 period, but as you would expect, Al Qaeda today is no longer the same beast.

And confusion still reigns over two of the most interesting, but most difficult, questions: Where does Al Qaeda begin and end, and how should we think about other jihadist thinkers, fighters, and groups that are not under Bin Laden's (or now Ayman al-Zawahiri's) discipline? Jihadists killed Ambassador J. Christopher Stevens and three other Americans in Benghazi, Libya, on September 11, 2012, and the Tsarnaev brothers used a homemade bomb at the 2013 Boston Marathon, killing three. Neither of these attacks was initiated by Al Qaeda or had any direct link to the organization—but they were part of the movement and the mindset that Al Qaeda seeks to inculcate.

These goals and frustrations shaped how I structured this book: I wanted not only to present an intelligent reader with an understanding of Al Qaeda's history, organization, goals, tactics, and other basic information, but also to place the group in the context of the broader jihadist movement. To understand the threat today, we also need to recognize the role of important affiliate groups like Al Qaeda in the Arabian Peninsula and Al Shabaab and new organizations like the Islamic State—a group that emerged during the Syrian civil war and is so brutal that even Al Qaeda rejects it and yet so influential that it now rivals Al Qaeda for leadership of the global jihadist community. Finally, understanding Al Qaeda requires recognizing the range of US counterterrorism responses, their limits and trade-offs, and the controversies they have engendered.

1

HISTORY

What Was the Impact of the Anti-Soviet Jihad on the Jihadist Movement?

When the Soviet Union invaded Afghanistan in 1979, it set in motion a chain of events that would eventually lead to the creation of Al Qaeda. The Soviet occupation of, and eventual defeat in, Afghanistan shaped the ideology, strategy, and organization of Osama Bin Laden's group, and it remains an important touchpoint for the entire jihadist movement today.

The Soviets invaded Afghanistan in December 1979 to prop up the local communist regime there. Afghan politics were already turbulent, and the Soviet invasion sparked a broad uprising, with a range of Islamist and tribal groups taking up arms—a motley assortment of fighters collectively referred to as the *mujahedin* (Muslims who take up arms in the name of Islam). The *mujahedin* fought fiercely. Casualty figures are at best rough estimates, but the Soviets lost perhaps 15,000 soldiers, with an additional 50,000 wounded. The *mujahedin* lost over 75,000, with at least that many wounded. But the Afghan civilians bore the biggest brunt—perhaps one million died and five million fled into exile as the Soviets launched a brutal counterinsurgency campaign. The Soviets burned crops and brutalized civilians in areas suspected of supporting the rebels, leading millions to flee the country. Pakistan was the largest sanctuary for refugees, and it became an important base for the anti-Soviet struggle.

Afghanistan was remote and obscure, and most observers believed that the Soviets would quickly squash any resistance. Yet as the *mujahedin* stubbornly hung on, the United States (in true Cold War fashion) saw the continuing fighting as an opportunity to bleed the Soviet Union and to check what William Casey, the director of the Central Intelligence Agency (CIA) at the time, saw as the Soviet Union's "creeping imperialism."[1] Cooperating with the staunchly anti-communist Kingdom of Saudi Arabia, President Carter approved requests from the CIA and some members of Congress, most famously Representative Charlie Wilson of Texas, to provide aid to the *mujahedin*. Covert aid, such as limited funding and arms to anti-communist forces, began even before the Soviets invaded but steadily grew under President Reagan throughout the 1980s. The United States and Saudi Arabia would ultimately provide billions in aid to the *mujahedin*, including relatively advanced portable Stinger surface-to-air missiles.

As Afghanistan became a pawn on the Cold War chessboard, it also became the taproot of the modern global jihadist movement. Abdullah Azzam, a Palestinian Arab who was a well-known Islamist activist, traveled to Pakistan to support the *mujahedin* and called for Muslims worldwide to rally in support of their brethren in Afghanistan. Azzam became the leading ideologue of the anti-Soviet struggle and issued a *fatwa* (religious decree) in 1984 titled "Defense of Muslim Lands." He argued that infidels had invaded Muslim territory and had subjugated powerless Muslims. He contended that fighting against the Soviets was not just the religious duty of Afghans but of all Muslims: both a communal duty (*fard kifaya*) and an individual one (*fard ayn*).

The brutality of the Soviet campaign proved to be ideal propaganda for Azzam, and the anti-Soviet struggle fed the burgeoning idea, whose seeds were planted well before the 1979 invasion, that all Muslims were part of one community (*ummah*). While preparing to fight the Soviets, the different tribal and Islamist groups cross-fertilized. Egyptian jihadists met Saudi fighters, and both in turn mixed with Pakistani and Libyan figures. Ideas and struggles that in the past had been limited to one community were now embraced by many nationalities. The Saudi government in particular exploited its own support for the *mujahedin* to enhance its legitimacy and welcomed the shift in jihadist sentiment away from fighting so-called apostate regimes and toward fighting the Soviet invaders.

Although the United States and Saudi Arabia supported the Afghan struggle financially, they did not support the flow of Arab foreign fighters. Because the Afghans themselves were long on numbers but short on equipment, encouraging raw recruits who did not speak the language to join the fray made little sense. As the scholar Thomas Hegghammer argues, "Arab Gulf states and Western governments acquiesced to foreign fighter recruitment, but they did not organize it or pay for it. The foreign fighters were funded by private donors and the nongovernmental Islamic charitable sector."[2] The most Saudi Arabia did was subsidize plane tickets to Pakistan, but this assisted relief workers as much as foreign fighters.

Contrary to later jihadist propaganda, the mobilization of foreign fighters did not happen overnight. Indeed, as the Soviet presence wound down, the number of these "Afghan Arabs" (or "Arab Afghans"), as they came to be known, grew. Perhaps 100 Arabs were fighting in 1985; by 1989, the year the Soviets departed, the number of foreign fighters had mushroomed to between 5,000 and 20,000. Most came from the Arab world, but a significant portion also came from Pakistan.[3]

The Afghan *mujahedin* groups cooperated with one another at times, but they remained divided or even hostile for much of the conflict. The Afghan Arabs were similarly divided: most came to fight the Soviets, but their attitudes toward their own governments, their interpretations of Islam, and their relationships with the myriad Afghan groups varied significantly. Pakistan, where most of the Arab Afghans were based, became a hothouse of competing ideas and personalities—all part of the same broad movement but often bitterly divided.

For the Afghan Arabs, the 1987 Battle of Jaji was a key moment. The battle itself was not conclusive, but the Arab foreign fighters, including Bin Laden, fought hard, and the story of the Arab fighters' courageous stand against the mighty Soviet army became a propaganda victory they exploited to gain new followers and build their reputation as battle-hardened soldiers of jihad. Such bold deeds, embellished and mythologized in the telling, stood in stark contrast to the historical defeats suffered by Arab armies at the hands of Israel and the political stagnation and corruption into which much of the Arab world seemed to have sunk. The Arab press covered the battle extensively, launching Bin Laden's reputation as the mighty warrior who stood up to a superpower.

The truth is that the Afghans liberated themselves; the handful of poorly-trained Arab volunteers did little more than die. Yet in addition to creating organizational structures and relationships that would endure long after the conflict was over, the anti-Soviet struggle also created a legend that would become a fundamental pillar of Al Qaeda's global appeal: the idea that a small band of committed fighters, strengthened by their faith in God, could stand up to a superpower and change the world. When the Soviets withdrew from Afghanistan—and, even more astounding, when the Soviet Union itself collapsed shortly thereafter—the Arab Afghans claimed credit. Indeed, they saw the anti-Soviet struggle as a model for future action: lure an infidel foe into a killing ground where the world's Muslims would converge and overwhelm the enemy, using their willingness to fight and die to defeat a foe that was technologically superior but morally inferior. This logic, and the idea that Muslims are bound together and must defend one another, would mobilize Muslims to fight in Bosnia, Chechnya, Iraq, Syria, and elsewhere.

Did the United States Fund Bin Laden and Al Qaeda?

Although the United States provided arms and billions of dollars to Afghan groups fighting the Soviets, Bin Laden and like-minded Arab Afghans "received little or no assistance from the United States," according to the 9/11 Commission.[4] To some observers, this blanket statement smacks of a whitewash. Even someone as esteemed as Robin Cook, a former British foreign secretary, wrote that Bin Laden in the 1980s "was armed by the CIA."[5] In addition, US money also found its way into the hands of *mujahedin* figures like Gulbuddin Hekmatyar, who was close to Pakistani intelligence and later to Bin Laden.

A closer look at US policy and goals make the 9/11 Commission's conclusion on the lack of support more logical. The influence of the Arab Afghans was miniscule in the fight against the Soviets, even though it grew in the telling. "A drop in the ocean" is how Abdullah Anas, an Afghan Arab who spent years fighting the Soviets and who was close to Bin Laden, described it in his account.[6] For anti-Soviet fighters, the problem was not manpower—plenty of Afghans opposed the Soviets and were eager to fight—but rather a lack of equipment and training. Washington had little need to encourage young, unskilled fighters from the Arab world to join the fray. Some fighters like Bin Laden came with their own (considerable) funds, but most did not know the language and were often zealous and intolerant in their religious beliefs. This did little to help the cause. Moreover, even though Bin Laden and other Arab Afghans were not focused on the United States at this point, most were highly anti-American in their views and would not have been eager for an alliance. Washington also gave the money to fight the Soviets to Pakistan, which handled much of the day-to-day details of support.

US officials, Al Qaeda leaders, and Pakistani intelligence officials have all made statements denying any relationship—an oddly convincing confluence. Reputable scholars such as Thomas Hegghammer also contend that while the American and Saudi governments supported the Afghan *mujahedin*, they did not directly aid the Arab foreign fighter movement.[7] Sometimes, however, a conspiracy theory that conjures up both hubris and nemesis is much easier to believe than the truth. As Al Qaeda expert Peter Bergen points out, "This is one of those things where you cannot put it out of its misery. The story about bin Laden and the CIA—that the CIA funded bin Laden and trained bin Laden—is simply a folk myth. . . . The real story here is that the CIA did not understand who Osama was until 1996."[8]

Why Was Al Qaeda Founded?

Moscow's declaration in April 1988 that its forces would leave Afghanistan in the coming nine months left Arab jihadists elated but divided. Hundreds, even thousands, of Arabs had flocked to Afghanistan and Pakistan throughout the late 1980s to fight the godless communists and, for some (such as the Egyptians and Libyans), to find a sanctuary from the hostile regimes they opposed back home. Now, suddenly, the anti-Soviet jihad was ending with an unexpected victory.

Some fighters returned home and never again took up arms. Others turned their ire against their own governments, fomenting violent revolution. A few continued to fight abroad—in Afghanistan against the post-Soviet regime or for one or more of the quarreling local Afghan factions, and in new lands such as Bosnia and Chechnya, where Muslims appeared to be under siege.

Bin Laden and Al Qaeda embarked on their own unique journey—one that would cross the paths of many jihadists but would ultimately have an altogether different destination.

The victory against the Soviets seemed miraculous: a ragtag group of fighters, armed with faith and seemingly little else, had defeated one of the most powerful militaries in history. Al Qaeda sought to capitalize on this enthusiasm and the infrastructure that had developed over the years to facilitate the Afghan jihad. To mobilize foreign fighters against the Soviets, Abdullah Azzam, the key ideologue of the anti-Soviet jihad, had established the "Services Office" with financial support from Bin Laden. The Services Office was a sort of central bureau or nerve center designed to facilitate logistics—transporting people to and from the battlefield, raising funds, issuing propaganda material, and much more. Bin Laden had also established a training camp in Afghanistan, called *Maasadat al-Ansar* (Lion's Den of Supporters), that was dedicated to training Arab fighters. Abu Ubaydah al-Banshiri, who became Al Qaeda's military commander, urged, "Now that the jihad has ended, we should not waste this. We should invest in these young men and we should mobilize them under [Bin Laden's] umbrella."[9] Indeed, more and more recruits were flowing in, even as the Soviets departed: in 1984, there were fewer than 20 Arab *mujahedin*; by 1989, this number had gone up to perhaps 500 fighters, along with thousands of others who did humanitarian work.[10]

However, the question of what exactly the Afghan Arabs should do next split Azzam and Bin Laden. The two had favored different Afghan leaders during the anti-Soviet struggle, and while Bin Laden took sides in the intra-Afghan struggle that followed, Azzam called for unity among the Afghan groups and thought the Arabs should stay out of it altogether. Outside the Afghan struggle, Azzam did not want to focus on apostate regimes or otherwise get involved in Muslim-on-Muslim violence—unlike Zawahiri and many other Afghan Arabs, who were still fixated on toppling their regimes back home. Instead, Azzam called for focusing primarily on post-Soviet Afghanistan, where the communist regime still held power, and—once that war was won—Palestine, where (in his eyes) non-Muslims had taken Muslim land. Zawahiri was openly critical of Azzam, even trying to smear him as a US and Saudi agent.[11] Accusations that the Services Office was financially mismanaged may also have played a role in Bin Laden's decision to move away from Azzam.[12]

Further complicating the picture was Bin Laden's personal wealth, which made him unique among the Arabs who had flocked to Afghanistan. As one Afghan *mujahedin* commander recalled to journalist Peter Bergen, "To be honest we didn't care about bin Laden. We didn't notice him much. The only thing he did have was cash. The only thing was that he was rich."[13] Egyptians—especially Zawahiri—pushed for the creation of Al Qaeda in part to exploit Bin Laden's wealth and connections in order to fund their own struggle against the Mubarak regime; it is perhaps no surprise, then, that Egyptians would eventually come to occupy positions as senior Al Qaeda officials and instructors in Al Qaeda training camps.

Regardless of the mix of personal, strategic, ideological, and financial motives that led to Al Qaeda's creation, Bin Laden's organization from the start planned to walk a path different from the one trodden by other Afghan Arabs.

Under Bin Laden's leadership, Al Qaeda was formally established at a meeting in Peshawar in August 1988. Bin Laden wanted to create a jihadist vanguard movement—a concept championed by jihadist thinkers such as Sayyid Qutb—that would support the struggles of Muslims across the globe, including uprisings against so-called apostate regimes in the Muslim world. Al Qaeda would fulfill three related, but distinct, goals: first, it would serve as a terrorist group in its own right; second, it would continue the Services Office's role of helping organize, train, and otherwise provide logistics for Muslim jihadists—but this time to assist struggles around the world, not just in Afghanistan; and third, it would try to unify, lead, and reorient the broader jihadist movement, giving it greater purpose and direction.

Minutes from this and other preliminary meetings provide an inside look at the birth of the group that would one day become the fearsome bogeyman of the West. The members called for only "the best brothers" to be chosen for Al Qaeda after having been tested in training camps—in the words of one early Afghan Arab, "they were very, very, very careful about choosing or recruiting anyone."[14] Members had to be willing to make a long-term commitment, be disciplined and obedient, and have good manners. Though Al Qaeda would support groups with thousands of members and causes with millions of sympathizers, this core organization would always remain small—a vanguard.

At first, Al Qaeda was small and of marginal importance. Figures like Omar Abd al-Rahman, the infamous "Blind Sheikh" currently serving a life sentence in prison in the United States for his involvement in the 1993 World Trade Center bombing (as well as other attacks), had far broader appeal and name recognition, and important operatives like Ramzi Yousef—the mastermind of the 1993 attack—maintained their operational independence from Al Qaeda. As the 9/11 Commission notes, it is misleading to apply the label "Al Qaeda operations" to many of the attacks by jihadist organizations in the early 1990s.[15] Indeed, Al Qaeda's focus on the United States would not come until several years after its founding. Yet the ambitions of Al Qaeda's founders and the organizational framework they envisioned continue to shape the group to this day.

What Did Al Qaeda Do in Sudan?

On June 30, 1989, Lieutenant General Omar Hasan Ahmad al-Bashir overthrew the regime of Sadiq al-Mahdi in a coup. The new Bashir government was in many ways a classic military dictatorship, but to shore up his power, Bashir made an alliance with Sudan's Islamists, particularly Hassan al-Turabi, a leading Islamic scholar tied to Sudan's Muslim Brotherhood. Until the mid-1990s, Turabi was the dominant ideologue and a key political figure in Sudan. He pushed for the Islamicization of Sudan and embraced Sunni Islamist radicals from around the world.

Turabi invited Bin Laden to set up shop in Sudan in 1990,[16] and he and Al Qaeda relocated to Sudan in the 1991–1992 period—a time when the Afghan jihad had descended into internal bickering and Pakistani pressure on Arab jihadists to leave the country was growing. (The organization still maintained some presence in Pakistan and continued to oversee the training of some militants there. Many jihadists at this time also went to their native countries or to other parts of the world.) Upon arrival in Sudan, Bin Laden made a multimillion dollar donation to Turabi and his political organization, the National Islamic Front; invested millions in Sudan's economy; assisted the Islamist government's efforts to subjugate the Christian south; and otherwise became closely integrated into Sudanese political and economic life. Some of the businesses set up by Bin Laden would prove to be profitable and provide financial support to local militant cells, but most showed a loss.

Al Qaeda was not the only group operating in Sudan during this period: Hamas, Hizballah, and a number of other terrorist groups were also active there. Egyptian Islamic Jihad (EIJ), Ayman al-Zawahiri's organization, had set up shop in Sudan in 1989. Iran also regularly sent representatives to Sudan to try to work with terrorists there in the early 1990s. Arabs were not required to have a visa to enter Sudan, enabling radicals whose passports had been seized to enter the country easily; Khartoum also issued Sudanese passports to members of various Arab groups who went to Sudan.

As its support for such a motley set of terrorist groups suggests, Sudan itself was a major state sponsor of terrorism at this time. Sudanese officials were involved in the planning and logistics of the 1993 attack on the World Trade Center in New York City and provided refuge, training, travel documents, and weapons to several terrorist organizations.[17] That same year, the United States placed Sudan on its state sponsors of terrorism list.

At first, the focus of Al Qaeda during its time in Sudan was on supporting jihadists in the Muslim world with training, money, and operational assistance. Bin Laden established the Islamic Army Shura Council to coordinate different jihadist terrorist and insurgent groups, bringing together leading figures from Al Qaeda with leaders of other groups from across the globe. Al Qaeda worked with fighters and groups throughout the Arab world, including in Algeria, Egypt, Iraq, Jordan, Lebanon, Libya, Morocco, Oman, Saudi Arabia, Tunisia, and Yemen. Bin Laden also supported militants and fighters in the broader Islamic world, including in Bosnia, Burma, Chad, Eritrea, Indonesia, the Philippines, and Tajikistan.[18] To be clear, these groups were not part of Al Qaeda, but rather of the global jihadist network that Al Qaeda sought to foster and strengthen.

Egypt was particularly prominent given the apparent progress being made there by EIJ and the Islamic Group (IG, or al-Gama'a al-Islamiyya) in their struggle against the Egyptian government, and because of the importance of Egypt to the Islamist movement in general and Egypt's proximity to Sudan. The long and unguarded border between the two countries that smugglers regularly traversed made it relatively easy for operatives to go from Sudan to Egypt. The leading Egyptian jihadist religious figure, Sheikh Omar Abd al-Rahman, lived in Sudan in the early 1990s before leaving for the United States (where he is currently imprisoned). According to one scholar's estimate, by the end of 1991, close to a thousand Egyptians affiliated with EIJ and IG lived in Sudan; many of these were Egyptian fighters who had previously fought in Afghanistan.[19] As these conflicts stagnated and as Bin Laden's anger at Saudi Arabia and the United States grew, Al Qaeda began to shift its focus toward the United States.

The interaction among jihadists in Sudan proved exceptionally important to the future of Al Qaeda's vision of global jihad. The groups cross-fertilized, with the teachings and ideas of one group finding a receptive audience with others. In addition, groups trained and learned how to organize in a clandestine manner in Sudan. In Sudan, Bin Laden formed—or "incubated," in the words of one scholar—a set of networks that later proved devastatingly effective for the terrorist organization.[20]

Sudan's support for terrorism began to change, eventually quite dramatically, in 1995. In June of that year, Egyptian jihadists sheltered in Sudan and supported by the Sudanese government attempted to assassinate Egyptian President Hosni Mubarak when he visited Ethiopia. Pressure from Saudi Arabia, Egypt, Libya, the United States, and other countries mounted when Sudan refused to turn over the assassins, leading the United Nations to impose sanctions in 1996. Over time, this pressure moved Khartoum to loosen its embrace of various radical groups. Sudan expelled many Libyan fighters after pressure from Muammar Qaddafi's government, banned Arab militants from preaching, and eventually moved to control or expel the Egyptian militant presence in the country. Bin Laden's wealth and prestige were not enough to protect these allies from the concerted campaign being waged to expel them.

Sudanese officials began discussions with the United States on ways to ease international pressure, and the United States pushed for the expulsion of Bin Laden to Saudi Arabia and an end to Sudan's support for terrorism in general. However, Saudi Arabia did not want Bin Laden to relocate there, fearing blowback from his many admirers if they were to imprison him. Instead, Turabi asked Bin Laden and his organization to leave the country, and Bin Laden and his cohorts returned again to Afghanistan in 1996. Sudan reportedly seized all of Bin Laden's properties and other assets within Sudan, which was a significant financial setback for the organization and limited its ability to shape the broader jihadist movement at the time.

What Were Al Qaeda's Initial Goals?

On its founding, Al Qaeda emphasized that "our agenda is that of war" and thus declared that it would not focus on humanitarian matters, in contrast to many Islamist groups. In addition, it pledged to be the "constant enemy" of the world's tyrants while supporting jihadists in Afghanistan. To these ends, Al Qaeda would "promote jihad awareness" and "prepare and equip" jihadist cadres, coordinating them to create "a unified international Jihad movement."[21] Notably absent from these initial goals is a declared focus on the United States.

Al Qaeda was born in Pakistan out of the anti-Soviet struggle in neighboring Afghanistan in the 1980s, and the organization retained an emphasis on Afghanistan and Pakistan even after the fall of the Soviet Union. Al Qaeda's first act of international terrorism was an unsuccessful assassination attempt on Afghanistan's former king, Zahir Shah, in Rome in 1991. Although most leaders agreed in the beginning that the focus should be on Afghanistan, they disagreed about which faction among the quarreling anti-Soviet Afghan groups Al Qaeda should support.

But as the struggle in Afghanistan began to transition from "holy war" to internecine slaughter among various Muslim contenders for power, international jihadist interest in the country began to wane. Al Qaeda's early years saw constant debates in jihadist circles about which enemy should be the primary focus of the movement. Bin Laden himself seemed unresolved, flitting from cause to cause and foe to foe. Many held up Palestine as a goal, but little was done to this end. Pakistani groups called for jihadists to join the fight against India. Bin Laden briefly returned home to Saudi Arabia from Afghanistan in 1989 and became infuriated when the Saudi government invited 250,000 American and other Western troops to defend the Kingdom's sacred ground against Iraq after the 1990 Iraqi invasion of Kuwait. After Saudi officials put him under house arrest, he fled back to Pakistan, but he retained an anger at the Saudi government that would only grow in the ensuing years.

Yemen, Bin Laden's ancestral home, was also repeatedly considered as a possible new base and focus, and he became active in supporting anti-communist efforts there. However, by 1994, the communist movement had been crushed. Nor were the locals welcoming or eager to embrace Al Qaeda. In fact, Al Qaeda's representatives found they were becoming enmeshed in Yemen's fractious tribal politics rather than bringing Muslims together under the banner of jihad.[22] When war broke out in Bosnia in 1992, many jihadists flocked to that conflict as the next arena of jihad.

Part of this irresolution is due to the unusual nature of the organization: because it was meant to defend Muslims everywhere, Al Qaeda had no single priority. And although it seemed a blessing to the struggling organization when Bin Laden found a sympathetic home in Sudan, this development ultimately made this worse. Bin Laden appeared distracted by the enterprises he was running there and unsure of where to take the organization; at one point, he reportedly told several of his associates that he had decided to give up jihad altogether and become a farmer. Unfortunately, this flight of fancy did not last, and he did continue to support jihad. But the organization remained unfocused: during this period, it claimed involvement in attacks on US forces in Somalia and Yemen, helped Egyptian guerrillas in their struggle against the Mubarak government, and supported fighters in Bosnia, Tajikistan, and the Philippines, among other places.[23]

The movement was also shaped in the early years by the backgrounds of its core leaders. Although the Egyptian cadre of leaders imparted their operational skills, they also helped push the broader movement toward a focus on the various "apostate" regimes in the Muslim world—of course, one of the worst of these apostates just happened to be in Egypt. Bin Laden's approach toward these Muslim leaders changed over time. In 1986, Bin Laden clearly rejected claims that existing Muslim leaders were apostates and thus must be overthrown. In Bin Laden's eyes, jihad was to fight infidel oppressors (the Soviet Union, Israel, India, and so on), not

Muslim regimes. However, Bin Laden's views of Arab regimes, especially the Al Saud, steadily darkened, and the September 1994 arrest of a group of dissident Saudi sheikhs who had been openly criticizing the Saudi monarchy for failing to defend Islam seems to have pushed him across the line toward open revolt. Only in 1995 did Bin Laden finally declare Arab regimes to be idol worshippers and thus not true followers of God. In 1996, he publicly issued a *fatwa* in which he scathingly criticized Saudi Arabia and "the occupying American enemy," linking the local struggle and the anti-US struggle in a way that would become an Al Qaeda hallmark.

Why Did Al Qaeda Focus on the United States?

Bin Laden had little interest in attacking the United States when he first journeyed to Afghanistan. Over time, a mix of anger at supposed US outrages, a shifting ideology, and changes in the strategic landscape altered his focus and that of Al Qaeda.

Although Bin Laden himself did not seem obsessed with the United States in the organization's early days, it clearly shaped his thinking. As terrorism expert Peter Bergen notes, as early as 1984, Bin Laden refused to eat or drink American products because of US support for Israel. In 1987, at the outbreak of the first Palestinian *intifada*, Bin Laden made his private habits more public by calling for a boycott of American products.

He was further angered by the US deployment to Saudi Arabia after the Iraqi invasion of Kuwait in 1990. The Gulf War—and the associated presence of "infidel" forces on the Arabian Peninsula—stoked his already considerable anger at the Americans. In 1992, Al Qaeda issued a *fatwa* urging jihad to fight the US occupation of Saudi Arabia and other Muslim lands.[24] Mamdouh Salim, a leading Al Qaeda ideologue and operator, issued rulings calling for strikes against the United States because of its continuing military presence in Saudi Arabia and its intervention in Somalia; he also ruled that civilian deaths were acceptable in such attacks.[25] It was around this time that planning for the 1998 East Africa embassy bombings, Al Qaeda's biggest attack before 9/11, began.

The move back to Afghanistan after he was expelled from Sudan freed Bin Laden to make his goals more public. In 1996, Bin Laden issued a lengthy public *fatwa* calling on Muslims to boycott US goods and expel American troops from the Arabian Peninsula. He declared the expulsion of the United States as the top priority for Muslims after affirming their faith in God. In this statement, he also celebrated various attacks on Americans, such as the 1983 bombing of the Marine barracks in Beirut, Lebanon; the 1992 bombing of a hotel supposedly patronized by US soldiers in Aden, Yemen; the 1993 "Black Hawk Down" incident in Somalia; and the 1995 and 1996 attacks on compounds housing large numbers of Americans and Westerners in Saudi Arabia (the first done by militants supposedly inspired by Bin Laden, the second by Iran).[26]

Yet even as Al Qaeda moved toward the United States, it did not abandon its focus on apostate regimes and the expulsion of other foreign occupiers. The 1996 *fatwa* lays out a bill of particulars against the ruling Al Saud regime, accusing them of suspending Islamic law, squandering the country's oil riches, ignoring the plight of the Palestinians, and allowing "crusaders" into the Holy Land, among other crimes. It also praises the conflicts in Chechnya against the Russians and in Bosnia against the Serbs. However, Bin Laden is also clear that Americans and Jews "represent the spearhead" and thus deserve top billing.[27]

Beyond a genuine hatred of the United States and its policies, a focus on the United States was a way to unify a movement that had long been divided over which local conflict(s) to emphasize. By Bin Laden's logic, defeating America—"the head of the snake," in Bin Laden's words—was the first step to winning any and all of these local struggles. When Al Qaeda decries what it sees as Israeli oppression of the Palestinians or Indian subjugation of Kashmir, the United States is painted as the puppetmaster. In his 2002 "Letter to the American People," Bin Laden wrote, "Our fight against these governments is not separate from our fight against you." Zawahiri also believed that Muslims understood the importance of fighting Israel and America and that this would be more widely accepted than other goals. Although Al Qaeda would be loath to admit it, the shift to the United States also occurred because of failures else-where. By 1996, jihadists in Algeria, Bosnia, Chechnya, Egypt, and other theaters of jihad appeared to be losing steam; focusing on the United States was a way to reinvigorate the movement.

However, many jihadists opposed this shift. In fact, the "far enemy" strategy championed by Bin Laden took years to become popular. Some argued that the United States was just too strong an enemy to be confronted. One jihadist remarked that "America knows everything about us. It knows even the label of our underwear."[28] Even more important, most militants reasoned (logically enough) that their most immediate problem was the local regime that imprisoned and oppressed them and that the United States was of secondary import.

What Was the Role of Egyptian Militants during Al Qaeda's Formative Years?

The struggles, experiences, and concerns of Egyptian jihadists shaped Al Qaeda in its formative years and continue to play an important role in Al Qaeda today. Two movements dominated the jihadist cause in Egypt: the IG (Islamic Group, also known by its Arabic name, al-Gama'a al-Islamiyya) and EIJ (Egyptian Islamic Jihad, also known as al-Jihad). The IG was the larger and far more important of the two in the domestic Egyptian context, but it was EIJ and its leader, Ayman al-Zawahiri, that would come to play an important role in Al Qaeda.

EIJ grew out of the followers of Muhammad Abd al-Salam Faraj, whose organization was responsible for the assassination of Egyptian President Anwar Sadat. When Zawahiri was only 15 years old, he organized a group dedicated to jihad; in the late 1970s, his organization encountered other cells and individuals linked to Faraj, and the groups eventually joined forces. Zawahiri embraced Faraj's focus on the Egyptian regime over other possible targets—quite different from Al Qaeda's later focus on the United States. To Zawahiri and others, the Egyptian government was spiritually bankrupt because it did not enforce Islamic law at home and worked with Israel, the United States, and other hostile infidel powers.

In the massive crackdown on Islamists that followed the assassination of Sadat in 1981, thousands were arrested, including many who were not involved in the attack. Zawahiri himself does not appear to have been involved in the assassination of Sadat (though he was still arrested), and he later criticized it as premature and thus a tactical blunder. Upon their release from prison, and still facing repression and harassment from Egyptian authorities, many Egyptian jihadists went to Pakistan and Afghanistan. Zawahiri fled, too, and sought to continue his clandestine activity, eventually ending up in Pakistan. There, EIJ was reborn as Zawahiri organized these strands in exile in Pakistan from 1986 to 1989. As Fawaz Gerges contends, "For Zawahiri and his cohorts, the Afghan jihad was a Godsent opportunity to heal their wounds and replenish their depleted ranks after being hunted down by government security services. They could plot and conspire against their ruling archenemies in safety and infiltrate hardened fighters back home to foment instability and disorder."[29]

Much of EIJ, along with the IG, returned to the struggle in Egypt in the early 1990s, using Sudan as the base for their activities. (EIJ's cadre in Afghanistan, Yemen, and elsewhere also focused on supporting the struggle in Egypt during this time.) For the next several years, the two groups, sometimes working in collaboration, conducted a wide range of terrorist and guerrilla attacks in a wave of violence that claimed the lives of over 1,000 Egyptians. The IG was responsible for 90% of the attacks in Egypt during the 1990s, and it had thousands of fighters and tens of thousands of supporters. As terrorism researcher Jennifer R. Williams notes, EIJ, which was much smaller and considered itself an elite organization, was more calculated and ambitious in its attacks, striking high-level Egyptians such as the interior minister and prime minister.[30] When many of the initial attacks on government targets failed, the jihadists began to attack tourist sites and other soft (that is, not heavily defended) targets, reasoning that destroying Egypt's economic lifeblood would hasten the collapse of the regime. The bloodiest of these attacks was the 1997 massacre of 62 people, 58 of them foreign tourists mostly from Japan, Switzerland, and Germany, at the Luxor Temple. But although Egypt lost perhaps one billion dollars in tourist revenue as a result of these attacks—a huge amount for this middling economy—the regime did not fall.[31]

Zawahiri's attachment to Bin Laden grew throughout this decade as EIJ suffered a series of devastating blows in Egypt. In the early 1990s, the Mubarak government arrested almost 1,000 EIJ members after a catastrophic operational security failure, when a sloppy EIJ operative allowed the organization's membership Rolodex to be captured by security forces. These arrests led EIJ to lash out and increase attacks, and although operations continued for several years, EIJ and the IG eventually alienated the Egyptian public. Tired of the constant violence and the disastrous effects it was having on the economy, the public turned on the jihadists and began supporting the efforts of the security forces to defeat them. Many Egyptian jihadists blamed Zawahiri for these setbacks.

By 1997, the Mubarak regime had effectively crushed the jihadist network inside the country, and leaders of the Islamic Group were calling for a ceasefire. Zawahiri, however, bitterly denounced the ceasefire and endeavored to keep what was left of his organization alive. To do this, he turned once again to Bin Laden.

Bin Laden's relationship with Zawahiri went back to the days of the Afghan jihad. In the period shortly after Al Qaeda was founded and both organizations were in Peshawar, Bin Laden provided $100,000 to "kickstart" EIJ. But by 1995, Zawahiri reportedly told another EIJ member, "These are bad times."[32] A computer found by a *Wall Street Journal* reporter that belonged to Zawahiri reveals a series of tense exchanges over small amounts of money, with the organization losing members and becoming unable to act due to financial problems. In 1996, Zawahiri lost his base in Sudan and traveled to Chechnya to try to establish a base there.

This period appears to be a turning point for Zawahiri. He failed to establish a base in Chechnya and was arrested and imprisoned for several months by Russia, returning to Afghanistan in 1997. The organization suffered further blows, with the disruption of EIJ cells in Albania and Azerbaijan in 1998. EIJ had thought locations far from Egypt were safe zones, but when security forces seized operatives (and their computer), it proved an intelligence bonanza to the Egyptian regime and led to individuals being sent back to Egypt for trial from Latin America, the former Soviet Union, the Arab world, and elsewhere.

By 1998, EIJ's finances were devastated, it did not have an independent base from which to operate, and its organization was disrupted both in Egypt and externally. Bin Laden, who had long pushed for EIJ to embrace a more global agenda, suddenly found that Zawahiri and much of EIJ were finally open to this message. In 1997, EIJ's own bulletins began to call for attacks on the United States. In 1998, Zawahiri signed on to the Al Qaeda-backed declaration of the "World Islamic Front for Combat Against Jews and Crusaders," marking what the US government argued was effectively a merger between the two groups. The 1998 attacks on the US embassies in

Kenya and Tanzania demonstrated how integrated the operational structures of the two organizations had become, with operatives from both cooperating in a seamless manner. Zawahiri rationalized this shift in targeting in part by claiming that the United States was at war with the group, the United States backed the Egyptian government, and the Jews controlled America.[33] In June 2001, Zawahiri's group formally merged with Al Qaeda.

Though Bin Laden pushed Zawahiri and other Egyptians toward a more global agenda, the EIJ cadre also played a key role in the Al Qaeda leadership. Gerges declares the Egyptians to be "the brain trust and nerve center within Al Qaeda."[34] Key Egyptians included Mohammed Atef, Al Qaeda's military commander until his death from a US attack in 2001; his predecessor Abu Ubaydah al-Banshiri, who established cells in Africa among other accomplishments until his death in an accident in 1996; and Seif al-Adl, another important military commander. EIJ had conducted suicide operations as early as 1993, and as the organization began to merge with Al Qaeda, that organization embraced suicide attacks—as seen in the 1998 embassy bombings. The Egyptians' dominance caused resentment among other nationalities and even led to some defections.

Al Qaeda learned much from its Egyptian members. They had long fought a bitter clandestine struggle against an implacable regime with a skilled (and brutal) intelligence service—a service supported by the United States.[35] This bitterness against pro-Western Arab regimes became ingrained in Al Qaeda. Zawahiri's and other EIJ members' losses due to security lapses also led Al Qaeda to emphasize clandestine tradecraft—teaching its operatives to use aliases, blend in with their neighbors, ensure secrecy, and keep the core organization small. Zawahiri would also push Al Qaeda and affiliated groups to seek out a sanctuary, having learned the hard way that a ruthless regime can crush a terrorist movement if it has no haven. Finally, EIJ's concept of a "vanguard"—a small group that would conduct skilled attacks on top targets—became one of Al Qaeda's hallmarks.

But Al Qaeda is much more than a creature of EIJ. Zawahiri now leads an organization that seeks to bring together all Muslims and that focuses on the United States, not Egypt—Bin Laden's vision, not Zawahiri's. Al Qaeda's use of charities, emphasis on propaganda, and support for insurgent movements and like-minded jihadists around the Muslim world—core parts of what the organization is and does—also come from Bin Laden's leadership and vision and represent a departure from EIJ's traditional approach. So although EIJ and other Egyptians shaped Al Qaeda, this was a two-way street.

What Was Al Qaeda's Relationship with the Taliban before 9/11?

The relationship between the Taliban and Al Qaeda was unprecedented. The Taliban allowed Al Qaeda more freedom of action than any state sponsor of terrorism before it, and it came to embrace much of Bin Laden's worldview as the relationship progressed.

The Taliban emerged out of the Afghan refugee camps located in Pakistan. Millions of Afghans fled to Pakistan during the anti-Soviet struggle in the 1980s, and a generation of Afghans grew up in the camps. Entering the Afghan civil war in 1994, the Taliban steadily became the dominant force in Afghanistan. After over a decade of carnage and the proliferation of warlords and criminals, many ordinary Afghans initially welcomed the respite from chaos that Taliban rule provided, despite its brutality. The Taliban also had ties to powerful religious organizations in Pakistan and to the Pakistani military and intelligence services.

The Taliban embraced Bin Laden when he and Al Qaeda relocated to Afghanistan in 1996, but the organizations initially had many differences. The Taliban leader Mullah Omar admired and respected Bin Laden for joining the fight against the Soviet Union, and Al Qaeda endorsed Omar's efforts to make Afghanistan into an Islamic state. However, the Taliban's religious worldview differed from that of Al Qaeda. The Taliban emerged from Deobandi groups in Pakistan and idealized a rural, and ethnic Pashtun, way of life that emphasized traditional values. Al Qaeda members embraced a Salafi credo and in general saw themselves as more modern and better educated. Al Qaeda members often disdained their hosts as religiously ignorant. More broadly, the Taliban was focused first and foremost on Afghanistan, while Al Qaeda saw Afghanistan as only part—and not even the most important part—of the broader struggle. Al Qaeda attacks and the ensuing condemnation and pressure from the United States and the international community also strained the relationship. Saudi Arabia in particular created discord: it was one of the few states that recognized the Taliban, but it also regarded Bin Laden as an enemy and pressed for the Taliban to expel him.

Over time, though, the Taliban and Al Qaeda moved closer together. By one estimate, as much as $20 million of the $30 million of Al Qaeda's annual pre-9/11 budget went to the Taliban, funding arms purchases, social welfare projects, and other support. Al Qaeda also put its own military units into the fray to fight against the Taliban's remaining enemies in Afghanistan: the "055 Brigade" was a unit of several hundred Arab fighters known for their bravery and military experience. As one Pakistani general observed, "The Arabs are the best fighters they have."[36] Al Qaeda even carried out terrorist attacks on the Taliban's behalf, the most notable being the assassination of legendary *mujahedin* (and anti-Taliban) commander Ahmad Shah Massoud on September 9, 2011.

US counterterrorism efforts also made the relationship stronger. Following the Al Qaeda attacks on the US embassies in Kenya and Tanzania in 1998, the United States under President Clinton launched cruise missiles against suspected Al Qaeda training camps in Afghanistan. The strikes did kill some militants, but they failed to kill Bin Laden or any of the other senior leaders. In addition to missing their targets, the strikes also backfired, as many Muslims celebrated Al Qaeda and Bin Laden for standing up to the United States. The Taliban, reluctant to be seen as craven in the face of US pressure, became even more resistant to international efforts to give up Bin Laden and more hostile to the United States in general. The worldviews of the two organizations gradually entwined, with Al Qaeda recognizing Mullah Omar as the "commander of the faithful."

From the haven the Taliban provided, Al Qaeda grew strong and became far more active. The Taliban allowed Al Qaeda to set up new camps that it fully controlled, like the Al Farouq camp, and to take over older camps like Khalden and Derunta that were previously controlled by multiple groups.[37] These camps gave Al Qaeda control over many foreign fighters who had come to Afghanistan to train, enabling it to greatly expand its influence and spread its ideology to these operatives. The Taliban put few restrictions on Al Qaeda, allowing its operatives to travel freely within the country and to transit in and out without restriction. The organization was able to conduct many of its most important attacks during this time period. In addition to the 1998 embassy attacks, Al Qaeda struck the US Navy destroyer USS *Cole* while it was refueling in the Yemeni port city of Aden in October 2000, killing 17 American sailors and wounding 39 others. And, of course, Al Qaeda launched the devastating 9/11 attacks in 2001. In each of these attacks, the haven the Taliban provided in Afghanistan was vital, giving Al Qaeda leaders the ability to plot and organize with relative impunity, protected by the Taliban's embrace.

Al Qaeda also used its training camps in Afghanistan to support various insurgent and terrorist groups throughout the Muslim world, helping fighters in Kashmir, Yemen, the Philippines, and elsewhere. US intelligence officials believe that between 10,000 and 20,000 foreign volunteers trained in Afghanistan after Bin Laden relocated there, many of them in Al Qaeda camps.[38] In these camps, fighters learned the basics of guerrilla tactics and how to use explosives, calculate artillery range fires, and other irregular warfare skills. A select few—hundreds, not thousands—were chosen to receive more advanced training in terrorism tactics and operations, such as surveillance, assassination, and recruitment of new members. As Michael Sheehan, the US State Department's former coordinator for counterterrorism, described it, "Afghanistan was the swamp these mosquitoes kept coming out of."[39]

Perhaps most critical, the haven in Afghanistan enabled Al Qaeda to knit together the various strands of the global jihadist movement. Different groups sent fighters to Afghanistan for training and sanctuary, and there they developed personal connections with members of other groups. Al Qaeda also proselytized in the camps, spreading its interpretation of jihad and vision of the global struggle for Islam, broadening the horizons of thousands of fighters from around the world.

2

KEY ATTACKS AND PLOTS

Why Were the 1998 Embassy Attacks So Important?

The bombings of the US embassies in Nairobi, Kenya, and Dar es Salaam, Tanzania, on August 7, 1998, killed 224 people—12 Americans and 212 Africans—and wounded thousands more. These bombings were a turning point in Al Qaeda's history and in the history of terrorism. Previous attacks had seen Al Qaeda facilitating local terrorists; now it was acting on its own, planning and executing the attacks, with Bin Laden himself playing a crucial role.

The embassy attacks were long in the making. Al Qaeda operatives began casing American, British, French, and Israeli targets in Nairobi, Kenya, in 1993, and Al Qaeda began to establish businesses to support its members in Kenya years before the attacks. Bin Laden himself also played a direct role in the attacks; looking at the surveillance photos his operatives had taken, he "pointed to where a truck could go as a suicide bomber."[1] Attacks on US embassies in Albania and Uganda were also planned, though US officials believe these did not occur because they were disrupted.

The US embassy in Nairobi was ultimately chosen because it "was an easy target."[2] The US State Department's Accountability Review Board, which investigated embassy security procedures before the attack, found that the building lacked a "setback" from the street, and determined that the State Department's procedures for evaluating the threat of terrorism were flawed.[3] Ambassador Prudence Bushnell, who had unsuccessfully sought better security for the facility before the attack, declared, "There just was no way to protect the building."[4]

The operation's planning proceeded slowly. The initial operational mastermind, Abu Ubaydah al-Banshiri, drowned in a ferry accident on Lake Victoria, and it took several years to acquire the necessary explosives. Al Qaeda's move from Sudan in 1996—and the loss of its assets there—as well as the surrender of Madani al-Tayyib, the head of Al Qaeda's finance committee, to Saudi authorities also led to delays, straining the organization's finances at a key moment. In 1997, the plot appeared to have been disrupted. Kenyan police, working with the CIA and the Federal Bureau of Investigation (FBI), raided the homes of several suspected militants.[5]

In 1998, with authorities believing they had eliminated the threat, the pressure eased, and planning for the attacks continued. Teams in Nairobi and Dar es Salaam rented residences and purchased materials for bombs and the trucks that would deliver them. Shortly before the bombings, the leaders skipped town, leaving the lower-level members behind to face the inevitable crackdown after the attacks. In Afghanistan, Bin Laden and other top leaders left their base in Kandahar and moved to the countryside in anticipation of a US military response.[6]

Concurrent with this operational activity, Al Qaeda launched a bold public relations campaign against the United States. On February 23, 1998, Bin Laden and Zawahiri published a *fatwa* in the name of the "World Islamic Front for Combat Against Jews and Crusaders" that laid out their bill of grievances against the United States and the West in general. The statement also proclaimed that "[t]he ruling to kill the Americans and their allies—civilians and military—is an individual duty for every Muslim who can do it in any country in which it is possible to do it." Bin Laden was making clear that he had moved away from military targets, declaring in an interview that "[w]e do not have to differentiate between military and civilian" and that "they are all targets."[7]

On August 7, 1998, at 10:35 a.m. local time in Nairobi and four minutes later in Dar es Salaam, the truck bombs detonated with catastrophic force. As Ambassador Bushnell recalled,

> The two tons of energy that hit the three buildings surrounding the parking bounced off and over the bricks and mortar with devastating effect. Two hundred thirty people were killed instantaneously. Over 5,000 people were injured, most

of them from the chest up and most of them from flying glass. Vehicles and their occupants waiting for the corner traffic light to change to green were incinerated, including all passengers on a city bus. The seven-story office building next to the embassy collapsed and the rear of our chancery blew off. While the rest of the exterior of our building had been constructed to earthquake standards, the windows shattered, the ceilings fell, and most of the interior simply blew up.[8]

Beyond the death toll, many Kenyans suffered eye injuries as a result. The casualty toll was far less in Dar es Salaam because the US embassy was on the edge of town and was not near other buildings.

The 1998 bombings were a truly global operation. In conjunction with the cell in Kenya, Al Qaeda's leadership planned the bombings from Afghanistan. Khalid Abu al-Dahab, operating from the United States, reportedly provided money and false travel documents to terrorists worldwide.[9] Cells in Yemen helped facilitate communication, and the cell in the United Kingdom did much of the publicity.[10] The members of Egyptian Islamic Jihad who had only recently joined Al Qaeda also played a significant role; indeed, the attacks can be seen as a "coming out" for the alliance of the two organizations.

The high death toll and relative sophistication required for the near-simultaneous strikes catapulted Al Qaeda to a top US security priority. As National Security Advisor Samuel ("Sandy") Berger testified about Bin Laden, "In 1996 he was on the radar screen; in 1998 he was the radar screen."[11] The bombings led to more aggressive US intelligence efforts against Al Qaeda—Director of Central Intelligence (DCI) George Tenet even sent a memo to subordinates declaring, "We are at war... I want no resources or people spared in this effort."[12] Nevertheless, the intelligence community and other US government agencies and officials would be criticized after 9/11 for not sufficiently recognizing the danger that Al Qaeda now represented.

The 1998 US cruise-missile strikes on Afghanistan and Sudan launched in response to the bombings, known as Operation "Infinite Reach," failed. In fact, they backfired. The attack on Afghanistan further pushed the Taliban into Al Qaeda's embrace, reinforcing the Taliban's perception that the United States was determined to remove it from power. In addition, the attacks played into

Afghan nationalism and a cultural emphasis on protecting guests, making it harder for Taliban leaders to back down and surrender Bin Laden. The strike on Sudan proved particularly controversial. The US claimed that the target, the Al-Shifa factory, produced chemical weapons and had links to Al Qaeda. The Sudanese government and some in the American media claimed it was merely a pharmaceutical plant that produced vital medicines like aspirin and tuberculosis drugs.[13] The strikes were also controversial because they occurred during President Clinton's domestic troubles related to an affair with White House intern Monica Lewinsky, and critics contended that Clinton used military force simply to look presidential—an allegation that the 9/11 Commission found to be unsubstantiated.

What Were Al Qaeda's Most Important Attacks before 9/11?

Although the 1998 embassy attacks put Al Qaeda on the terrorism map, and 9/11 was Al Qaeda's most dramatic and lethal attack ever, during the preceding decade it carried out attacks that demonstrated its growing skill and ambition.

Al Qaeda's operations started off modestly. In 1992, Yemeni jihadists who were part of the Al Qaeda-sponsored Islamic Army Shura Council bombed two hotels in Aden, unsuccessfully targeting US troops transiting Yemen en route to Somalia as part of Operation "Restore Hope."[14] In 1993, Al Qaeda trainers claimed they assisted Somalis in downing two American helicopters—the infamous "Black Hawk Down" incident. In 1995, a group of Saudis who claimed to have been inspired by Bin Laden bombed a joint US-Saudi facility in Riyadh used to train the Saudi National Guard.[15] In all these cases, it appears that local groups and figures, not the Al Qaeda core, took the lead. Al Qaeda had perhaps a minor supporting role, assisting with logistics and training, but did not direct the actual attacks.

Many of the most lethal jihadists active during this period operated independently of Al Qaeda. In 1993, jihadists in the United States inspired by the so-called Blind Sheikh (Omar Abd al-Rahman) bombed the World Trade Center, in part because of the absurd belief that "the majority of people who work in the World Trade Center are Jews."[16] Followers of the Blind Sheikh also plotted to destroy other landmarks in New York City, including the United

Nations headquarters, the Lincoln and Holland Tunnels, and the George Washington Bridge. Bin Laden and Al Qaeda played little if any direct role in planning any of these attacks.

Ramzi Yousef, an independent jihadist, was the operational mastermind behind the 1993 World Trade Center bombing, and he and his uncle, Khalid Sheikh Mohammad, would be behind a number of important subsequent plots. In 1994 and 1995, they organized the "Bojinka" plot, a plan to bomb 12 American passenger jets over the Pacific Ocean. They constructed bombs and cased flights, even doing a successful trial run, detonating a small bomb on one plane and killing a passenger, proving they could smuggle the bomb successfully. Due to an accidental fire, Philippine security officials found their bomb-making lair in Manila, and the Bojinka plot fizzled out. Yousef was eventually arrested in Pakistan in 1995 after an extensive manhunt and was sent for trial in the United States.

Even in many of the pre-9/11 attacks in the Middle East that are often attributed to Al Qaeda, it did not actually play a direct role. In 1995, Egyptian jihadists attempted to assassinate Egyptian President Hosni Mubarak when he was visiting Addis Ababa, Ethiopia, and two years later they would slaughter 62 people, 58 of them foreign tourists, in an attack at the ancient Temple of Queen Hatshepsut in Luxor, Egypt. Though some of the individuals involved in these attacks would go on to become important members of Al Qaeda, few had ties to Bin Laden at the time, and the attacks themselves were part of a long campaign of domestic terrorism within Egypt. In 1999, a then-relatively unknown jihadist, Abu Musab al-Zarqawi, attempted to bomb the Radisson hotel and various Jewish and Christian religious sites in Amman, Jordan. Again, although Zarqawi had ties to Bin Laden from his time in Afghanistan in the late 1980s and would later found Al Qaeda in Iraq, these attacks do not seem to have been directed in any way by Bin Laden or his organization.[17] Part of the confusion in attributing these early attacks to Al Qaeda versus other groups stems from Al Qaeda's willingness to support other groups and independent jihadists in carrying out their attacks and to use non-members for its own operations.

However, Al Qaeda became far more active as the decade wore on, and its direct role in attacks increased. In addition to the 1998 embassy bombings in Kenya and Tanzania, the group sent Algerian jihadist Ahmed Ressam to Canada, where he plotted to bomb Los

Angeles International Airport at the end of 1999 but was arrested trying to cross the border.[18] In January 2000, Al Qaeda attempted to bomb USS *The Sullivans* and failed; 10 months later, the group successfully used a boat laden with explosives to conduct a suicide bombing against USS *Cole*, killing 17 Americans. Al Qaeda also attempted to bomb the US embassies in Rome and Paris in early 2001, but US and European security officials thwarted the attacks.[19]

The ambition and innovation characterizing many of the attacks of Ramzi Yousef, Khalid Sheikh Mohammad, and other jihadists would characterize Al Qaeda's own operations by the end of the decade. Yousef wanted to kill tens of thousands in the 1993 World Trade Center attack as revenge for supposed US atrocities, and the 1995 Bojinka plot was unprecedented for the simultaneous mass attacks involved. Al Qaeda's 1998 embassy strikes, in which two prominent, symbolic targets were hit almost simultaneously in attacks designed to inflict mass casualties, reflected the ambition and dramatic flair of the 1993 World Trade Center attack and the 1995 Bojinka plot, and the attacks on USS *Cole* and USS *The Sullivans* revealed that Al Qaeda had the audacity to directly strike US warships—a remarkably bold target—using a simple yet innovative method: suicide bombers aboard a ship.

Yet without the benefit of hindsight, Al Qaeda and its jihadist fellow travelers at times seemed more like the gang that couldn't shoot straight than an unstoppable terrorist juggernaut. Yousef's plan for the 1993 World Trade Center attack was to topple the North Tower into the South Tower to bring both down, an approach that works better with Legos than with real buildings. (Sadly, the second attempt by terrorists to strike the towers would prove to be successful at bringing them down.) Operational security for this mission was also primitive—many of the perpetrators were caught simply because one of them decided to pretend the rental van used to carry out the attack had been stolen so he could get the deposit back, leading to prompt arrests. The attempt to destroy USS *The Sullivans* failed because the boat used for the bomb sank—it turned out the attackers had neglected to factor in the weight of the explosives.

Yet Al Qaeda proved persistent. Unlike most terrorist groups, Al Qaeda proved willing to try and fail when conducting spectacular attacks, to be patient, and to learn from mistakes. So having been stopped once did not mean they would not try again.

In the 1990s, the broader jihadist movement also revealed a disturbing willingness to inflict mass casualties. Although terrorists rightly have a bloodthirsty reputation, most groups fear that too much killing would prompt a crackdown or would discredit their cause. As terrorism expert Brian Jenkins noted in 1975, "Terrorists want a lot of people watching and a lot of people listening, but not a lot of people dead."[20] With the first World Trade Center strike, the Bojinka plot, the 1998 embassy attacks, and other plots, the jihadist movement revealed not just a willingness but a true desire to kill thousands—a goal that would soon be clear to the whole world.

How Did Al Qaeda Carry Out the 9/11 Attacks?

The 9/11 attacks were the deadliest terrorist attacks in history by an order of magnitude: never before had the world seen a thousand people die from terrorism in a single day, let alone almost three thousand.

Khalid Sheikh Mohammad, the mastermind of 9/11 (later known to intelligence officials by his initials, KSM), was a terrorist of singular ambition and creativity. A Pakistani national of Baluchi descent born and raised in Kuwait, KSM earned an engineering degree from North Carolina's Agricultural and Technical State University in 1986. KSM turned against the United States due to his anger at US policy in the Middle East, particularly US support for Israel, and after graduating embarked on the peripatetic life of a modern jihadist. As the 9/11 Commission noted, KSM "applied his imagination, technical aptitude, and managerial skills to hatching and planning an array of terrorist schemes" beyond the 9/11 plot, ranging from reservoir poisoning to assassination.[21]

KSM's nephew is Ramzi Yousef. Three years younger than KSM, Yousef was the mastermind of the 1993 World Trade Center bombing, and the two at times worked together. The celebrity Yousef gained in jihadist circles for carrying out the 1993 attack inspired his uncle to focus more on attacking the United States; just eight years later, KSM's infamy would dwarf that of his nephew.

Though KSM and Bin Laden had probably fought together against the Soviets in Afghanistan in the 1980s, their relationship did not develop until much later, when they both relocated to the Afghanistan-Pakistan region in 1996. KSM presented Bin Laden with an array of plots and sought Al Qaeda's financial and logistical support, but turned down Bin Laden's request that KSM join Al Qaeda, as the organization at that point had done little against the United States. It was around this time that KSM first presented the idea of having pilots hijack planes and crash them into buildings in the United States—the genesis of the 9/11 plot. KSM reconsidered joining Al Qaeda after the 1998 embassy bombings proved to him that Bin Laden was serious about attacking the United States, and in late 1998 or early 1999, Bin Laden approved what Al Qaeda labeled "the planes operation." Al Qaeda would eventually provide as much as $500,000 to fund the operation.[22]

KSM believed that America's economy was its Achilles' heel and New York, as America's economic capital, became his primary target. His original plan was vastly ambitious: nine aircraft would be hijacked and crashed into targets on America's East and West Coasts. KSM himself would be on a tenth plane. After landing this plane, KSM would first execute all the male passengers and then denounce US support for Israel and for repressive governments in the Arab world, among other crimes. Bin Laden, however, saw the plan as unworkable, and targets such as the CIA and FBI headquarters, nuclear power plants, and tall buildings in California and Washington state were struck from the list.[23] The two World Trade Center towers, the Pentagon, and the US Capitol building all remained. (Bin Laden had initially pushed to attack the White House over the Capitol, but was eventually dissuaded because the White House was a harder target to strike than the Capitol.)[24]

Bin Laden himself selected the initial four candidates to lead the operation, and he played a direct role in choosing other important operatives as the plot progressed. In Afghanistan and Pakistan, several of the key 9/11 operatives received advanced training on commando tactics, night operations, shooting from a motorcycle, and other advanced techniques. KSM also instructed the operatives on Western culture, key English phrases, and clandestine tradecraft such as how to use codes; most important, KSM provided details on how to hijack airplanes as well as basic flight training using flight-simulator software.[25]

Mohamed Atta, an Egyptian, was the overall operational leader of the 19 hijackers, and he piloted the plane that struck the North Tower of the World Trade Center. The other three pilots were

Marwan al-Shehhi, from the United Arab Emirates; Hani Hanjour, from Saudi Arabia; and Ziad Jarrah, from Lebanon. Most of the remaining 15 hijackers came from Saudi Arabia—it was far easer for Saudis to get visas to the United States than for Yemenis or Arabs from other poor countries, as border officials did not worry that the comparatively wealthy Saudis would overstay their visas and illegally find jobs. The non-pilots acted as "muscle" whose job was to control the passengers and overpower any resistance. They did not know the operational details of the plans, only that they had volunteered for a suicide mission in the name of jihad.

After leaving Afghanistan, the attackers returned home and tried to make themselves inconspicuous. They avoided associating with known jihadists, fearing that they would come on the radar screen of security services. Atta shaved his beard and no longer went to extremist mosques. Several of the hijackers "lost" their passports in order to avoid the additional scrutiny that might come with the Pakistani visas and acquired new, clean ones that enabled them to enter the United States.

Because the hijackers had valid visas, they were able to enter the United States—in some cases, multiple times—without suspicion. After the attack, this ease of entry attracted considerable criticism. For example, two of the key operatives, Khalid al-Mihdhar and Nawaf al-Hazmi, were already suspected of being involved in terrorism, and the CIA had learned in early 2000 that Mihdhar had a US visa and that Hazmi had flown to the United States. However, they were not placed on a watchlist, and thus were not flagged for consular or border officials to stop them from entering the United States. Nor was their presence disclosed to the FBI until August 28, 2001—very late in the game—and even then, the request to find more information was labeled "routine."[26]

Mihdhar and Hazmi entered the United States in January 2000 and, after settling in, began to take pilot training courses. Their poor language skills in particular proved a barrier, making flight training difficult. Neither Hazmi nor Mihdhar would be pilots in the end, becoming instead part of the team of muscle hijackers. But while Hazmi and Mihdhar flailed in the summer of 2000, Mohamed Atta, Ziad Jarrah, and Marwan al-Shehhi arrived in the country, where they would train to fly airplanes successfully in Florida. Hani Hanjour, the fourth pilot, had already earned his pilot's license in the 1990s; he was included in the plot after he went to Afghanistan for military training and identified himself as a trained pilot in his background information. He did refresher training in the fall of 2000 and the spring of 2001.[27]

The muscle hijackers arrived in the United States beginning in April 2001, with all but one arriving by the end of June. Author Terry McDermott writes that "[f]rom the arrival of the muscle on through early September, the hit teams lived on the suburban fringes of America, inhabiting a series of seedy apartments and motels. They bought memberships at gyms and worked out regularly. Jarrah even signed up for martial arts lessons. . . . The pilots booked surveillance flights across the continent, examining operations and security on board different airlines."[28]

On the morning of September 11, every one of the 19 hijackers passed through airport security and boarded their flights. The knives, Mace (or similar debilitating spray), and other weapons they carried also made it through security, as officials were focused on detecting firearms and explosives—the tools that had been used to hijack and blow up airplanes in the past. To seize control of the planes, the hijackers stabbed several crew members and passengers and also used Mace to overcome resistance. The hijackers claimed to have bombs, but the FBI later found no evidence of explosives, and the 9/11 Commission contended that the bombs were a bluff.

Part of the hijackers' success came from the innovative nature of their tactics. No one at the time expected that attackers would seize a plane with weapons like knives or that they would deliberately crash it, so the passengers had good reason to avoid a confrontation and hope for a rescue attempt after the plane landed.

This advantage of surprise evaporated quickly. The passengers on United Airlines Flight 93, which had departed 25 minutes later than scheduled, used their cell phones to contact friends and relatives after the hijacking began. After learning the fate of the other flights, they attempted to seize control of the airplane. Audio later recovered from the plane's cockpit voice recorder revealed that the hijackers feared the passengers might succeed and deliberately rolled and crashed the plane. The heroic actions of the passengers saved an unknown number of innocent lives at the Capitol, the intended target of Flight 93.

The other three hijacked planes were flown into two of the World Trade Center towers and the Pentagon. At the World Trade Center, fireballs engulfed parts of the buildings, killing several hundred people and trapping hundreds more. The heat from the explosions and fires weakened the buildings' structures, leading the two towers to collapse; falling debris started a fire at a third tower, 7 World Trade Center, causing it to collapse as well. The Pentagon also sustained significant damage. In total, the attacks killed 2,977 people and caused roughly $10 billion in direct damage to property and billions more as the US and world economies reeled. The destruction exceeded even Bin Laden's imaginings, for Al Qaeda's leaders, like US engineers, had not expected the towers to collapse.

In hindsight, the 9/11 attacks led to an overestimation of Al Qaeda's strength. Numerous reports persisted of an imminent second wave of attacks, while pundits and politicians competed to imagine what horrible thing Al Qaeda might do next. US officials, from the president on down, made fighting Al Qaeda their top priority.

Could the 9/11 Attacks Have Been Prevented?

For most Americans, the 9/11 attacks came out of the blue, compounding the shock produced by the destruction and staggering death toll. Post-attack solidarity eventually gave way to finger-pointing, with many blaming the intelligence community for failing to prevent the attacks while politicians and bureaucrats vied to absolve themselves or their organizations of any fault. Although there is plenty of blame to be shared, hindsight is 20/20, and much of this criticism does not reflect the perspectives and political realities of the pre-9/11 era.

Al Qaeda was not lucky on 9/11—the plot's success reflects Al Qaeda's audacity, skill, dedication, organizational strength, unusual assets, and approach to terrorism. Al Qaeda sees itself as a vanguard organization and has always sought out creative and dedicated operatives like Khalid Sheikh Mohammad and Mohamed Atta. In addition, Al Qaeda was willing to put time and resources behind its operatives: the plot itself cost perhaps $500,000, and few terrorist groups could afford such a costly single operation. Most terrorist groups are operationally conservative, but Al Qaeda had already proven willing to innovate, using a suicide boat bomb to attack USS *Cole*, seeking out nuclear and other unconventional weapons, and otherwise trying to find new ways to fight and terrorize. Finally, Al Qaeda stresses operational security, making it difficult for intelligence agencies to penetrate it.

Yet despite Al Qaeda's skill and dedication, it is possible the 9/11 attacks could have been prevented. After the attacks, a host of recriminations consumed the country. Conspiracy theorists offered a mix of bizarre theories, most of which blamed President Bush (or, as some believe, his puppet-master, Vice President Cheney) for either knowingly allowing the attacks to occur or even staging the attacks themselves and using Al Qaeda as a fall guy in order to justify invading Iraq. According to the latter theory, the World Trade Center towers collapsed due to a controlled demolition, not from the damage caused by the planes. And, of course, no conspiracy would be complete unless Jews could somehow be blamed, and one theory—especially prevalent in the Muslim world—is that Israeli intelligence bombed the towers in order to spur the United States to go to war against the Muslim world.

More credible criticism focused on the performance of the intelligence agencies tasked to prevent such attacks, particularly the CIA. The 9/11 Commission, a bipartisan set of wise men and women formed to investigate the failure to stop the attacks and advise on next steps, found that the CIA and FBI lost track of several suspects and that a number of the hijackers were known to US intelligence, yet watchlists were not updated to stop them from acquiring visas to enter the country.[29] The CIA, FBI, and National Security Agency all possessed useful information relevant to the 9/11 plot, but this information was not fully shared and, as a result, chances to disrupt the plot were missed. More broadly, the 9/11 Commission found that the intelligence community, and the US government as a whole, did not exercise sufficient imagination, failing to anticipate a tactic like a suicide bombing with an airplane or the scale of the carnage.

Before 9/11, counterterrorism was given only fitful senior-level attention, and it lacked money and manpower. After the 1998 embassy bombings, DCI Tenet wrote an internal memo declaring, "We are at war. I want no resources or people spared in this effort."[30] Yet the CIA and other intelligence agencies continued to emphasize more traditional intelligence collection over counterterrorism. As one intelligence officer responsible for Al Qaeda later wrote, he and other lower-level intelligence officials "knew a runaway train was coming at the United States, documented that fact, and then watched helplessly—or were banished for speaking out—as their senior leaders delayed action, downplayed intelligence, [and] ignored repeated warnings. . . ."[31] Moreover, the CIA feared that risky covert actions such as working with Afghan opponents of Al Qaeda could later discredit the CIA when the political pendulum shifted; this fear would manifest a decade later as the memory of the 9/11 attacks faded and CIA efforts to get tough on Al Qaeda, including the torture of detainees, were criticized by lawmakers and others in the government as excessive and illegal, even though the Agency had extensive White House authorization.

The CIA was widely blamed because many of its covert action and collection attempts yielded little, but compared to other government bodies, the Agency was fighting hard. Indeed, legal scholar and polymath Richard Posner contends that the CIA in particular, as well as other voices in government, offered up a range of what at the time seemed like daring and creative options, such as increasing the authority the president gives the CIA, including more latitude to kill Bin Laden should a capture operation not be feasible; covertly aiding the anti-Taliban Northern Alliance; and other measures.[32] Only looking back do these measures seem paltry.

The FBI, in contrast, was a disaster. Like the CIA, the FBI made obvious mistakes that can be faulted in hindsight, such as failing to follow up on reports that suspected jihadists were seeking flight training and that several of the hijackers were in touch with Islamist radicals in the United States who were already being monitored. Beyond these particular errors, though, the FBI as an institution was flawed from a counterterrorism perspective. The FBI devalued analysis, did not train its operatives properly on intelligence collection, did not adequately resource counterterrorism, and paid more attention to investigating past attacks than preventing future ones. In addition, FBI knowledge in the field was not shared with headquarters or other local offices, let alone with the rest of the US government.

The US military was not seriously involved in going after Al Qaeda before 9/11, despite the armed forces' impressive intelligence and strike capabilities. Senior military and defense officials did not seriously consider military operations in Afghanistan, special operations forces raids, or other measures that became standard after 9/11. The 9/11 Commission found that "[a]t no point before 9/11 was the Department of Defense fully engaged in the mission of countering Al Qaeda."[33]

Blaming an "intelligence failure" or government bureaucrats is always politically easier than blaming political leaders, and many criticisms of the intelligence community are deserved, but the deeper problems that allowed the 9/11 attacks to happen stemmed from US counterterrorism policy itself. Before 9/11, the US government as a whole remained passive on counterterrorism, despite superb strategic warning. Even the 1998 embassy attacks did not elicit a strong response: the cruise-missile strikes on supposed Al Qaeda-linked targets in Sudan and Afghanistan did not damage Al Qaeda in any meaningful way, and in fact made it look stronger for successfully defying the United States. The CIA regularly warned that Al Qaeda would attack, and in February 2001, DCI Tenet testified that Bin Laden and Al Qaeda posed "the most immediate and serious threat" to the United States.[34] However, as long as Al Qaeda enjoyed a haven in Afghanistan, its leadership was free to arm, train, organize, and build a mini-army. It could plot attack after attack, and it only needed one operation to remain undetected in order to be successful. Similarly, the United States did not aggressively target potential Al Qaeda cells (at home or abroad), thus enabling the group to recruit and send operatives around the world with little risk of arrest or disruption. Nor did Washington have coherent counterterrorism policies toward Pakistan and Saudi Arabia, both key countries when it came to Al Qaeda. Political leaders did not force better intelligence cooperation, demand that the military become more engaged, or otherwise remedy the institutional problems.

Yet even with all these mistakes, it is tough to see how the 9/11 attacks could have been easily prevented. Our thinking on 9/11 suffers from hindsight bias: the intentions and clues seem obvious after the strike, but if we put ourselves in the place of analysts and policymakers at the time, the reality was far more complex. Posner points out that the United States had not suffered a successful airplane hijacking for 15 years before 9/11, making it difficult to justify increasing airline security. As the 9/11 Commission explains, "Before 9/11, al Qaeda and its affiliates had killed fewer than

50 Americans, including the East Africa embassy bombings and the *Cole* attack. The US government took the threat seriously, but not in the sense of mustering anything like the effort that would be gathered to confront an enemy of the first, second, or even third rank."[35] CIA analysts tracked Al Qaeda plots all over the world, but the available clues pointing to a strike in the United States were lost in the vast sea of threat information about other possible attacks. Investigations into past attacks, such as the Al Qaeda bombings of US embassies in Africa in 1998 and Hizballah's attacks on the US Marine barracks and embassy in Beirut in 1983, found that tactical warning is often likely to be lacking when it comes to terrorism—that's just the reality. And some problems are almost impossible to solve. US policy toward Pakistan remains muddled well over a decade after 9/11. President Bush's aggressive measures in going after terrorists are now criticized as excessive. In short, the risk of terrorism remains, but so too does the risk of wasting money and creating new problems with excessive counterterrorism methods.

How Did Al Qaeda Justify the 9/11 Attacks?

Although some in the Muslim world cheered the attack on the United States, seeing it as comeuppance for a brutal imperialist power, strong criticism came from a surprising quarter: Islamists. Forty-six leaders from a wide assortment of Islamist groups, including the Muslim Brotherhood in Egypt, Hamas, and the Jamaat-e Islami in Pakistan, signed a letter condemning the attacks, declaring them "against all human and Islamic norms."[36] Muhammad Hussein Fadlallah, the spiritual guide of Hizballah in Lebanon (a group that had itself killed hundreds of Americans in suicide attacks in the 1980s), said he was "horrified" by these "barbaric. . . crimes" that were "forbidden by Islam."[37] Leading religious authorities in the region, including Abdulaziz bin Abdullah al-Ashaykh, the chief mufti of Saudi Arabia, and Mohamed Sayyid al-Tantawi, the rector of Cairo's Al-Azhar University, also denounced Al Qaeda's actions.

These Islamist leaders and religious scholars rejected the legitimacy of Al Qaeda's actions based on several criteria that have foundations in Islamic legal tradition, including that Al Qaeda leaders did not have the authority to declare jihad; that the United States is not a legitimate target because Muslim regimes had made treaties with it; and that Islam forbids killing civilians.

In response, Al Qaeda issued a detailed statement in 2002 laying out the religious justifications for 9/11. The rejoinder—which was specifically directed at the Muslim scholars and Islamist leaders who had denounced the attacks, rather than at a Western audience—demonstrated how much this criticism from Islamists stung. In their analysis of the 2002 Al Qaeda statement, scholars Quintan Wiktorowicz and John Kaltner explain that Al Qaeda started by challenging the credentials of their critics, claiming they were corrupted by apostate governments: at best, they were ignorant of Islam; at worst, mouthpieces for US-dominated regimes. The authors of the Al Qaeda statement argued that these Islamic scholars were "giving the Crusaders the green light to exact revenge on Muslims."[38] In contrast, the jihadist leaders (i.e., themselves) were pure. In other words, the clerical leaders had sold out, leaving it to non-scholars to defend the faith.

To counter arguments that the attacks on the United States were unlawful because the United States had entered into treaties with several Muslim countries (under Islamic law, it is illegal to wage jihad against someone with whom you have signed a treaty), Al Qaeda claimed that the United States was already engaged in a war on Islam and that the jihadists were merely taking up arms in defense. US sanctions against Iraq and the bombing of Iraq in the 1990s, and, of course, Washington's close relationship with Israel, were cited as examples of American perfidy. Any treaties that had been signed were therefore invalid because the United States broke the treaty first. And, in any event, apostate regimes were not empowered to make treaties in the first place.

The critique about the unlawful killing of civilians was particularly important to the jihadists. Numerous verses in the Qur'an and sayings of the Prophet Muhammad unequivocally reject the killing of civilians. After 9/11, Yusuf al-Qaradawi, an influential and highly respected Islamic scholar, quoted Qur'an 5:31: "Whosoever kills a human being for other than manslaughter or corruption in the earth, it shall be as if he has killed all mankind."[39] Al Qaeda leaders countered with the Qur'anic admonition: "And one who attacks you, attack him in like manner as he attacked you" (2:194). As the United States, in their eyes, had already violated the rules of war by killing Muslim civilians with sanctions in Iraq and by supporting the killing of Palestinian civilians, Muslims need have no inhibitions about killing civilians in return. Based on this "norm of reciprocity," the Al Qaeda leaders argued that "[i]f believers have targeted Muslim women, children and elderly, it is permissible for Muslims to respond in kind."[40]

In case that argument did not quite satisfy the legal scholars, Al Qaeda further argued that American civilians are not really civilians: factory workers make the weapons used to wage war, journalists serve as propaganda mouthpieces for the government, and so on. Indeed, they claimed that because the United States is a democracy, the American people are responsible for their government's actions.

As Wiktorowicz and Kaltner conclude, "The sheer breadth of these conditions leaves ample theological justification for killing civilians in almost any imaginable situation."[41] Although Al Qaeda and like-minded groups rely on these and other similar arguments to defend their actions and to continue to justify killing to this day, they have never fully escaped the mainstream Islamic consensus that their actions are not justified under Islam.

What Was the Fallout from the 9/11 Attacks for Al Qaeda?

The 9/11 attacks shocked the world and made Al Qaeda and Bin Laden household names. Yet they were also a disaster for Al Qaeda, as the US-led response sent the organization reeling.

Over 80 countries lost citizens on 9/11: New York in particular is an international city, and the World Trade Center buildings were global workplaces. Over 130 countries offered basing, overflight rights, troops, and other forms of military assistance to the United States, and even more helped target the finances of suspected Al Qaeda and Taliban assets. The world, at least temporarily, rallied behind America's leadership.[42]

The most immediate loss for Al Qaeda was the toppling of the Taliban government. After 9/11, the United States worked with the Northern Alliance, a collection of anti-Taliban fighters that was on the ropes as the Taliban steadily consolidated control of Afghanistan. This force was supported by US airpower and, with additional assistance from the CIA and US special operations forces, in a matter of months captured the capital city of Kabul and drove the Taliban from much of Afghanistan. Bin Laden had hoped that the United States, like the British and the Soviets before it, would become bogged down in Afghanistan—which has the reputation of being the "graveyard of empires"—but in 2002, it looked like the US victory was complete.

The loss of the Taliban regime was a particular blow to the broader jihadist cause. Bin Laden himself had accepted the Taliban as a true Islamic government and Mullah Omar as the "commander of the faithful." Many jihadists believe that creating an Islamic state is the first step to victory and thus felt strongly that the Taliban's attempt should have been nourished rather than risked in such a cavalier way. They argued that such a state should grow powerful and either conquer or revolutionize other Muslim states and that only when the Muslim world was under "true" Islamic leadership would it become strong enough to confront enemies like the United States.

Al Qaeda itself lost key leaders, such as Mohammed Atef, its military commander, in the initial onslaught. Lawrence Wright reports that Al Qaeda lost almost 80% of its members in Afghanistan in the final months of 2001.[43] Even more important, though, it lost its safe haven. No longer could it bring recruits from around the world to its training camps, train them to fight insurgencies, select the best recruits for terrorist attacks, and indoctrinate them to its interpretation of Islam. After 9/11, its leaders were on the run, and the training camps were closed. The United States discovered hundreds of documents, videotapes, and phone numbers that led to innumerable additional leads on the location and activities of Al Qaeda members, enabling further arrests. Terrorism analyst Peter Bergen notes that "following 9/11 al-Qaeda—whose name in Arabic means 'the base'—lost the best base it ever had in Afghanistan."[44]

At the same time, the CIA orchestrated a massive campaign of arrests and disruptions around the globe. Jihadists were arrested or at least monitored in much of the world, and their recruiting and fundraising attempts were disrupted. This roundup went well beyond a narrow focus on the Al Qaeda core, bringing in members of like-minded groups from Algeria, Libya, Yemen, and elsewhere. President Bush, in his address to the nation on September 20, 2001, declared, "Our war on terror begins with Al Qaeda, but it does not end there. It will not end until every terrorist group of global reach has been found, stopped and defeated."[45]

As would be expected, US allies and moderate Muslims condemned the attacks, but what was even more damaging for Al Qaeda was the criticism within jihadist circles. Journalist Jason Burke quotes the jihadist strategist Abu Musab al-Suri, who lamented that the 9/11 attacks cast "jihadists into a fiery furnace. ... A hellfire which consumed most of their leaders, fighters and bases."[46]

By the end of 2002, Al Qaeda was on the ropes: it had lost its base, its global presence was disrupted, and many potential supporters and sympathizers criticized both its message and the wisdom of its leaders.

What Attacks Has Al Qaeda Done Since 9/11?

After the 9/11 attacks, the United States and its allies hit Al Qaeda hard, removing its sanctuary in Afghanistan and putting its global network under siege. But Al Qaeda did not stand still. Despite having been declared "on the run" multiple times by US officials, Al Qaeda has carried out several high-profile attacks since 9/11 that have killed hundreds of people. Fortunately, alert security officials disrupted many more plots in Europe, Asia, the Middle East, and the United States. Some of these were quite ambitious: in 2006, Al Qaeda supported a cell in Britain in its attempt to detonate bombs on as many as 10 flights over the Atlantic Ocean (a replay of the failed 1995 Bojinka plot). Many, however, were smaller endeavors, and the plotters were arrested before the plots were close to completion.

Some failures were really near-misses. On December 22, 2001, Richard Reid attempted to ignite a bomb hidden in the soles of his shoes while on a flight from Paris to Miami; an alert flight attendant noticed the smell of the matches he was using, passengers and crew members overpowered him, and the flight was diverted to the Boston airport, where it landed safely. In 2009, Umar Farouk Abdulmutallab, who had ties to Al Qaeda's Yemeni affiliate, hid a bomb in his underwear and tried to detonate it as his plane was landing in Detroit; he too was subdued by passengers after setting fire to his clothes and a blanket. Although technically failures, these attacks showed that Al Qaeda was able to penetrate Western security measures despite the intense post-9/11 efforts to secure civil aviation.

Where Al Qaeda did succeed, it was often against undefended civilian targets. In 2002, Al Qaeda bombed a historic synagogue in Djerba, Tunisia, killing 21 people. In October of that year, Jemaah Islamiyya, a Southeast Asian group whose leaders worked with Al Qaeda, bombed a nightclub on the Indonesian island of Bali, killing 202 people, most of them foreign tourists. On March 11, 2004, jihadists in Spain with direct links to Al Qaeda conducted the deadliest modern terrorist attack in Europe, killing over 190 people when they bombed four commuter trains. The next year, on July 7, four Al Qaeda–supported suicide bombers detonated themselves aboard subway trains and a double-decker bus in London nearly simultaneously, killing 52 people and wounding over 700.

Despite these successes, Al Qaeda suffered several problems after 9/11 that limited its effectiveness. The loss of its safe haven in Afghanistan dramatically lowered the overall competence of its operatives. Some recruits were still able to be trained in Pakistan and elsewhere, but volunteers were far more likely to be disrupted while en route to or inside Pakistan, and they and Al Qaeda in general had to lie low. Leaders and trainers had to stay on the move to avoid being captured or killed in a drone strike. Jihadists were not safe back in their home countries, either: US and allied security services were now on full alert, thus requiring operatives to exhibit a higher level of professionalism than in the past to keep from being caught. Jihadist plots, whether directly supported by Al Qaeda or not, were often bungled by inexperienced recruits who made foolish mistakes or compromised operational security, drawing the attention of alert counterterrorism officials. Defensive measures like more advanced airport security screening, while never perfect, also made attacks harder. Together, these challenges made a "spectacular" attack like 9/11, which took years to plan and organize and required cells around the world to pitch in, far harder to pull off.

Less noticed in the West, but far more deadly, were Al Qaeda's efforts to support and exploit conflicts in the Middle East, Africa, and South Asia by backing jihadist insurgencies—a return to its early role as "Quartermaster of Jihad."[47] In Saudi Arabia, Al Qaeda founded a new branch that began a sustained terrorism campaign in 2003 that took several years for Saudi authorities to beat. More commonly, though, Al Qaeda worked with existing local jihadist groups, insinuating itself into a conflict and helping its local allies become stronger. War zones in Iraq, Syria, and elsewhere saw repeated acts of terror (as well as guerrilla war) carried out by Al Qaeda-linked groups.

As it stands today, a mix of aggressive efforts abroad, better intelligence, and improved defenses at home has made conducting a successful terrorist attack in the United States far harder; at the same time, conflict in the Muslim world has captured the passions of many and enabled the jihadist movement to remain relevant and dangerous.

3

STRATEGY AND TACTICS

What Are Al Qaeda's Goals Today?

Beginning in the mid-1990s, and becoming firm in February 1998 with the release of a *fatwa* from the Al Qaeda-backed umbrella group, the World Islamic Front for Combat Against Jews and Crusaders, Al Qaeda coalesced around a set of goals.[1] They include:

- *Ending the US presence in the Middle East.* In Al Qaeda's eyes, the United States is an imperial power bent on dominating the Muslim world. Its military presence in particular—whether in Saudi Arabia and the rest of the Arabian Peninsula ("the holiest of places"[2]), Iraq, or Afghanistan—is seen as a desecration, as is the broader US political influence in the region. The United States is blamed for bolstering repressive regimes, supporting Israel, condoning or encouraging the slaughter of Muslims, artificially depressing oil prices and thus robbing Muslims of their patrimony, and otherwise oppressing the region. Other "crusader" powers, particularly those that contribute military forces to places like Afghanistan and Iraq, are also seen as oppressive powers to be opposed.
- *Destroying Israel.* Israel is regarded as a colonial Western outpost that has stolen Muslim lands, and Al Qaeda seeks to destroy the Jewish state completely. Much of its rhetoric and some of its attacks (e.g., on Jewish religious sites in Djerba, Tunisia, in 2002 and in Istanbul in 2003) suggest that it sees international Jewry and Israel as interchangeable. The group's

rhetoric is also viciously anti-Semitic, in addition to being anti-Israel.

- *Reorienting the jihadist movement.* Al Qaeda also seeks to convert Muslim fighters (and Muslims in general) to its Salafi-jihadist worldview. Few of the Saudis who went to Afghanistan to join Al Qaeda before 9/11 were anti-American when they arrived: this was cultivated in Al Qaeda-controlled camps.[3] Al Qaeda pushes the idea that jihad is obligatory on young males and that the community in general must back the fighters. It tries to spread this credo to Muslims everywhere through propaganda and by example.

- *Opposing "apostate" regimes in the Muslim world.* Bin Laden, Zawahiri, and other Salafi-jihadists reject the Islamic credentials of the rulers of Muslim states based on various interpretations of *shari'a* (Islamic law). Moreover, they believe that the policies (peace with Israel, relations with the United States, repression at home, and so on) and personal behavior (corruption, profligacy, etc.) of these leaders indicate that they are not true Muslims and thus must be overthrown. Since 9/11, Al Qaeda has supported struggles against Muslim governments in Afghanistan, Algeria, Egypt, Iraq, Jordan, Pakistan, Saudi Arabia, and elsewhere.

Although the above goals appear specific, in practice they include a host of potential countries and targets, and these goals themselves are linked to a broader set of struggles. In Zawahiri's *Knights Under the Prophet's Banner*, partly a history of the Egyptian jihadist movement and partly a treatise meant to inspire others, he includes not only the United States, Israel, and apostate regimes in the Muslim world, but also the United Nations, multinational companies, international news agencies, and even relief organizations on his list of enemies. Other enemies of Al Qaeda include India and Russia as powers occupying Muslim lands.

In the long term, Al Qaeda also seeks to create a true Islamic state: a caliphate. This state might start off weak, but even a small state would allow jihadists to govern. Governing would enable Al Qaeda to impose its version of Islam on those under its control and, more important for this fighting group, create a base from which it could expand its control. Al Qaeda leaders are vague, however, on when such a state should be declared or what it would actually look like in practice, falling back on the comforting idea that if Islamic law is implemented, there will be pious leaders and a just society, and the details will largely work themselves out.

This stands in sharp contrast to the Islamic State, Al Qaeda's rival in Iraq and Syria that broke from Al Qaeda in 2014 and declared a new caliphate. Al Qaeda leaders reject this as presumptuous, claiming that the group's current leader, Abu Bakr al-Baghdadi, lacks the religious credentials to declare a caliphate and that, in any event, doing so is premature. Al Qaeda's statement denouncing the move refers to Baghdadi's organization as a "group that calls itself a state" and snidely declares, "we do not hasten to declare emirates and states. . . that we impose on people, then declare whoever disapproves of such entities to be a rebel. . ."[4] Al Qaeda in the past urged its affiliates in Yemen and Somalia not to go down this road. Perhaps to Zawahiri's surprise, Baghdadi's declaration was a popular one, with many foreign Muslims flocking to Iraq and Syria to join the Islamic State, some even bringing their families along with them.

The specific interpretation of these goals is often done opportunistically. When opportunities for new jihads against the United States or other "crusader" powers arise, as in Iraq in 2003, these become priorities. Instability in Syria, Iraq, Pakistan, and Yemen are among the opportunities that the movement is helping exploit today. This opportunism also guides the movement's tactics. Killing civilians, particularly Jews and Americans, is deemed acceptable when other targets are too difficult to attack. At times, the group tries to link up with local groups when the local groups want to become operational.

The potential targets and goals also vary within the Al Qaeda core and between the Al Qaeda core and its affiliate organizations, sympathetic insurgencies, individuals it has trained, and its broader admirers. The Al Qaeda core focuses more on criticism of US and "crusader" policies in the Middle East, whereas local groups in Muslim countries often focus on anti-regime violence. The Islamic State focuses on consolidating and expanding its position in Iraq and Syria.

Some jihadists in the West are more concerned about social issues than about foreign policy. Incidents such as Mohammed Bouyeri's 2004 attack on Theo Van Gogh, a Dutch filmmaker who produced a documentary that blasted the treatment of women under Islam, and the violent demonstrations over the cartoons ridiculing the Prophet Muhammad in a Danish newspaper demonstrate that for many European Muslims, social issues are often more salient than US support for corrupt regimes in the Arab world. Even so, the Al Qaeda core is trying to reach out to these would-be followers. Although Bin Laden historically focused on policy more than values, and at times even mocked US claims that Al Qaeda is at war with Western freedoms, Al Qaeda released a videotape in March 2006 that railed against the Danish cartoons.[5]

Many groups that work with or admire Al Qaeda but are not part of it organizationally also focus on social issues, not US policy. The Taliban in Afghanistan, Boko Haram in Nigeria, and Jemaah Islamiyya in Indonesia are concerned about the penetration of Western popular culture and ideas, as suggested by the 2002 attack on a Bali night club and Boko Haram attacks on Christian schools. In Egypt and Southeast Asia, terrorists with links to Al Qaeda have burned churches and attacked Christian businesses.

Sectarianism also has emerged as an important driver of jihadist recruitment. Al Qaeda in Iraq initially gained support because it championed fighting American soldiers there, but over time, the Shi'a-led government and the Shi'ite community became the group's focus. In Syria, which has attracted many jihadists, Al Qaeda's rivals, including the Islamic State, have done well emphasizing the fight against the minority 'Alawite community and its Shi'ite backers, Iran and Hizballah, rather than an anti-Western agenda. The eruption of the Syrian civil war and its spillover into Iraq and beyond have only served to inflame sectarian tensions even further.

Though Al Qaeda emphasizes its ideological objectives in its rhetoric, the group is also motivated by a thirst for vengeance. The American response that followed 9/11 resulted in the death and arrest of thousands of jihadists, many of whom were friends and family of Al Qaeda members. Zawahiri lost his wife and four-year-old daughter after a US bombing in Afghanistan.[6] This thirst for vengeance has led to an acceptance, and at times a desire, for mass casualties. In his book, Zawahiri urges his readers to "inflict the maximum casualties against the opponent, for this is the language understood by the West."[7]

Al Qaeda's broad agenda is both a strength and a weakness. Al Qaeda can always find a grievance, seizing on popular causes as they arise and fitting them into its broader agenda. However, the jihadist Abu'l Walid charged in the 1990s that the organization changes targets too much, and as a result "every action is tactical and improvised."[8] Though Al Qaeda today shifts its focus less than in the past, by having many enemies, it cannot concentrate its energies on one.

Does Al Qaeda Have a Strategy?

Although jihadists' ideology and tactics often seem primitive, their strategic thinking is not. There are several jihadist intellectuals who devote themselves to what they call "strategic studies" (al-dirasat al-istratajiyya), and William McCants, an expert on jihadist thinking, notes that these intellectuals are equally comfortable citing Western political theorists and the Qur'an to explain how the jihadist movement can end American hegemony and establish Islamic states. In both their statements to the world and their internal correspondence, Bin Laden and Zawahiri have repeatedly put aside lofty rhetoric and have offered several concrete ideas on how Al Qaeda can achieve its goals of expelling the United States from the Muslim world, overthrowing apostate regimes, replacing them with Islamic governments, and creating a society of true Muslims.

In practice, though, Al Qaeda has pursued several strategies simultaneously to defeat its enemies, and its preferred approach has varied during its long history. Making this more confusing, the jihadist movement as a whole is divided over the best approach, and Zawahiri's command over affiliate groups today, let alone the broader movement, is uneven at best.

Al Qaeda seeks to exhaust its enemies though a strategy of attrition. Part of the motive for 9/11 was to bog the United States down in Afghanistan—this had worked for the mujahedin against the Soviets, after all. Bin Laden long argued that the United States—and the West in general—was unwilling to pay the price in blood to maintain its dominant role in the Middle East. For example, Bin Laden claimed that after attacking US forces in Somalia in 1993, jihadists "realized that the American soldier was just a paper tiger."[9] They view the US withdrawal from Iraq in 2011 and the drawdown from Afghanistan in 2014 as proof that the United States lacks staying power: the strength of the jihadists, in contrast, is their willingness to die for their cause and their understanding that this fight may last for generations.

Attacks on the US homeland and on Western targets in general are meant to undermine morale, reinforcing the point that a US presence in the Middle East will never succeed. Al Qaeda sees the battlefield as global: US and other enemy targets can be hit anywhere.[10] Indeed, attacks outside war zones often are more likely to grab attention and to inspire Muslims while frightening enemies than attacks inside war zones. The 9/11 attacks are one such example. In a 2004 statement, Bin Laden trumpeted the ease of this approach, noting that the *mujahedin* had "bled Russia for 10 years, until it went bankrupt" and that to bait the Bush administration "[a]ll we have to do is send two mujahedin to the furthest point east to raise a piece of cloth on which is written al-Qaida, in order to make the generals race there to cause America to suffer human, economic, and political losses."[11] Because of the difficulty of one single group being able to maintain pressure on the West in the face of a concerted counterterrorism campaign, influential jihadist thinker Abu Musab al-Suri calls for a decentralized approach in which disconnected cells attack Western countries until those countries are so overextended that they are forced to pull back their forces from Muslim countries.

Another aspect of the attrition strategy is financial: after 9/11, Bin Laden bragged that by spending just half a million dollars on the attack, he forced the United States to spend trillions of dollars in defense—"bleeding America to the point of bankruptcy," as Bin Laden put it.[12] He claimed credit for the financial crisis in the United States and other economic problems. Al Qaeda also seeks to divide the United States from its allies. By conducting attacks in Europe, Al Qaeda is hoping to divide the North Atlantic Treaty Organization (NATO). The model here is the attacks in Madrid in 2004, which led Spain to withdraw its forces from Iraq.

Yet though the United States understandably focuses on terrorist attacks in the West, Al Qaeda also wants to create mini-Islamic emirates throughout the Muslim world and weaken or overthrow US allies there. By striking the "far enemy," the United States, Al Qaeda believes it is weakening the foundation on which local regimes stand. But it also wants to build up jihadist forces on the ground to attack these regimes directly; thus, Al Qaeda seeds new groups or aids existing jihadist insurgents in their struggles against governments in Algeria, Iraq, Pakistan, Syria, and Yemen, among other countries. Assistance may involve propaganda, fundraising, training, and the provision of foreign fighters.

Strategic thinking extends to the local level as well. For example, Abu Bakr Naji (a pseudonym for an unknown author) has advocated a strategy for creating security vacuums in Muslim countries by attacking infrastructure tied to national wealth, such as tourism and oil pipelines. When the security services redeploy their forces to protect that infrastructure, jihadists can take over the unprotected territory and begin providing rudimentary government services. These "administrations of savagery" can then combine with one another to form Islamic emirates.[13]

Supporting local groups fits in with Al Qaeda's broadest goal: spreading its interpretation of Islam. In its propaganda and through its training and actions, Al Qaeda aims to promote a sense of Muslim unity and Salafi values. When one of these groups captures territory and begins to offer services and provide local governance, or if a group actually succeeds in taking over a country, the group notionally advances these teachings. In time (and if left unchecked), this control of territory provides Al Qaeda and its allies a safe haven that enables them to organize, train, and fight more effectively, further spreading their influence. Reverses that result in a loss of controlled territory, like the loss of a haven in Afghanistan after the fall of the Taliban in 2001, thus deal a tremendous blow to the group.

Dramatic attacks like 9/11 bring Al Qaeda's goals together. In addition to believing that such attacks can intimidate the United States, Al Qaeda believes that they inspire Muslims worldwide, shaking them out of their apathy. Such attacks also prompt a US response, such as the invasions of Afghanistan and Iraq, that Al Qaeda believes forces the United States to show its true colors as a hegemonic power. This, in turn, further inspires Muslims while at the same time bringing American troops into killing zones where Al Qaeda's skill in fostering insurgency will help it win out.

Nevertheless, though Al Qaeda has strategies that on paper may seem relatively well thought out, in practice these strategies have limits or are flawed. The 9/11 attacks did not intimidate the United States but rather led it to redouble its efforts to fight Al Qaeda and Salafi-jihadists around the world. The attacks did compel the United States to go to war in Afghanistan and contributed to the decision to go to war in Iraq in 2003—both expensive endeavors in both lives and dollars—but this hardly bankrupted the United States, and it remains active in the Middle East (though certainly less eager to intervene than in the past). Many of the affiliate organizations Al Qaeda has sponsored continue to emphasize the fight against their local enemies, not the United States. Still other groups call for killing Shi'a or otherwise "purifying" the Islamic community, which Al Qaeda generally opposes. In its efforts to be seen as the leader of the global jihadist movement, Al Qaeda has often found itself spending precious resources on the relatively minor goals of its affiliates instead of on the bigger fight against its primary enemies and embracing tactics that have at times put its organizational survival at risk. At the local level, tactical concerns—such as seizing an opportunity to attack a vulnerable target, even if that target is not a particularly important one from a strategic standpoint—or even simple revenge often dominate thinking. So while Zawahiri and other leaders have a strategic outlook, in practice the group, its allies, and its followers are often opportunistic and inconsistent.

How Did Al Qaeda Become a Suicide Bombing Factory?

Suicide bombings have gone from an unusual tactic to a commonplace one. Muslims historically have rejected suicide bombings, and many still do today. Islam strictly prohibits suicide: "And do not kill yourselves," instructs the Qur'an, "Indeed, Allah is to you ever Merciful."[14] It was not until Hizballah used suicide bombings against the US Marine Corps barracks and US embassy in Lebanon to devastating effect in 1983 that Islamist groups embraced them. Even then, support for suicide bombing was lukewarm for many years and was more about the need to defeat Western infidels than endorsement of the tactic. According to the Chicago Project on Security and Terrorism, the 1980s saw only a handful of suicide attacks; the number increased to dozens for much of the 1990s: 1995 was the worst year with 27 attacks. During this period, few of the suicide bombers were Salafi-jihadists. One of the biggest perpetrators, the Liberation Tigers of Tamil Eelam (LTTE), was a secular-nationalist group fighting for an independent Tamil homeland.[15]

As Palestinians embraced the tactic against Israel in the 1990s, some leading Sunni scholars began to support suicide attacks. A prominent and relatively mainstream Sunni theologian, Yusuf al-Qaradawi, claimed, "Suicide is an act or instance of killing oneself intentionally out of despair, and finding no outlet except putting an end to one's life. On the other hand, martyrdom is a heroic act of choosing to suffer death in the cause of Allah, and that's why it's considered by most Muslim scholars as one of the greatest forms of jihad."[16]

Zawahiri, back when his focus was on Egypt as leader of Egyptian Islamic Jihad, initiated suicide bombing there in 1993, in a failed attempt to kill Egypt's interior minister. His group subsequently used a suicide bomber to target the Egyptian embassy in Islamabad in 1995. Not surprisingly, the many Egyptian members of Al Qaeda shaped Bin Laden's thinking on suicide bombing.[17] Al Qaeda also gained help from an unlikely ally: the Lebanese Hizballah. Though the Shi'a-dominated organization differs in its ideology from Al Qaeda, and Shi'a are loathed by many Salafi-jihadists (the two are currently fighting each other in Syria), the leadership of both organizations can be pragmatic, and the two share many enemies, including the United States. Jihadists linked to Al Qaeda traveled to Lebanon to study with Hizballah in 1994, and Bin Laden told them specifically that he wanted them to study the Marine barracks bombing.[18] Suicide bombings marked Al Qaeda's first major attack, the 1998 embassy bombings, as well as the 9/11 operation, and have become the organization's hallmark.

Although Al Qaeda used suicide bombings in the 1990s, the tactic went critical when Hamas and other Palestinian groups used it during the second *intifada*, which began in 2000. Adding further momentum, the US invasion of Iraq in 2003 triggered a massive wave of suicide attacks as Al Qaeda-linked forces embraced the tactic to fight the American occupiers, their Iraqi government allies, and the broader Shi'ite community, whom many jihadists saw as the true enemy. The tactic spread throughout Al Qaeda's network, and Sunni jihadists would use suicide bombings in almost every theater they fought in, including Pakistan, Chechnya, Algeria, Somalia, Syria, and elsewhere—over 35 countries in all. Over the last decade, Salafi-jihadists have launched hundreds of suicide bombings each year that in total have killed tens of thousands of people, the vast majority of them Muslims.[19] Today, suicide bombings in war zones barely make the news.

Al Qaeda seeks to spread an ethos of martyrdom: if Muslims in general rejected suicide bombing, Al Qaeda would lose recruits, money, and public support in general. So it was not enough for Al Qaeda members to want to die for the cause; they had to convince others that this tactic was acceptable, even glorious. Al Qaeda long pushed the same message as Qaradawi, stressing that dying while fighting Islam's enemies was cause for martyrdom. Its propaganda and public statements are replete with calls for martyrdom; mixing God with practicality, Zawahiri declared that "martyrdom operations" (i.e., suicide bombings) were "the most successful way of inflicting damage against the opponent and the least costly to the mujahedin in terms of casualties."[20]

As Zawahiri suggests, suicide bombings have a tremendous advantage over most other terrorist tactics: they are effective. Terrorism scholar Bruce Hoffman found that, on average, suicide attacks are four times as lethal as other methods. He explains, "Suicide bombings are inexpensive and effective. They are less complicated and compromising than other kinds of terrorist operations. They guarantee media coverage. The suicide terrorist is the ultimate smart bomb."[21] The bomber can evade many simple defenses, and because he plans to die, the problem of protecting or extracting an operative—a constant issue for Western military organizations—goes away. Suicide bombings also helped Al Qaeda differentiate itself from other groups, demonstrating its commitment and zealotry.[22]

Most mainstream Muslims still reject suicide bombing, particularly when used to slaughter other Muslims or innocent civilians. One London-based Muslim organization described suicide bombing as "anathema, antithetical, and abhorrent to Sunni Islam... an act which has consequences of eternal damnation."[23] Most Muslims condemn suicide bombings today, though roughly half of Palestinians say it is at least "sometimes justified," and significant percentages in Egypt, Bangladesh, Lebanon, and other countries also accept its validity.[24] To justify killing Muslims, some Salafi-jihadists have had to embrace the doctrine of *takfir*—essentially, that some of their Muslim victims are not "real" Muslims because they support an enemy regime, consort with infidels, and so on, and that therefore they are legitimate targets.[25] These rationalizations, however, place the groups in opposition to the population and make them even less popular.

How Dangerous Are Lone Wolves?

Lone Wolves have perpetrated some of the deadliest attacks since 9/11. Lone Wolves—or, as FBI Director James Comey prefers to call them, "lone rats"—are individuals who carry out terrorist attacks on their own without the explicit direction of an established group or leader. In the jihadist context, Lone Wolves are individuals who have been radicalized by Al Qaeda or Islamic State propaganda but are not acting under the direction of the Al Qaeda core or any other established group. Army Major Nidal Malik Hasan, though in communication with Al Qaeda-linked figures such as Anwar al-Awlaki, largely acted on his own in 2009 when he shot and killed 13 people at Fort Hood, Texas, in the worst jihadist-related terrorist attack on US soil since 9/11. Four years later, Dzhokhar and Tamerlan Tsarnaev detonated crude homemade bombs at the Boston Marathon, killing three people, injuring over 250, and setting off a massive manhunt that shut down the city of Boston for several days. Lone Wolves have also acted throughout Europe. In England in May 2013, Michael Adebolajo and Michael Adebowale, two British Muslim converts of Nigerian descent, killed Lee Rigby, an off-duty English soldier home on leave, with a knife and a cleaver—they claimed they attacked Rigby "because Muslims are dying every day" at the hands of British soldiers.[26]

These and other attacks have led to tremendous concern about Lone Wolf terrorism. Shortly before the tenth anniversary of the 9/11 attacks, President Obama stated in a *CNN* interview that a terrorist attack perpetrated by a Lone Wolf was more likely to occur in the United States than a large, coordinated attack like the one we saw on 9/11.[27] Terrorism scholar Jeff Simon argues that with the growth of the Internet, it is easier for Lone Wolves to find propaganda, self-radicalize, and even find bomb-making instructions and material. Even more important, Lone Wolves are an intelligence nightmare. Intelligence agencies cannot learn their identities by infiltrating the meetings of a terrorist group, searching the computer of a leader and finding personnel records, or monitoring suspicious communications.[28] Many Lone Wolves are impossible to detect until after they have committed an attack. The phenomenon of Lone Wolves is not just limited to extremist Muslims like Al Qaeda and those it inspires: individuals motivated by extreme right-wing ideology have perpetrated several Lone Wolf attacks, including the 1995 bombing of a federal building in Oklahoma City, which killed 168 people.

Some Al Qaeda figures have recognized the potential of Lone Wolf attacks. In 2005, Abu Musab al-Suri, an influential Al Qaeda strategist, published a 1,600-page treatise online titled *The Call to Global Islamic Resistance.*[29] In it, Suri calls on Muslims to establish terror cells on their own without linking up to Al Qaeda and to use the Internet to learn how to conduct attacks.[30] The Al Qaeda core's role, in Suri's vision, is to produce propaganda and to give general strategic guidance that isolated cells will follow on their own.

The Syrian conflict and the growth of the Islamic State make the Lone Wolf danger stronger. The Islamic State's propaganda has appealed to thousands of Westerners, and some of these individuals may simply choose to act at home rather than traveling to Iraq and Syria; Westerners who have returned home from waging jihad in Syria and Iraq may also strike. In 2014, Mehdi Nemmouche, a French citizen who had spent the previous year fighting in Syria, walked into the Jewish Museum in Brussels and opened fire with a pistol and an AK-47, killing four people in just seconds.[31]

Though Lone Wolves are frightening, it is easy to overstate the danger they present. They are feared because they are almost impossible to stop, but in general, their success rate is low.[32] This should not be surprising: they are untrained, and because they are not in contact with more experienced jihadists, they often fail to make bombs properly, fail to keep their preparations hidden, or make other beginners' mistakes.[33] British jihadists in 2012 sought to attack marchers from the anti-Muslim English Defense League, but they showed up after the march ended, and one of their cars was impounded for having no insurance. A search at the impound lot later revealed weapons and explosives. "Spectacular" attacks like 9/11 are usually beyond the capabilities of Lone Wolves. According to Sidney Alford, an explosives expert from the United Kingdom who has personally examined many of the bomb-making manuals published by Al Qaeda and its sympathizers, these manuals often contain numerous errors—which, given the volatility of some of the materials involved in making a bomb, can be potentially disastrous for amateurs using these manuals to make a homemade bomb.[34] Many would-be Lone Wolves also publish online rants or otherwise make their intentions known; though given the large number of fools and lunatics who post on the Internet, it is difficult to know which ones to pay attention to in advance.

When they do strike, Lone Wolves often have difficulty attacking again and thus sustaining the terror. Hasan, for example, probably assumed he would die in a hail of bullets during his attack at Fort Hood. (He was shot five times but survived.) The Tsarnaev brothers had no safe house where they could hide out after the bombing, no escape route out of Boston, and no ability to carry out additional attacks.

Al Qaeda itself seems to have little use for Lone Wolves, despite its propaganda. In a letter to Bin Laden, Al Qaeda media spokesman Adam Gadahn explained that many jihadist forums were "repulsive to most Muslims" and that their participants were ignorant fanatics.[35] Al Qaeda wants to hurt the West, but random one-off attacks do not enable the organization to direct resources to whatever the current priority is, to raise or lower pressure on governments it seeks to coerce, or to otherwise fit the violence into a broader strategy. Not surprisingly, Al Qaeda puts little faith in Lone Wolves, and its leaders have prioritized training and top-down control and coordination whenever possible.

However, this may be changing. In 2013, to mark the twelfth anniversary of the 9/11 attacks, Zawahiri issued an audio message calling for Lone Wolf attacks on the United States: "Keeping America in a state of tension and anticipation does not cost us anything but [organizing] dispersed strikes here and there. In other words, just as we defeated it in a war of nerves in Somalia, Yemen, Iraq and Afghanistan, we must afflict it with a similar war in its own home. . . . These dispersed strikes can be carried out by one brother, or a small number of brothers." He also praised the Boston Marathon bombers.[36] Some analysts have suggested that this call for smaller-scale attacks carried out by lone operatives acting independently from the Al Qaeda core is a sign of just how weak and impotent the core organization has become.

What Do You Learn in an Al Qaeda Training Camp?

Training is at the heart of Al Qaeda: as part of its mission to fight its enemies in the West and in the Muslim world, it has trained its own operatives, members of other groups, and jihadists in general. Perhaps 20,000 recruits went through Al Qaeda's camps between 1996, when Bin Laden returned to Afghanistan, and 2001. As its relationship with the Taliban grew tighter in the late 1990s, Al Qaeda received permission to expand its training efforts there. Thousands more have trained since then in Pakistan or in the camps of Al Qaeda-linked affiliates.

Upon meeting an Al Qaeda or other jihadist facilitator, recruits would fill out forms describing their health, age, family, and education. Religiosity was also measured, with recruits asked how much of the Qur'an they had memorized. This being a terrorist group, recruits were asked about military experience and whether they could safely return to their home countries. Recruits had to promise to abide by camp rules, follow orders, and otherwise obey their new leaders.[37] To monitor these recruits, designated members kept track of guns and ammunition, spending, and travel.[38] This specialization allowed Al Qaeda to take advantage of individuals with unusual skills and to build a broader organization to support jihad worldwide, but it also presented an operational security risk for the organization: when discovered, these records were a gold mine for counterterrorism officials.

Most training is the jihadist version of boot camp. One schedule showed that the recruits woke up before sunrise for morning prayers, followed by calisthenics at 6:00 a.m. Recruits did push-ups and sit-ups before going off for a run. Training then commenced in small-arms handling and anti-armor or anti-aircraft operations—but not terrorism. Before 9/11, most recruits who trained in Afghanistan were sent to fight with the Taliban against its enemies. As one US official said, "The vast majority of them were cannon fodder."[39]

Yet Al Qaeda also assessed volunteers as they went through its camps. As one internal document noted, "The training military camp will have a big role in appraising and categorizing the Mujaheedeen [sic] brothers."[40] A far smaller elite group—often made up of recruits with prior military experience, though at times just those with the right language skills or nationality—was selected from this large pool to train to observe foreign embassies, conduct assassinations, learn codes, gather intelligence, and recruit spies. Ahmed Ressam, who tried to bomb the Los Angeles airport in 2000, testified that he received not only light-weapons training in a camp in Afghanistan but also training on explosives, surveillance, tradecraft for blending in with a population, destroying infrastructure, and striking government targets.[41]

Indoctrination was also at the core of the camps. Recruits were told that by fighting they would be establishing God's rule on earth and that should they die, they would be seen as martyrs. A substantial portion of time was reserved for instruction in the basics of the Qur'an and *hadith* (reports of the sayings of the Prophet Muhammad) and the associated duties of jihad, with additional instruction focusing on the ways of the Prophet and more advanced theological concepts.[42] Al Qaeda pushed its vision of Islam on recruits, using propaganda ranging from poems and videos to talks by hardened fighters with "street cred" to inspire recruits. Training materials reflected all of these goals. Constant exhortations to follow God's will and engage in jihad were mixed in with instructions on how to set up a camp for soldiers and the proper equipment for each holy warrior (which includes a handkerchief and soap).[43]

Indoctrination themes ranged from the Israeli occupation of Jerusalem and US occupation of Saudi Arabia to calls for helping the Chechens fight the Russians to how Islam will help economic development. Indeed, Al Qaeda was skilled at taking recruits who went for training in order to fight for one cause (like Chechnya) and redirecting them to new fights, such as Al Qaeda's struggles against Saudi Arabia and the United States. In short, Al Qaeda was knitting together the various grievances into one coherent whole, making Muslims from Europe, Africa, the Middle East, and Asia see their individual concerns and struggles as part of a broader whole.

The individuals running the camps gained considerable control over the fates of the recruits. Some "secured" (i.e., confiscated) the passports of new recruits to prevent desertions, though in truth many individuals were hesitant to return home anyway for fear of arrest. Even more important, by tying different struggles together, camp leaders could convince an individual to abandon his original goals and focus on another target. Omar Khyam, a British jihadist who was arrested for plotting to explode a fertilizer bomb at a nightclub in London, had originally planned to join the Taliban but was convinced by an Al Qaeda member while in Pakistan to act back home instead.[44] Mohamed Atta, who led the 9/11 operation, originally planned to fight in Chechnya but was redirected when he came to Al Qaeda's attention in Afghanistan.

The camps also seasoned recruits, separating jihadist blow-hards from those committed to action. One jihadist recalled that after attending a camp, his gang of friends became far more seri-ous: "[Before] they were joking around and using slang. After the camp the guys were talking jihad, praying, and quoting the Koran."[45] In the camps, the recruits also formed relationships and networks that they could draw on in the years to come.

For many volunteers, particularly Westerners unaccustomed to the difficulties of living in a remote part of a developing country, the camps could be too much. Recruits in Somalia, for example, con-tracted diseases like malaria and received little medical treatment. Most of the "Lackawanna Six"—a group of Yemeni-Americans from outside Buffalo who in 2003 were convicted in the United States of providing material support for Al Qaeda because they had attended training camps in Afghanistan before 9/11—never actually com-pleted their training. One faked an injury to leave early. A girlfriend of one recruit recalled, "They slept on rocks, and there were ants crawling all over them. He really didn't talk about it."[46] She claims he returned home less religious as a result of the experience.

Some trainers deliberately used especially painful or humiliating exercises, both to build esprit de corps and to weed out the weak. For Western recruits, the results at times could be comical. Omar Hammami, an American who went to train with Al Shabaab in Somalia, recalls having to do the "wheelbarrow" (walk on his hands with a comrade holding his feet) across broken glass and digging his own "grave" in the sand—he was then made to lie in it while a trainer jumped on his stomach. His trainer also "believed that beat-ing the muscles with a stick would hasten the workout process." A Western jihadist comrade of Hammami's protested to the instruc-tor, but the protest went nowhere as neither understood the other's language. Many recruits simply left because of the painful and silly workouts.[47]

The disruption after 9/11 of the haven Al Qaeda enjoyed in Afghanistan made it far harder for the organization to continue its extensive training of jihadists. Local movements in Yemen, Iraq, and elsewhere took on some of the training, but because these organizations had a more regional agenda than the core, their training and indoctrination was tailored accordingly. Al Qaeda continued to train operatives in Pakistan, but the scale of activities was greatly diminished. Indeed, because Al Qaeda's finances were being squeezed by US and allied counterterrorism efforts, some Western recruits were asked to purchase their own weapons and ammunition or were otherwise fleeced when they went abroad to train.[48]

From the start, Al Qaeda recognized that not all potential recruits and terrorists could be trained in its camps and made a concerted effort to disseminate training materials and propaganda videos far beyond the confines of the training camps. In 2000, British police found what is commonly referred to as the "Manchester Manual" in the home of Al Qaeda member Abu Anas al-Libi. In addition to religious exhortations, the manual explains important techniques such as how to establish a safe house, how to handle forged documents, how to maintain secure communications, and how to respond when being interrogated.[49]

Though the specifics of the propaganda and training have changed over time—Al Qaeda now uses the Internet to disseminate much of its material—Al Qaeda still tries to improve the skill and dedication of would-be jihadists from afar. Training camps, however, remain vital to the overall experience, building skills and establishing networks that transform otherwise bumbling jihadists into far more skilled terrorists.

Could Al Qaeda Get a Nuclear Weapon?

In 2009, President Obama declared nuclear terrorism to be "the immediate and extreme threat to national security," a view shared by many US politicians in both parties as well as many prominent government officials and outside experts.[50] This consensus, however, overstates the danger. Al Qaeda has repeatedly sought a nuclear capability—and its leaders have shown a desire to slaughter thousands of their enemies—but the terrorist group appears never to have gotten close to acquiring a nuclear weapon. If anything, Al Qaeda today is further away than ever from going nuclear.

Although terrorists rightly have a bloodthirsty reputation, few terrorist groups in history have expressed any interest in nuclear weapons: acquiring them is too hard, and using them would probably backfire, alienating potential supporters and leading to a manhunt that would make the post-9/11 US blitz against Al Qaeda look like a pinprick. Unfortunately, Al Qaeda is an exception to this happy rule: its leaders have long had an interest in nuclear weapons. In 1993, while in Sudan, some reports indicate that Al Qaeda attempted to buy uranium to use in a nuclear weapon;[51] instead, it was sold "Red Mercury"—basically, irradiated junk passed off as nuclear fuel. Zawahiri himself took control of Al Qaeda's nuclear program in 1998, the year that marked the beginning of Al Qaeda's more serious efforts to go nuclear. In 1999, Bin Laden declared in an interview with *Time* magazine that acquiring nuclear and other unconventional weapons was "a religious duty."[52] Shortly before 9/11, Al Qaeda operatives were in touch with Pakistani nuclear scientists, and although the conversations never went very far and did not involve a specific plan, they nevertheless are worrisome as a sign of intent. Zawahiri reportedly told a Pakistani journalist in 2001 that "if you have $30 million, [you can] go to the black market in central Asia, contact any disgruntled Soviet scientist and... dozens of smart briefcase bombs are available;" he then went on to claim that Al Qaeda had done so—a claim experts dismissed as braggadocio.[53]

While in Afghanistan, Al Qaeda also experimented with biological and chemical weapons, though the types of pathogens and agents it used were not highly lethal ones like smallpox or bubonic plague. However, in the various post-9/11 plots (all disrupted) that involved crude versions of such weapons, such as ricin and cyanide, local leaders—not Al Qaeda's top bosses—appeared to be the ones who decided to use these weapons. Some plots, such as the purported "ricin ring" tied to Abu Musab al-Zarqawi and Iraqi jihadists, generated sensationalized media reports that were often based on initial government exaggerations.[54]

Muslim theologians often condemn weapons of mass destruction as against Islam because such weapons are indiscriminate and thus could kill civilians, including Muslim civilians, in addition to killing the enemy. Jihadists, however, cite a *hadith* about a siege in which the Prophet Muhammad used a catapult to attack a city and justified it because the non-combatants chose to live among fighters. For jihadists, unconventional weapons are like the catapult: indiscriminate but militarily necessary (and therefore permissible).[55] In 2003,

Nasir al-Fahd, a radical Saudi cleric, wrote a legal treatise titled "On the Legal Status of Using Weapons of Mass Destruction Against Infidels."[56] Fahd argued that conventional weapons already kill tens of thousands but are allowed, so there is no "humane" reason to avoid nuclear weapons—and, indeed, those who are the first to condemn them, like the United States, already possess them. In Fahd's view, because Westerners have already killed so many Muslims, both necessity and reciprocity justify a mass-casualty response.

Losing Afghanistan was catastrophic for Al Qaeda's nascent nuclear program, eliminating the secure base from which it could experiment and organize for the long term. Today, several barriers stand in Al Qaeda's way, each formidable on its own, and even more daunting when taken together.

First, Al Qaeda lacks access to fissile material, of which there are few sources in the world. Al Qaeda could attempt, as it has in the past, to buy or steal this material—or even an entire weapon—from a state: a possibility that produces endless scaremongering and the occasional fun movie. Perhaps the most plausible approach would be to get the materials from Pakistan or the former Soviet Union. These states, however, fear that terrorists might use nuclear weapons against them and, in any event, rightly view their nuclear stocks as a top national security priority. So they guard them well. Stephen Younger, who headed nuclear-weapons research at the Los Alamos National Laboratory and ran the Defense Threat Reduction Agency after 9/11, cautions, "regardless of what is reported in the news, all nuclear nations take the security of their weapons very seriously."[57] Journalist William Langewiesche similarly notes that there is no known case in which a large amount of highly enriched uranium has gone missing.[58] Al Qaeda has tried to buy nuclear weapons, but as terrorism expert Bruce Hoffman points out, "Each time they tried, they got scammed."[59]

Even if Al Qaeda somehow obtained fissile material, building a nuclear weapon requires a critical mass of scientists, engineers, and managers. Such expertise is not widespread among jihadists, and the more widespread the circle of confederates, the greater the risk of detection—especially when the group is being hunted.[60] Some knowledge is available from the Internet and other public sources, but not enough to build a real device.[61] Even if the group did manage to construct a weapon, it would weigh over a ton and would contain delicate mechanisms and radioactive materials that require extremely careful treatment. Conservatively, the cost would be in the millions—a high cost for a group whose resources are already stretched. Even a stolen nuclear weapon is no guarantee. As Charles Ferguson, an expert at the Council on Foreign Relations, contends, "You don't get it off the shelf, enter a code and have it go off."[62] The skeptical John Mueller points to these and other difficult tasks—a total of 20 in all—that terrorists must accomplish before using a nuclear weapon successfully, making the odds prohibitive.[63]

Al Qaeda has alternatives when it comes to less lethal but still unconventional attacks, such as those that might involve chemical weapons or non-contagious biological weapons. But the fact is that Al Qaeda has used guns and bombs (and passenger jets) to kill thousands; many unconventional weapons, while scary, would do less damage and could easily fail. Even the post-9/11 attempt by Al Qaeda terrorist Jose Padilla to use a radiological weapon ("dirty bomb") bolsters the case for skepticism. The US Justice Department eventually determined that the radiological device "was still in its initial planning stage" (i.e., not ready to use); the Justice Department also noted that the Al Qaeda leadership had been skeptical of Padilla's plan and instead told him to blow up apartment buildings using natural gas—in other words, to keep it simple and stick to proven techniques.[64]

If Al Qaeda or a like-minded group has even a small chance of acquiring a nuclear weapon, we should be concerned. But concern should not mean panic. Intelligence agencies and diplomats should continue to focus on the risk of terrorist nuclear acquisition, keeping the barriers between Al Qaeda and the bomb high.

Should We Laugh at Al Qaeda?

Abu Musab al-Zarqawi, the founder of Al Qaeda in Iraq who made his name by personally beheading captives, had a less than successful start to his terrorism career. According to Jordanian intelligence, his first operation was in 1993, when he sent an operative to bomb a theater showing a pornographic film. However, the bomber became distracted by the film, and after planting the bomb under a theater seat, he sat down and stayed to watch.[65] The bomb detonated underneath him, and the bomber eventually bled to death.[66]

Given the carnage, fear, and suffering associated with even small terrorist attacks—let alone massive strikes like 9/11 or the steady stream of car bombs that countries like Iraq face—laughing at terrorist mishaps like this seems at best insensitive and at worst a form of hubris, soon to be corrected by the next bloody attack. Yet terrorists do many stupid things, and it is important to recognize, and exploit, these mistakes when weighing both the threat and the response.

Some terrorists are steady and skilled. Mohamed Atta, the 9/11 plot leader, was focused and determined, staying below the radar screen while moving inexorably toward his ultimate goal of bringing death to thousands. Al Qaeda leaders, recruiters, and senior operatives are usually smart and dangerous. Many of the foot soldiers, however, are untrained fools, and this frequently leads them to disaster.

The list of stupid terrorist actions is long and appears to grace all nationalities. In Afghanistan, would-be suicide bombers gave their comrades a last embrace before heading out on their mission—a bad move if you are all wearing suicide vests. The whole group went up in smoke as the bombs detonated. This foolishness occurs outside war zones, too. In 2007, a group of Americans planned to attack Fort Dix in New Jersey. To prepare for the assault, they went to the local shooting range and, while practicing, screamed anti-American slogans and called for jihad—and filmed themselves doing so. Because they looked so cool, they decided to turn their video into a DVD at the local Circuit City. The tech guy there promptly reported them.

A plot in the same year that got closer to success in the United Kingdom was undone by the idiocy of the plotters. Two men, one a doctor and another a PhD student, schemed to crash their Jeep Cherokee, loaded with fuel and propane tanks, into the Glasgow airport terminal. Instead, they crashed into the security barrier (apparently, they thought that the barrier could be easily driven through, just like in the movies). The bomb did go off—too far from the airport to do any damage—and immolated the two terrorists, one of whom later died from his burns. The same men had also planned to use a car bomb to blow up a London nightclub. They parked the car illegally and it was towed—but fortunately for investigators, the men left their cell phones in the car, revealing all their possible accomplices to the security services.

Terrorists in the United States have proven woefully inept at acquiring or setting off a bomb (though quite good at acquiring fake bombs from FBI informants or agents). With the exception of the crude bomb set off at the Boston Marathon, terrorists have not set off *any* bombs in the United States since 9/11. And lest we think that this is because bomb design is particularly difficult, contrast this to the 1970s, when groups as diverse as Puerto Rican separatists, left-wing radicals, and the Jewish Defense League set off dozens of bombs in the United States.[67] As far back as 1919, a group of anarchists managed to detonate massive bombs nearly simultaneously in seven different US cities—and they did not have YouTube videos or online how-to articles to learn from.[68]

Islamic terrorists' false piety also deserves scorn. Some, perhaps many, are true believers who try to live an exemplary life (at least according to their own warped version of it). Yet hypocrisy is common in the ranks of terrorists. Pornographic files are commonly found on the computers captured when terrorists are arrested or killed—including computers found in the Bin Laden compound. Nor are animals safe: a sniper rifle sight using thermal imagery captured two Taliban fighters satisfying themselves with a donkey.

Besides the joy of snickering at evil fools, recognizing the weaknesses of the terrorists can serve several purposes. First, it should help us recalibrate the threat. Watching out for another 9/11 or similar mass spectacular remains vital, but many of the dangers are mundane and low-level: the terrorists are too poorly trained and incompetent to do much more. It should also help us put terrorism in perspective: Al Qaeda remains a danger, but it is not always the 10-foot-tall terrorist giant we feared on September 12, 2001.

Terrorists' missteps should also remind us of the importance of stopping terrorists from going abroad to train. The Glasgow bombers were not idiots: they were well educated and highly motivated. Rather, it was their lack of training and guidance that made them seem so hapless. Zarqawi, who dispatched the bomber to the theater showing adult films in Jordan, later went to Afghanistan and fought in Iraq, becoming a fearsome threat.

Finally, terrorists' mistakes and their penchant for porn also offer an opportunity to undermine their support. No one wants to join a group of panting fools, and the more we can paint these groups as a hypocritical gang that can't shoot straight, the less appealing they look to potential recruits.

4

IDEAS AND INFLUENCES

What Are the Key Schools of Thought That Influence Salafi-Jihadism?

Al Qaeda and the broader Salafi-jihadist movement it seeks to lead are influenced by several overlapping schools of thought within Islam that have millions of adherents. However, few of these adherents embrace terrorism.

Salafism

The first three generations of Muslims were known as the *Salaf* ("forefathers" or "predecessors"), and their practice of Islam is considered to be exemplary. Contemporary Salafis seek to return to the practices of these early Muslims and embrace a literal and puritanical interpretation of Islam. They emphasize the oneness of God (*tawhid*) and reject what they see as religious innovations that emerged after this early period, such as many popular religious practices, compromises with local customs, and the philosophical contemplation of religious issues. Instead, they favor a narrow focus on the Qur'an and on the life of the Prophet Muhammad (*sunna*) and his sayings and teachings (*hadith*). They believe that Islamic law is a complete system that skilled scholars can understand: there is no need to analogize or otherwise apply logic to understand the truth, and indeed, there is no room for different interpretations. A broad array of smaller movements and groups, including several described below, fall under the umbrella of Salafism.

Wahhabism

Wahhabism is a form of Salafism that emerged in central Arabia in the mid-eighteenth century. It is based on the teachings of the religious scholar Muhammad Ibn Abd al-Wahhab and his alliance with the Saud family. The movement came to dominate the Arabian Peninsula and resulted in the founding of the Saudi state. Drawing on the Hanbali school of Islamic law, Wahhabis embrace a conservative and puritanical form of Islam. Wahhabism stresses the oneness of God, rejects Islamic legal scholarship that does not draw narrowly on the Qur'an, *sunna*, and *hadith*, and questions the legitimacy of interpretations of Islam that are more accepting of practices such as visiting the tombs of saints and adopting foreign dress. It is particularly hostile to Shi'ite Islam. The spread of the Wahhabi movement in Arabia thus resulted in the movement's warriors destroying local religious shrines and even massacring Shi'a.

The Wahhabi alliance with the House of Saud has proven mutually beneficial. The Saudi royal family enjoys legitimacy and commands religious fervor, while Wahhabi scholars have their teachings enforced by the state, which has put the Wahhabi interpretation of Islam and Islamic law at the heart of the Kingdom's educational and legal establishment. As Saudi Arabia's wealth surged in the 1970s due to the oil boom, the Saudi government and individual Saudis spent billions of dollars a year promoting Wahhabism abroad, building mosques, schools, and other institutions to propagate their interpretation of Islam.

Deobandism

The Deobandi seminary was founded in northern India in the nineteenth century in reaction to two powerful forces: British colonialism and Salafi preaching, much of it originating from Wahhabi circles. The seminary sought to oppose British colonialism and Western culture by reviving Islamic scholarship and practice in India while remaining peaceful colonial subjects. It also furthered Salafi teachings with its own clampdown on local superstitious practices and a conservative understanding of the Hanafi school of Islamic jurisprudence (the school of law followed by the majority of South Asian Muslims).[1] Deobandism spread to what is now Pakistan and Bangladesh as well as Afghanistan. Important Islamic movements in Pakistan, like Sipah-e

Sahaba Pakistan, Jamiat Ulema-e-Islam, and Lashkar-e Jhangvi, as well as the Taliban in Afghanistan have a Deobandi orientation.

Ahl-e Hadith

The Ahl-e Hadith ("the people of the *hadith*") is another prominent Salafi movement in South Asia, with many Pakistani jihadist groups embracing its ideas. The school grew out of the same Salafi teachings as the Wahhabi movement and has retained close ties to Wahhabi scholars and Saudi donors, though they are not tied to the Saudi state. As the name suggests, the Ahl-e Hadith movement emphasizes a return to the Qur'an and the sayings of the Prophet Muhammad as the sole sources of Islamic law and orthodoxy, rejecting later developments and local customs. The movement exemplifies the tension in Salafi thought between jihadist ideology on the one hand and obedience to the state on the other. The followers of the Ahl-e Hadith have at times embraced jihad, as with the Lashkar-e Taiba, an important Ahl-e Hadith jihadist organization in Pakistan that works closely with Pakistani intelligence. The Ahl-e Hadith in India, however, have remained rigidly quietist.

A common theme among these Salafi and Salafi-influenced movements is an emphasis on returning to the authentic, foundational sources of Islam. As such, they not only reject other Islamic religious traditions but are also hostile to veneration of Muslim holy men, mysticism, or other ideas that move away from a focus on the oneness of God and in their eyes smack of idolatry. They emphasize the study of the Qur'an and *hadith* and oppose importing foreign philosophies or practices, including secular Western ideas. Each of these movements began as reformist projects that endeavored to strip away the impurities introduced over centuries of religious ignorance.

Yet though Salafis all agree that Islam is a complete system, scholar Quintan Wiktorowicz points out that applying dogma to new issues and problems "is a human enterprise and therefore subject to different interpretations of context."[2] For example, Islam clearly prohibits attacks on civilians. But different scholars might have different takes on whether, say, civilian workers on a military compound are combatants or not. The result is division, even though Salafis claim to be a single school of thought.

Most of these movements' adherents are not jihadists, let alone members of Al Qaeda or the Islamic State. Although many embrace ideas about the proper role of Islam in society and have a hostility toward non-Sunnis and non-Muslims that jihadists also share, these movements have many members who focus on social welfare, accept the political authority in their state even if authoritarian or democratic (and thus not theocratic), and favor political quietism over violence. Many Salafi leaders are highly conservative in their willingness to oppose Muslim governments, contending that if a ruler claims to believe in God and allows such minimal activities as letting Muslims pray and practice Islam, he should be accorded the benefit of the doubt as to whether he is a true Muslim—no matter how repressive, corrupt, and dictatorial he may be. In addition, most believe that the best way to spread Islam is through proselytizing, not violence.

Many Salafi religious leaders reject Al Qaeda or at least some of its activities and attacks. Al Qaeda and like-minded groups, in turn, reject traditional religious leaders, believing they are at best misled by corrupt governments or at worst willing agents of apostate regimes. However, because Al Qaeda and associated movements recruit and fundraise primarily among communities that embrace Salafi ideas, the good opinion—or at least not the open hostility—of important Salafi religious figures is vital for both Al Qaeda's operational longevity and its continued ideological influence.

Who Are the Key Thinkers Jihadists Admire and Read?

Although Bin Laden and Zawahiri were not trained as theologians or recognized as religious leaders, they and other Al Qaeda members draw on a long and rich tradition of Islamic political thought to justify their actions. As with all great religions, Islam has many interpretations—and like all great religions, passions run high over theological disagreements. There are many figures, both significant and minor, on whom the jihadists draw. Their relative importance varies according to the concerns of the moment, but several stand out because of their historical importance, their veneration by modern jihadists, or the influence of their arguments.

Taqi al-Din Ibn Taymiyya was a thirteenth-century theologian whose teachings form the core of modern jihadist ideology. A regular critic both of political leaders for not enforcing Islamic law and of the religious establishment for neglecting the Qur'an and the beliefs and practices of the earliest Muslims, Ibn Taymiyya was an early model of conservative Islamic reform. At the time, the Mongols were rampaging throughout the lands of Islam—in 1258, Mongols captured and devastated Baghdad, the center of one of the great dynasties in Islam, pillaging the city and murdering hundreds of thousands. Ibn Taymiyya argued that the Mongol leaders, some of whom professed to be Muslims, were actually apostates because they frequently used Mongol customary law instead of Islamic law. The duty of obedience to a true Islamic ruler became a duty of rebellion against someone who rejected the word of God. In such circumstances, jihad was a religious obligation, akin to the "five pillars" of faith that all Muslims must accept and practice. From Ibn Taymiyya's teachings, jihadists today argue that political resistance is required if a leader does not enforce Islamic law.

Five centuries later, Muhammad Ibn Abd al-Wahhab preached similar ideas in the Arabian Peninsula, leading to the growth of Wahhabism—an austere form of Salafism. Ibn Abd al-Wahhab allied with an emerging political leader, Muhammad Ibn Saud. Ibn Saud's forces conquered the Arabian Peninsula, spreading Wahhabism and destroying shrines—including the tomb of the Prophet Muhammad (because they believed it represented a form of idolatry)—as they went. Contemporary Wahhabis are highly critical (to put it gently) of Shi'a, those who are Westernized, and non-Salafis in general, believing all to be deviant in their beliefs and behavior. The Saudi religious establishment, which educates Salafis from around the world, continues to embrace many of Ibn Abd al-Wahhab's ideas, and they are particularly important in shaping the worldview of Al Qaeda and the Islamic State.

One of the most important influences from the modern era on the global jihadist movement is Egyptian writer and activist Sayyid Qutb. In the early 1950s, Qutb headed the Muslim Brotherhood's propaganda department and was editor in chief of its newspaper. He was a visceral anti-Semite and was deeply contemptuous of the United States (and the West in general), believing it to be immoral due to its materialism and sexual and personal permissiveness. After Gamal Abdel Nasser came to power, Qutb was arrested, tortured, and eventually executed by the Egyptian regime in 1966.

One of Qutb's most important contributions to Al Qaeda's ideology comes from his discussion of *jahiliyya*, a term traditionally used to describe the period of ignorance before the birth of Islam. As Quintan Wiktorowicz contends, Muslims believe this was "a time when unbridled human desire ruled with unfettered brutality, resulting in abhorrent practices such as female infanticide."[3] In Qutb's influential book *Social Justice in Islam*, he argued that modern societies, including many supposedly Muslim countries (especially Egypt, where he lived), were in a state of *jahiliyya* because they emphasized materialism over true Islam. To remedy this, Qutb declared that faithful Muslims must take up arms and fight, forming a vanguard that would grow in power and strength and ultimately bring down the foundations of the entire *jahili* system (starting with the Egyptian regime, of course). Once the corrupt system was removed—and only then—the way would be clear for the establishment of a true Islamic society.

Qutb's views on social justice, Western cultural imperialism, and political activism influenced the thinking of Islamist groups around the world. But his influence on Al Qaeda was more than just ideological—it was personal: Zawahiri's uncle, Mahfouz Azzam, represented Qutb at his trial, and Muhammad Qutb, Sayyid Qutb's brother, was an associate of Abdullah Azzam, who was perhaps the most influential ideologue in the anti-Soviet jihad in Afghanistan and who had taught Bin Laden at King Abd al-Aziz University in Jeddah, Saudi Arabia.

Another key thinker was Muhammad Abd al-Salam Faraj, a jihadist active in Egypt in the late 1970s who briefly led and unified the movement that included Egypt's Islamic Group and Islamic Jihad (Zawahiri's organization). Around 1980, Faraj authored a pamphlet titled *The Neglected Duty*, which drew on the work of Ibn Taymiyya and continued Qutb's rejection of the legitimacy of the Egyptian regime. The "neglected duty" Faraj was referring to was jihad: in his view, Muslims should treat jihad the way they treated other obligations of the faith, such as prayer and charity, because practicing true Islam required an Islamic society and state. Faraj declared that the Egyptian government's Western-derived laws and brutality rendered it un-Islamic. For Faraj, fighting the near enemy—the Egyptian regime—was more important than fighting the far enemy—the imperialist powers (namely, the United

States and Israel). Faraj proclaimed: "There is no doubt that the first battlefield for *jihad* is the extermination of these infidel leaders and to replace them with a complete Islamic Order. This is the start."[4] Only once a true Islamic government had been installed could external enemies like Israel and the United States be fought. Faraj also believed that a dramatic act, such as the assassination of Egyptian President Anwar Sadat, would spark a popular revolution, and in 1981 his followers killed the Egyptian president. The Egyptian regime executed Faraj shortly after. Though Al Qaeda would come to embrace the opposite strategy—prioritizing the fight against the far enemy—Faraj's emphasis on defeating the near enemy first resonated strongly within the broader jihadist community; in addition, the influence of his ideas about the propaganda value of dramatic acts can be seen in the attacks Al Qaeda carried out on 9/11 as well as the beheading videos currently being produced by the Islamic State.

Abdullah Azzam is the ideological and organizational father of the "foreign fighter movement," from which Al Qaeda draws many of its recruits. Ibn Taymiyya, Ibn Abd al-Wahhab, Qutb, and Faraj all emphasized establishing a proper Islamic society and government and saw false Muslim leaders as the threat. Azzam, on the other hand, saw foreign enemies as the primary threat. As Thomas Hegghammer explains, Azzam was strongly influenced by the burgeoning pan-Islamic movement emerging in Saudi Arabia in the 1970s.[5] He believed that all Muslims were truly one people and that when infidels occupied Muslim lands, as happened when the Soviet Union invaded Afghanistan in 1979, Muslims everywhere had a duty to fight to expel the infidels. Azzam preached and wrote numerous works that inspired Muslims to fight in Afghanistan, raised money, and developed organizations, such as the Services Office, to facilitate the flow of foreign fighters to and from the battlefield. Unlike earlier jihadist ideologues (and many jihadists today), Azzam did not consider other Muslim governments to be illegitimate, urged fighters to focus on narrow theaters of war rather than all foes everywhere, and emphasized conventional military tactics, not terrorism. Azzam was assassinated in Pakistan in 1989—who was behind the assassination remains unclear to this day.

Abu Muhammad al-Maqdisi is perhaps the most important living ideologue in the Salafi-jihadist world today—far more influential than even Ayman al-Zawahiri. Maqdisi—whom Jordan jailed for many years but released in early 2015—has been praised by his supporters as the "Ibn Taymiyya of our age."[6] However, as Joas Wagemakers points out, Maqdisi's views are quite distinct from those of Al Qaeda.[7] Maqdisi focuses on the struggle against illegitimate regimes in Muslim countries, whose overthrow he justifies on the basis of their apostasy and their alliances with non-Muslim powers. Maqdisi has criticized jihadist groups for focusing on the Shi'a, as in Iraq, or on the United States and Israel, as Al Qaeda emphasizes. Maqdisi is also more tolerant—by Salafi-jihadist standards, at least—of the Muslim Brotherhood and other more mainstream political Islamist movements. He rejects their Islamic legitimacy, but he calls for preaching and other peaceful means to show them the light, rather than taking up arms against them when they are in power, as they were briefly in Egypt and are currently in Tunisia and the Gaza Strip.[8] Like Faraj, Maqdisi contends that all these other struggles can wait until there is a true Islamic government that can unify believers and harness the power of the state. The purpose of fighting is to create areas that are de facto Islamic states. In these areas, even as they fight, jihadists should also proselytize and otherwise try to change the behavior of those in the territory they control, rather than using force to compel proper behavior.

Maqdisi's teachings influenced Abu Musab al-Zarqawi, the founder of Al Qaeda in Iraq, though Maqdisi would later criticize Zarqawi's emphasis on killing Iraqi Shi'a. Later, Maqdisi would also rebuke the Islamic State, Al Qaeda in Iraq's successor, for its brutality against fellow Muslims. Indeed, though the Islamic State would seem to be following Maqdisi's emphasis on controlling territory and instituting Islamic governance, Maqdisi rejects the Islamic State's harsh treatment of Muslims under its control and calls for the group to use preaching, not punishment, to sway people to the true path.

Many other contemporary thinkers influence the modern Salafi-jihadist movement, and fighters often seek out those whose views support whatever it is they already plan to do. Even so, the ideas and support of these thinkers are vital for the jihadist cause—inspiring them to take up arms, guiding them as they decide whom and what to target, enabling them to justify their actions, and helping them raise recruits and money.

How Does Al Qaeda Differ from the Muslim Brotherhood?

The Muslim Brotherhood is the oldest modern Islamist political movement in the Arab world, and perhaps the most important. Founded in Egypt in 1928, it now has branches or spinoffs in Kuwait, Jordan, Libya, Morocco, Sudan, Yemen, and other Muslim countries, and its thinkers and teachers have influenced Islamist movements around the world. Although Brotherhood members share a common outlook, the movement itself is organized by country, and one branch does not control another.

The Brotherhood rejects Western political and social models and calls for the application of Islamic law (*shari'a*) and the Islamicization of society. At times, different branches have engaged in violence: Hamas, the Palestinian terrorist group, grew out of the Muslim Brotherhood in Gaza; in the late 1970s, the Brotherhood in Syria led a bloody revolt against the regime of Hafez al-Asad, and its members became prominent in the struggle against Hafez's son Bashar as Syria descended into civil war in 2011; after World War II, the Muslim Brotherhood in Egypt was also behind several terrorist attacks.

Salafi-jihadists draw on Brotherhood thinkers, particularly Sayyid Qutb, and some strands of Brotherhood thinking overlap considerably with the ideas of the global jihadists. Yet at their core, Salafi-jihadists and the Muslim Brotherhood are fundamentally different and vehemently at odds. Unlike Salafis, Muslim Brotherhood thinkers accept a role for human reasoning in interpreting the Qur'an. Unlike jihadists, the Brotherhood, in most countries most of the time, has rejected violence—most notably in Egypt, where by the 1980s the Brotherhood had accepted a modus vivendi with the Mubarak regime and, while never fully legalized, participated in the country's (largely powerless) parliament. In Kuwait, Jordan, Yemen, and elsewhere, Brotherhood groups have also participated in peaceful politics. Unlike Al Qaeda, the Muslim Brotherhood embraces missionary work and social welfare projects—such as establishing free primary schools and low-cost community health clinics—as part of their strategy of grassroots activism and their efforts to Islamicize society from the bottom up.

Such pragmatism and willingness to accommodate those in power angers Al Qaeda and other global jihadists. In his book *The Bitter Harvest*, Zawahiri sharply criticizes Brotherhood leaders in

Egypt for rejecting violence and participating in politics. Hamas has also been on the receiving end of vitriol from Al Qaeda, which denounced its ceasefires with Israel and refusal to fully impose Islamic law in Gaza. Hamas has even bloodily repressed jihadists in the Gaza Strip whose ideology is akin to that of Al Qaeda.

The Brotherhood is both a potential bridge and a potential barrier for Salafi-jihadist terrorist groups like Al Qaeda. On the one hand, the Brotherhood propagates the call for a true Islamic society and fosters a religious and politicized worldview that shares similarities with the Al Qaeda worldview. Many Al Qaeda members, including Zawahiri, who briefly joined the Brotherhood as a teen, went through the Brotherhood's ranks. On the other hand, the Muslim Brotherhood's willingness to accommodate rulers whom Al Qaeda deems apostates, its general rejection of violence, and its openness to electoral participation offer an alternative vision of how to create an Islamic society that is far more popular than the vision Al Qaeda promotes—largely because the Brotherhood's vision is less extreme and does not involve violence. Thus, Al Qaeda sees the Brotherhood and its activities as a threat to the terrorist group's ability to fundraise and recruit, and indeed as a fundamental threat to the jihadists' very legitimacy.

The Muslim Brotherhood holds up participation in the electoral process as a peaceful and more effective alternative to the Salafi-jihadist call for violence; as such, the success or failure of peaceful politics will have a profound impact on their rivalry. Jihadists have long pointed to the Brotherhood's failure to gain power as proof that Brotherhood leaders were making compromises with no hope of success. The emergence of Brotherhood-affiliated regimes after the Arab Spring countered this argument, but the 2013 coup in Egypt that saw the democratically-elected Brotherhood government overthrown by the military was viewed by Salafi-jihadists as vindication that force is the only path to victory.

Why Do Other Jihadists Criticize Al Qaeda?

Appalled by the carnage in Iraq after the post-2003 anti-US resistance morphed into a sectarian civil war and other setbacks to the jihadist cause, former supporters in Egypt, Saudi Arabia, and elsewhere excoriated Al Qaeda for misinterpreting Islam and killing innocent Muslims. The criticism came from a powerful mix of imprisoned jihadists, rival group members, and clerics once considered sympathetic to Al Qaeda.

In 2002, Egypt's Islamic Group, the more numerous and politically important organization that for many years had both collaborated and argued with Zawahiri's Islamic Jihad faction, began to publish a series of works titled "Series for Correcting Ideas" (*Silsilat Tashih al-Mafahim*) that painstakingly addressed all of the ways in which Al Qaeda has misinterpreted jihad and resolutely condemned the use of violence against civilians. In 2007, leaders of the Libyan jihadist movement, one of the most important during Al Qaeda's formative period in the early 1990s, also denounced Al Qaeda. Salman al-Ouda, the Saudi sheikh who gained wide popularity for his criticism of the Saudi royal family's ties to the United States in the 1990s, also condemned Al Qaeda: "My brother Osama, how much blood has been spilt? How many innocent people, children, elderly, and women have been killed... in the name of Al Qaeda? Will you be happy to meet God Almighty carrying the burden of these hundreds of thousands or millions on your back?"[9]

Rank-and-file jihadist sympathizers have also raised concerns. During a 2008 "open meeting" Zawahiri held online, in which he took electronically submitted questions, questioners angrily criticized the group for killing innocent Muslims.[10] One critic demanded:

Excuse me, Mr. Zawahiri, but who is it who is killing with Your Excellency's blessing the innocents in Baghdad, Morocco and Algeria? Do you consider the killing of women and children to be Jihad? I challenge you and your organization to do that in Tel Aviv. Why have you—to this day—not carried out any strike in Israel? Or is it easier to kill Muslims in the markets? Maybe it is necessary [for you] to take some geography lessons, because your maps only show the Muslims' states.

Perhaps the most damning criticism came from the theologian and former Egyptian Islamic Jihad (EIJ) leader Sayyid Imam al-Sharif (known as Dr. Fadl), who had been present at the meeting that founded Al Qaeda. Fadl and Zawahiri, both doctors, had been young revolutionaries in Egypt together, lived in exile in Pakistan in the 1980s, and otherwise spent years as comrades in arms. In 1988, Fadl published *The Essential Guide for Preparation*, a 500-page guidebook for aspiring jihadists that would eventually be translated into nine languages and read by militants from Afghanistan to Indonesia; later he would author *The Compendium of the Pursuit of Divine Knowledge*, another important tract. Fadl was extreme: he initially argued that Muslims are always in conflict with non-Muslims and that Arab rulers are apostates—and so too are the many who support them or acquiesce in their rule. Fadl's teachings damned millions rather than just a few corrupt regime leaders.[11]

Fadl was captured after 9/11 and eventually jailed in Egypt. In 2007, Fadl blasted Al Qaeda in his broadside of a book, *The Document for Right Guidance for Jihad Activity in Egypt and the World*. Fadl, writing from inside prison, proclaimed that EIJ had "erred enormously from an Islamic point of view" by allowing "killing based on nationality, color of skin and hair or based on religious doctrine" and that those who target innocent people, including Bin Laden, Zawahiri, and their cohorts, "place their own desires and will before that of Allah's."[12] In a press interview, he called Zawahiri a "charlatan" and declared Al Qaeda attacks "a catastrophe for Muslims."[13] Many other EIJ members also in prison signed their names to Fadl's book as well, effectively making it a ceasefire declaration by some of Zawahiri's—and Al Qaeda's—earliest supporters.

Critics like Fadl blame the group for the growth of the doctrine of *takfir*, in which Muslims arrogate the right to declare others non-believers—a stance that the vast majority of conservative Islamic scholars reject. "It is not permissible for a Muslim to condemn another Muslim," writes Fadl.[14] The irony is that Al Qaeda has tried to limit the *takfiri* influence in the broader jihadist movement; for instance, Zawahiri warned Zarqawi, leader of Al Qaeda in Iraq, not to kill ordinary Shi'a and especially not to kill Sunni religious and tribal figures—but to no avail, as Al Qaeda in Iraq even killed members of rival Sunni insurgent groups. However, Zawahiri issued his warnings in private, as he did not want to alienate this important segment of the cause, and the result was that Al Qaeda was tarred with the brush of its affiliated group.

Al Qaeda's detractors also argue that the scope of violent jihad is actually much more narrow than Al Qaeda has made it out to be and believe that the slaughter of civilians—for example, in Algeria in the 1990s and Iraq after 2003; the 2005 attacks by Al Qaeda in Iraq on three hotels in Jordan that killed at least 67 people, including members of a wedding party that according to the groom included no Westerners; and similar atrocities—has led jihadists into the abyss, going far beyond the level of killing that Islam sanctions. They assert that knowingly killing civilians, inherent in attacks on targets like hotels and public transportation, is always wrong. Fadl stresses that even killing Christians and Jews is wrong: "They are the neighbors of the Muslims. . . and being kind to one's neighbors is a religious duty." He also argues that Muslims living under non-Muslim rule in the West have been given an opportunity to work, study, and live and rejects any "betrayal" of this by using violence.

Finally, Al Qaeda's critics make practical arguments. They point out that the killing of ordinary Muslims has alienated the population: rather than being seen as heroes, jihadists are painted as criminals, and brutal regimes gain support. In addition, taking on the United States has led to the death or imprisonment of thousands of jihadists and the overthrow of the Taliban, a true Muslim government. As Fadl wrote, "Ramming America has become the shortest road to fame and leadership among the Arabs and Muslims. But what good is it if you destroy one of your enemy's buildings, and he destroys one of your countries? What good is it if you kill one of his people, and he kills a thousand of yours?. . . That, in short, is my evaluation of 9/11."[15]

Al Qaeda's leaders pointed out that Fadl was in jail when he wrote his criticism: In a video message, Zawahiri sarcastically asked, "Do they now have fax machines in Egyptian jail cells? I wonder if they're connected to the same line as the electric-shock machines," and announced the publication of a massive tome he had written as a refutation of these critics titled *The Exoneration*.[16] However, although Al Qaeda can dismiss these and other critics as sellouts, the credibility of these figures, some of whom have struggled and bled for the jihadist cause, others of whom are highly respected religious scholars—and the fact that they are not alone—makes them hard to ignore.

More than any "public diplomacy" or propaganda from the United States and allied regimes, these critiques decrease the appeal and power of Zawahiri's movement. Government appeals to provide information and to cease offering these groups money gain more support. The criticisms also hinder recruitment when young Muslims no longer believe that violence is religiously sanctioned and realize that their communities will not see them as heroes.

How Does Al Qaeda Justify Killing Civilians?

Al Qaeda did not always target civilians. Bin Laden in 1991 had drawn a distinction between the American people and the American government, noting that the former "don't even vote, they are totally apathetic" and thus could not be legitimately targeted.[17] Early suicide attacks by EIJ operatives were widely condemned, even in extremist circles, because suicide operations were seen as contrary to Islam. The EIJ's attack on the Egyptian embassy in Islamabad in 1995, which killed 16 people, was criticized—even by Bin Laden—because it killed innocents. Bin Laden himself considered bombing the US embassy in Saudi Arabia in the early 1990s but rejected the operation because many civilians would die. Even Bin Laden's 1996 *fatwa* calling for attacks on the United States emphasizes attacks on soldiers, not civilians. For most of this period, Al Qaeda focused on supporting jihadist insurgencies, not international terrorism. However, by 1998, Bin Laden and his supporters would declare that "to kill the Americans and their allies—civilians and military—is an individual duty for every Muslim who can do it in any country in which it is possible to do it."[18] Over 15 years later, Al Qaeda continues to call for the killing of American civilians.

When addressing Western audiences, as in Bin Laden's 2002 "Letter to the American People," Al Qaeda justifies killing American civilians by arguing that because America is a democracy, "the American people are the ones who choose their government by way of their own free will; a choice which stems from their agreement to its policies."[19] Thus, the American people are complicit in America's policies in the Muslim world. To avoid Al Qaeda attacks, Americans can and should elect a new government that will change these policies. Similarly, Al Qaeda asserts that American civilians are legitimate targets because "[t]he American people are the ones who pay the taxes which fund the planes that bomb us in Afghanistan, the tanks that strike and destroy our homes in Palestine, the armies which occupy our lands in the Arabian Gulf, and the fleets which ensure the blockade of Iraq."[20] Al Qaeda also justifies its actions by pointing to the legitimacy of its cause: in a 1998 interview, Bin Laden argued that "the terrorism we practice is of the commendable kind as it is directed at the tyrants and the aggressors and the enemies of Allah."[21] Bin Laden also contended that America is simply getting a taste of its own medicine, claiming that the United States does not differentiate between civilians and soldiers or children and adults in its targeting and citing the atomic bombs dropped on Japan as a perfect example. Only "retaliation in kind" can stop America.

In the wake of the 9/11 attacks, prominent Islamic legal scholars and even the founder of Hamas issued a scathing condemnation of Al Qaeda for attacking civilians. The attacks were denounced as "un-Islamic," "against all human and Islamic norms," and "gross crimes and sinful acts."[22] After six months of noticeable silence, Al Qaeda finally issued a response, laying out in detail its religious justification for killing civilians.

As Quintan Wiktorowicz and John Kaltner explain in their remarkable analysis of the Al Qaeda statement, "al-Qaeda argues that the prohibition [against killing civilians] is not an absolute one and that there are conditions under which killing civilians becomes permissible." Using a combination of cherry-picked Qur'anic verses, medieval legal rulings, and creatively interpreted examples from Islamic history, Al Qaeda addresses each of the seven conditions under which, according to Islamic legal tradition, one can legitimately target civilians.

The first condition is reciprocity: since America has targeted Muslim civilians in Iraq and elsewhere, it is now legal for Muslims to target American civilians. Condition two is the inability to distinguish civilians from combatants: as long as enemy fighters are present and the target (that is, the building or fortification) is a legitimate one, it can be attacked, even if it means civilians may also be killed. This is related to condition three: assistance of civilians in "deed, word, or mind." According to this condition, anyone who helps the war effort is a legitimate target—that includes journalists and academics, who contribute by providing knowledge useful to the war effort, as well as people who work for companies that supply the government or military. Condition four is the necessity of war: if civilians will be killed in the act of taking out an enemy stronghold that is critical to the enemy's war effort, then it is permissible to kill civilians. Condition five is heavy weaponry: Al Qaeda refers to a story in which the Prophet Muhammad allowed Muslim fighters to use a catapult against the enemy, claiming that the planes used in the 9/11 attacks are the modern-day equivalent of such "heavy weaponry," and are thus allowed. (It's a bit of a stretch.) Condition six is human shields: "Al Qaeda argues that it is permissible to kill women, children and other protected groups if the enemy uses them as human shields (*turs*)."[23] The seventh and final condition is violation of a treaty: Al Qaeda claims, "It is allowed for Muslims to kill protected ones among unbelievers if the people of a treaty violate their treaty and the leader must kill them in order to teach them a lesson."

As Wiktorowicz and Kaltner correctly note, "The sheer breadth of these conditions leaves ample theological justification for killing civilians in almost any imaginable situation."[24] However, despite their best efforts to legitimize their atrocities, Al Qaeda largely failed to convince the vast majority of credible Islamic legal scholars that the killing of thousands of American civilians on 9/11 was anything but an act of barbarism, way beyond even the outermost limits of what is permissible in Islam. In the eyes of the elite scholars of the Islamic legal establishment, Al Qaeda's arguments are seen as sophomoric and are quickly dismissed. And although Al Qaeda has proclaimed time and again that it unequivocally rejects the authority of the Islamic religious establishment, the fact that it felt the need to issue a formal, detailed rebuttal in response to the condemnation of the establishment suggests that even if Al Qaeda itself does not recognize the legitimacy of the establishment, it at least recognizes that much of the Muslim world still does, and that to remain silent in the face of criticism from such respected authority figures would be to risk losing the admiration and support of many potential recruits and supporters.

What Themes Does Al Qaeda Push in Its Propaganda?

Propaganda and proselytizing have been part of Al Qaeda's core mission from the start. Al Qaeda leaders believe they should teach potential followers not only how to fight, but also how to think. Unlike many jihadist groups, Al Qaeda wants to shape the ideological vanguard as well serve as its instrument. In its use of terrorism and fighting in general, Al Qaeda tries to follow Zawahiri's statement that "more than half of this battle is taking place in the battlefield of the media."[25]

Al Qaeda promotes the idea of jihad as the "neglected duty," to use the words of Egyptian radical Muhammad Abd al-Salam Faraj. According to this view, jihad is incumbent upon all Muslims because Muslim lands are under attack from apostate rulers and Western powers (particularly the United States). All able-bodied young men are commanded to join the fight directly, and the rest—including women, children, and the elderly—are charged to contribute financially or otherwise support and encourage the jihad.

As a natural complement to efforts to change the discourse within the jihadist movement, Al Qaeda recognized early on the value of propaganda and how it might be used to attract supporters and undermine enemies. Al Qaeda's parent organization, the Services Office, took an important early stride by publishing the magazine *Al Jihad* in 1984—a move that Bin Laden himself sponsored. The inaugural issue set the tone for later themes of the jihad: the heroism of the *mujahedin*, the atheism and satanic nature of the foe, the glorification of martyrdom, and the requirement of jihad as a fulfillment of religious duties. In addition to *Al Jihad*, the Services Office used pictures and movies from the battlefield in its fundraising and recruiting drives—an approach that Al Qaeda later made into an art form. Similarly, the 1986 publication of the "will" of a martyr in *Al Jihad* and Zawahiri's 1993 videotaping of the testimony of a suicide bomber before his failed attempt to kill the Egyptian Interior Minister are tactics that eventually became staples of the Al Qaeda propaganda machine.

The media has always been an instrument that Al Qaeda has used to great effect. In the years before 9/11, Bin Laden occasionally gave interviews, and Al Qaeda videotaped operations and statements by would-be martyrs for future use. When John Miller of *ABC News* interviewed Bin Laden before 9/11, Zawahiri anticipated Miller's need for background footage and even used technical jargon such as "B roll" that indicated his familiarity with modern media practices.[26] Since 9/11, Al Qaeda's information operations have exploded in scope. *As-Sahab* (The Clouds), Al Qaeda's media arm, offers near-constant commentary on major events in the West and the Muslim world, using solid production skills.

As technology has evolved, so has Al Qaeda propaganda. Al Qaeda first created print magazines and issued press releases. Later it released its own videos to be shown on satellite television. As the Internet spread, Al Qaeda propaganda showed up online. At first, there were only a handful of Internet sites promoting a jihadist message; now there are thousands, though many appear and disappear according to the interests (and freedom) of their sponsors. Social media platforms like YouTube, Twitter, and Facebook spread jihadist content, with individual members reaching out to friends and followers as mini-propagandists (something the Islamic State has mastered).

Affiliates also develop their own propaganda. The most remarkable example of this is the online magazine *Inspire*, created by Al Qaeda in the Arabian Peninsula. *Inspire* is a stylish, professional-looking jihadist news and lifestyle magazine written in idiomatic English that is designed to appeal to a younger, Western, media-savvy audience (though Arabic translations of the magazine are published online as well).[27] The magazine, which as of spring 2014 had produced 12 issues, features high-quality, full-color photographs, letters from the editor, advice columns, interviews with prominent jihadist thinkers, and how-to articles, such as the one that garnered much attention in the Western media when it came out, titled "Make a bomb in the kitchen of your Mom."

The quality and sophistication of the magazine, both in terms of design and content, shocked many Western observers who still clung to outdated notions of Al Qaeda terrorists as backward, semi-literate savages hiding in remote mountain caves. Even more frightening, perhaps, was the realization of just how closely they were watching everything that was happening in the West, and especially the United States. Every issue of *Inspire* magazine so far has included a section titled "Hear the World," which features a list of quotes from "friend and foe." In addition to the obligatory quotes by Al Qaeda leaders and sympathetic quasi-religious figures, there are also quotes from prominent Western politicians, intelligence and law enforcement officials, and terrorism scholars talking about Al Qaeda and related issues, including the successes and failures of various counterterrorism strategies.

These media efforts target multiple audiences. First, they seek to threaten or cajole the United States and other Western enemies.

Second, they try to inspire the broader Muslim world, including Muslims in the West, to support the movement. Third, they try to influence those already in militant organizations to join Al Qaeda and adopt its agenda. Zawahiri, with his focus on media and communications, appears to have learned his lesson from EIJ's failure to act as a vanguard in Egypt where it shunned grassroots action, and he now warns that the movement must not "get isolated from its nation."[28] When a terrorist group becomes isolated from popular support, funding and recruits dry up. Even more dangerous, the population is more likely to cooperate with intelligence and police services, making it harder for the terrorist group to operate without disruption.

Through its attacks and propaganda, Al Qaeda has moved the narrative in the Muslim world away from what it was in the early days of the group's founding. Powerful jihadist cadres from Yemen, Algeria, and elsewhere now focus on Americans and other Westerners as well as on their local problems, and attacks on US forces, once considered ancillary (or even detrimental) to the goals of militant Sunni movements in the Middle East, are widely seen as both legitimate and essential. So too is the glorification of violence as part of jihad. The spread of these ideas is a core part of Al Qaeda's mission and one that ensures that its influence spreads far beyond the organization itself.

5

ORGANIZATION AND RECRUITMENT

Why Was Bin Laden Such an Effective Leader?

Perhaps no terrorist in history has created, nurtured, and managed a terrorist group as effectively as Osama Bin Laden. His success lies both in his personal story and in the unusual mix of traits he embodied, many of which he imbued in Al Qaeda.

Bin Laden grew up a scion of one of the wealthiest families in Saudi Arabia. A poor Yemeni in origin, his father Mohammad bin Awad bin Laden immigrated to Saudi Arabia and worked as a porter. He then founded his own construction company and eventually grew staggeringly rich as Saudi Arabia boomed from oil wealth. Osama Bin Laden himself was the seventeenth son: Mohammad fathered over 50 children to over 20 wives, though as a pious Muslim he maintained only four wives at a time, the marital limit according to Muslim scholars.

Mohammad's son Osama grew up pious and, despite his family's wealth, traveled relatively little. While a student at a university in Saudi Arabia, Osama was inspired to join the anti-Soviet jihad in Afghanistan. Because of his wealth and connections, Pakistani and Afghan leaders welcomed him, as did other Afghan Arab volunteers. Working with Abdullah Azzam, whose writings and propaganda helped create the Arab influx to Afghanistan, Bin Laden founded the Services Office to assist Arabs coming to fight with the *mujahedin*. He soon joined the fray himself, fighting bravely, if rather ineffectively, at the Battle of Jaji. While in Pakistan and Afghanistan, his unusual story—a man who could be enjoying every luxury but who chose instead to live in poverty and risk his life to help other Muslims—inspired other volunteers. Here, it seemed, was a man truly committed to his faith.

Bin Laden's personal wealth was vital to his initial success. Generous with his own fortune, he attracted attention from a range of jihadist groups, all of which were perennially cash strapped. The thousands of dollars Bin Laden gave to various groups and individuals from his own purse helped these movements sustain themselves and led some experienced jihadists, such as his partner and eventual successor Ayman al-Zawahiri, to work with Bin Laden by necessity. When Al Qaeda moved to Sudan, Bin Laden invested much of his personal fortune there, which helped him gain entrée with the Sudanese regime. However, relations eventually soured, and in 1996, the regime in Khartoum seized all of Bin Laden's assets within the country and forced him out, leaving him in a much weaker financial position. It was also during his time in Sudan that the Saudi regime persuaded his family to cut him off financially. Nevertheless, because of his family connections and over time his growing prestige, he also had access to the so-called Golden Chain of financiers in the Gulf states, particularly in Saudi Arabia.

Wealth made Bin Laden an asset, but it was his charisma that made him a leader. Bin Laden did not have the fiery charisma of revolutionary figures like Iran's Ayatollah Khomeini, and unlike terrorist leaders such as the Liberation Tigers of Tamil Eelam's Velupillai Prabhakaran or Sendero Luminoso's Abimael Guzmán, Bin Laden did not foster a cult of personality among his followers. Journalist John Miller, who interviewed Bin Laden in the spring of 1998, had this description of the enigmatic leader:

> He had a kind of calm in him that I did not expect. What I expected was somebody in the mold of the "Blind Sheikh" (the Egyptian cleric Omar Abdel Rahman), a fiery orator who would be pumping his fist and saying a lot of things at the top of his lungs. If you didn't lean into bin Laden, you couldn't hear him. . . . His deputies looked up to him as a great leader and a guy that they would follow into anything. There is that

charismatic aura or a scent that make people follow him; either you have it or you don't. They spoke of him with god-like reverence. . . .[1]

His bearing was calm and quiet, but he proved able to inspire his followers and, as time went on, a broad swath of the Muslim world. Bin Laden also had a vision. In his rhetoric, Bin Laden mixed religious and historical references and identified a host of problems that Muslims, especially Arabs, had to contend with around the world. Bin Laden blamed the Muslim world's problems on a turn away from Islam. Over time he became convinced that the West, and the United States in general, was the Muslim world's primary enemy. This view, which few held in the early 1990s, would become far more mainstream in large part because of his influence. Zawahiri, who had long focused his efforts exclusively on Egypt, even became a convert. Noman Benotman, a former Libyan jihadist interviewed by Peter Bergen, told him, "Osama influenced Zawahiri with his idea: Forget about the 'near enemy'; the main enemy is the Americans."[2]

Bin Laden also proved an excellent manager. In creating Al Qaeda, he established a movement that could operate in both a centralized and decentralized manner, taking advantage of what each approach had to offer. From the start, Bin Laden's organization stressed the need for team players and experienced operatives, striving to become an elite organization. This made it far more formidable. Bin Laden took advantage of his wealth, using it to seed and nurture organizations and proselytize through propaganda, training camps, and Al Qaeda's own attacks, effectively spreading his message among his followers and to a much larger audience. The jihadist movement was (and remains) riven by ideological battles and personality divisions, but he used his money and good offices to try to build bridges and otherwise unite this fractious movement.

In contrast to the eagerness of most terrorists, Al Qaeda's leaders are unusually patient—a quality Bin Laden sought in his lieutenants.[3] Al Qaeda is willing to promote operations that take years to bear fruit, such as the 1998 embassy bombings, which took five years from start to finish. Bin Laden was also willing to double down and renew an attempt after a plot was apparently disrupted, as happened in East Africa before the 1998 embassy bombings. Other terrorist leaders, in contrast, fear failure and demand constant action.

In the end, Bin Laden's greatest accomplishment is what lives on after him: Al Qaeda survived his death, and like-minded organizations have sprouted up throughout the Muslim world. Perhaps even more important for Bin Laden, his views—especially his call to fight the United States and other "far enemies"—are no longer fringe ideas and continue to this day to inspire young Muslims, many of whom have never met an Al Qaeda member, to take up arms.

How Does Ayman al-Zawahiri Differ from Bin Laden?

Whereas Bin Laden's father was a staggeringly wealthy self-made man, Ayman al-Zawahiri's childhood was less opulent but more established, as he was born into Egypt's elite. As Lawrence Wright reports, Zawahiri's father was a doctor, as were many of his relatives, and a great uncle had been the Grand Imam of Al-Azhar, the venerable center of Islamic learning in Egypt. On his mother's side, his grandfather had been the president of Cairo University. Yet despite their social class, Ayman's parents did not seek out other elites in Egypt or try to Westernize their family. They were pious Muslims at a time when many Egyptian elites embraced a more secular identity.

Ayman al-Zawahiri himself was a brilliant student—he would eventually continue the family tradition and become a doctor—but he also was aloof.[4] He quickly became involved in politics and formed his first revolutionary cell at the age of 15. Inspired at first by the execution of Sayyid Qutb, the radical Egyptian Islamist thinker, and drawing on the resurgence of religiosity in Egypt in the 1970s, Zawahiri joined with other young Egyptian radicals who sought to turn the country into an Islamic state and who were critical of Egyptian President Anwar Sadat's peace deal with Israel, embrace of the United States, and eagerness to Westernize the country. In the late 1970s, Zawahiri's group eventually merged with other like-minded cells to form Egyptian Islamic Jihad (EIJ). Members of the cell would assassinate Sadat in 1981 (a move Zawahiri wisely opposed as "emotional" and "poorly planned"[5]), provoking a massive crackdown that led to many executions and arrests, including the arrest of Zawahiri. Zawahiri was tortured while in prison and was forced to inform on his comrades, further radicalizing him. He was released from prison in 1984 and fled the country in 1985.

Zawahiri had first gone to help the anti-Soviet struggle as a doctor in 1980, staying for several months as part of the relief effort in Pakistan. When he eventually returned there after leaving Egypt, though, Zawahiri's main goal was to rebuild EIJ, not to fight the Soviets (unlike most other Arabs). While in Pakistan, he restored EIJ's leadership, communications, and operations networks, none of which could be done in Egypt given the strong police state there.

Zawahiri appeared unlikely to be a leader of Al Qaeda. For many years, Zawahiri focused on overthrowing the Egyptian government, not Al Qaeda's broader war against the United States. In 1993, he declared establishing an Islamic state in Egypt to be his group's primary objective—more important even than the struggle to liberate the Palestinian territories, going so far as to declare, "The Road to Jerusalem passes through Cairo."[6] The near enemy—apostate regimes in the Middle East—were his focus, not the far enemy (the United States).

Despite the initial differences in ideology between Zawahiri and Bin Laden, much of what we associate today with Al Qaeda actually began with Zawahiri and his Egyptian comrades. In 1993, Zawahiri's group used a suicide bomber to try to kill Egypt's hated Interior Minister, even though at the time Sunni religious figures uniformly rejected suicide attacks because they violated Islam's taboo against taking one's own life. Zawahiri also had his followers make martyrdom videos that would be disseminated after their deaths to inspire others, a technique Al Qaeda would also embrace.[7] Having watched Egyptian groups repeatedly fail to orchestrate a coup, spark a popular uprising, or create an insurgency, Zawahiri developed a respect for the need for secrecy, planning, and training as keys for success. As Essam Deraz, an Egyptian filmmaker who documented the *mujahedin* in Afghanistan, told Wright, Zawahiri's people "had experience in secret work. They knew how to organize themselves and create secret cells. And they became the leaders."[8] Zawahiri also became skeptical that the population would play a major role, advocating a "vanguard" strategy instead.[9]

Zawahiri's followers would form the initial core of Al Qaeda's leadership. The purpose at first appears to have been to exploit Bin Laden (and his resources) to bolster EIJ. Through Al Qaeda, EIJ had access to Bin Laden's money and to training camps, but access to a safe haven was particularly important. Being in Sudan, on Egypt's border, in the early 1990s offered excellent access to Zawahiri's main enemy at the time. As EIJ began to wither under the assault of the Egyptian government, Zawahiri found it hard to pay operatives, care for their families, and otherwise sustain the organization. By cultivating ties with Bin Laden, Zawahiri and his organization were able to live to fight another day.

As EIJ itself faded, Zawahiri became more closely associated with Al Qaeda and its distinct goals, first as an artifice to exploit Bin Laden, then by necessity due to financial woes, and finally by conviction. One Egyptian jihadist testified that Bin Laden argued that attacks in Egypt were too costly in terms of lives and money as the government was too strong and that Zawahiri should instead turn his organization's guns on the United States and Israel. Over time, Zawahiri would come to embrace this argument. Part of this change may have been due to a genuine ideological shift, but the collapse of the effort in Egypt, along with the aggressive US assistance to disrupt EIJ networks outside Egypt, also made Zawahiri more willing to change his lifelong goal. In 1998, EIJ allied with Al Qaeda, changed its organizational goals to match those of Bin Laden, and ceased all attacks inside Egypt; in 2001, the two groups officially merged.

In contrast to Bin Laden, Zawahiri is not charismatic. In person and in his rhetoric, he is more plodding than inspiring. A friend and revolutionary mentor told him early in his career, "Remember, if you are a member of any group, you cannot be the leader."[10] Nor does he have Bin Laden's personal story to inspire others. Although respected for his dedication to jihad, he did not directly fight the Soviets, and his betrayal of other EIJ members under torture further diminishes any attempts to cultivate a heroic myth.

Zawahiri, while different in style from Bin Laden, shares his pragmatism. Though more pedantic and dogmatic than Bin Laden in tone, Zawahiri has repeatedly shown that he can learn from his mistakes and has proved willing to work with groups that are not ideological bedfellows. Having learned firsthand how poor tradecraft can doom a revolutionary movement, he and his deputies in Al Qaeda constantly stress the critical importance of communications secrecy and compartmenting information. When offering guidance to groups in Syria and Yemen, he notes the mistakes the organization made in

Iraq and calls on them to work better with the population. Zawahiri also proved willing to work with Iran, despite what is probably a personal loathing for the Shi'ite regime, because both share common enemies and Al Qaeda needs any help it can get.

In the end, Zawahiri is a steely professional: he perseveres rather than triumphs. Though some thought Al Qaeda would collapse after Bin Laden's death, Zawahiri has held it together and in some ways has even improved its position despite the formidable US-led counterterrorism campaign.

How Is Al Qaeda Organized?

Al Qaeda has had multiple organizational structures in its over 25-year history, but in general, it has sought to be highly structured—not, as often portrayed, a loose network. However, outside pressure and the nature of the global jihadist movement have sometimes led it to become more decentralized and network-based. Making this picture even more complex, Al Qaeda has at times used centralized and decentralized methods simultaneously. In the end, this mix of organizational styles makes it difficult to speak of one form of Al Qaeda organization and blurs the line between where Al Qaeda begins and ends.

When Al Qaeda was created, members were required to swear loyalty to its *emir* (leader)—Bin Laden—and this requirement continued when Zawahiri took the helm. The *emir* is responsible for all of Al Qaeda's activities, and according to internal Al Qaeda documents, he should be "fair, speaks the truth, not greedy, intelligent, discerning, patient, treat people equally, farsighted, not a sinner, without the appearance of affluence, bold and resolute." Experience fighting jihad, leadership experience, and some Islamic legal knowledge were also necessary. University graduates were preferred.[11] In the beginning, the organization comprised individual committees charged with managing specific aspects of the organization, including military operations, foreign affairs, finances and administration, political issues, religious matters, intelligence and internal security, and propaganda and media affairs (at first headed by a jihadist nicknamed "Abu Reuter"). Al Qaeda also has an advisory committee, which is the second-highest decision-making body within the organization, below the *emir*, and is composed of its top members.

Since 9/11, when operations were more centralized, Al Qaeda's activities have varied along the spectrum of control and coordination, with some involving little role for the core beyond strategic guidance and others involving far more participation. Terrorism experts Bruce Hoffman and Fernando Reinares found that Al Qaeda core's command and control was "uneven" but that senior Al Qaeda leaders "appeared to have had a direct hand in the most important and potentially high-payoff operations."[12]

Despite its many formal bureaucratic structures, Al Qaeda is also highly informal and networked. Veterans of the anti-Soviet jihad and subsequent jihadist struggles formed close personal ties, including marriage bonds between fighters and the daughters and sisters of their comrades. Al Qaeda itself historically had resources, particularly money and control of training camps, and legitimacy, enabling it to build on these ties and connect different individuals and groups around the world. Thus it became a "hub" of the broader jihadist movement, often working with individuals and groups outside the core organization while at the same time planning its own attacks.

Today, Al Qaeda's organizational structure is more decentralized. Leah Farrall explains:

> Due to its dispersed structure, al Qaeda operates as a devolved network hierarchy, in which levels of command authority are not always clear; personal ties between militants carry weight and, at times, transcend the command structure between core, branch, and franchises. For their part, al Qaeda's core members focus on exercising strategic command and control to ensure the centralization of the organization's actions and message, rather than directly managing its branch and franchises. Such an approach reduces the command-and-control burden, because al Qaeda need only manage centralization on a broad level, which, with a solid *manhaj* [program] already in place, can be achieved through strategic leadership rather than day-to-day oversight.[13]

The Al Qaeda core (though often not its affiliates and sympathizers) usually maintains a high level of operational security. Key leaders use multiple aliases and try to limit the wide use of their names.[14]

The so-called "Manchester Manual," a pre-9/11 internal document captured in a raid that describes many Al Qaeda procedures, warns that apartments should not be rented as safe houses if there is a risk of the security services knowing about them and that when members are discovered by security services, suspicious "activity is stopped for a while, all matters related to the activity are abandoned."[15] Operatives are ordered to blend in with local populations, and members are told to be wary of intelligence and police services, to speak only in code, and to avoid mentioning specifics unless absolutely necessary. One member of the cell in Kenya that carried out the bombing of the US embassy in Nairobi in 1998 noted, "We, the East Africa cell members, do not want to know about the operations plan since we are just implementers."[16] Similarly, Bin Laden said that the September 11 hijackers did not know the details of their mission until "just before they boarded the planes."[17] To bolster its long-term position, the organization tries to penetrate local military and intelligence services, where operatives often receive advance information about pending arrests from sympathetic police members.

Yet another of Al Qaeda's organizational strengths is its skill in adapting to changing circumstances: to use management consultant speak, it is a "learning organization." Operatives are allowed to criticize leaders, including Bin Laden and Zawahiri, though as *emir*, Bin Laden (and now Zawahiri) retains ultimate authority. The "Manchester Manual" calls for evaluating operations after they are carried out in order to learn from them. This willingness to confront mistakes gives the organization the ability to recuperate quickly from an operation gone awry or from successful government counterterrorist measures.

Finally, Al Qaeda has a deep bench of leaders and is able to quickly replace those captured or fallen on the battlefield. For instance, Al Qaeda's number three leader, Mohammed Atef, was killed by a US airstrike in Afghanistan in November 2001. A little over a year later, his successor, Khalid Sheikh Mohammad (the mastermind of the 9/11 attacks), was captured in Pakistan. The next guy to take the number three slot was Abu Farraj al-Libi—he was captured in Pakistan in May 2005. His replacement, Hamza Rabia, did not even last eight months. (He was killed by an American missile strike in December 2005.) The whack-a-mole situation with respect to the number three position in Al Qaeda actually became something of a joke among observers in the United States, with one journalist quipping that "some jobs just seem impossible to keep filled."[18] After yet another "Al Qaeda number three"—Mustafa Abu al-Yazid—was killed in 2010, satirist Andy Borowitz announced on Twitter, "For those keeping score, we have now killed Al Qaeda's number three 9000 times."[19] Although such high-level losses have hurt Al Qaeda, they have not led to the organization's collapse. This resilience allows local operations to continue. For example, the initial coordinator of the July 7, 2005, London bombings was captured and his successor killed; a replacement, however, kept the plot moving. Even after the death of Osama Bin Laden—not just Al Qaeda's number one, but also its founder and public face—in 2011, the group has persevered.

Why Does Al Qaeda Make So Many Mistakes?

Al Qaeda faces numerous pathologies related to the nature of its recruits, its ideology, and the difficulties of running an underground organization. This leads to self-defeating or seemingly foolish behavior by its leaders and members.

Al Qaeda seeks out young men and encourages them to fight. Some of these young men are genuine sociopaths, while others are hardened or embittered by war and, if left to themselves, act brutally. Others go to war in the name of sectarianism or purifying Muslim society, a sure recipe for slaughter. Although the United States focuses on Al Qaeda's use of terrorism as proof of its brutality, for many Muslims the proof is in the way Al Qaeda or its affiliates behave when they wage war or attempt to govern a territory. Beheadings, floggings, and other atrocities are common. In 2012, members of Al Qaeda in the Islamic Maghreb (AQIM), working with fighters from other Islamist groups, seized control of a huge piece of territory in northern Mali and swiftly instituted an extremely harsh interpretation of Islamic law. Reports soon surfaced of vicious beatings, amputations, summary executions, mass rape, and the recruitment of child soldiers by the extremists.[20] These actions were evidently not sanctioned by the leadership of AQIM—the group's leader, Abdel-malik Droukdel, wrote a letter to his fighters in Mali chastising them for their "hasty" application of *shari'a*.[21] Yet AQIM's deeds spoke louder than Droukdel's rebuke.

This inability to control the fighters on the ground and prevent them from engaging in activities that undermine the broader jihadist project is less a result of poor leadership and more a result of the nature of Al Qaeda's current organizational structure. By allowing increasingly far-flung jihadist groups to become formal affiliates and take on the Al Qaeda brand name, Al Qaeda has expanded its reach and influence, but it has also dramatically limited its ability to supervise the actions that are being carried out in its name.

Al Qaeda stresses its zealotry in its propaganda, so it is no surprise that many recruits are uncompromising in their behavior and alienate others, including potential supporters. A constant problem is the question of who is a true Muslim and who is an apostate (and thus a legitimate target). Is it simply the ruler who has broken God's laws? Does it include the regime's forces of repression? What about ordinary individuals who are going about their lives without rebelling against the corrupt leader? Jihadist movements have often taken this question to extremes. Shukri Mustapha, an Egyptian jihadist leader in the 1970s, even declared, "if one religious obligation is missed, the rest are nullified. . . every Muslim who the call reached but turned away is an infidel. . . infidels deserve death."[22] Al Qaeda leaders recognize this danger and have criticized moves to "turn our weapons against Muslims."[23] Many jihadists, however, are less forgiving.

This enthusiasm for declaring fellow Muslims apostates hinders Al Qaeda's ability to recruit fighters and accomplish its strategic goals. We have already seen this happen in Syria, where in 2013 and 2014 infighting between rival jihadist groups escalated to the point that groups began labeling each other apostates and openly targeting one another. Some foreign fighters who had come to Syria to fight alongside their jihadist brethren became disillusioned after witnessing their fellow jihadists turning their weapons on one another over petty rivalries and decided to go back home. Zawahiri reminded fighters that their efforts should be focused on removing Syrian President Bashar al-Asad from power, not on fighting and killing each other. Zawahiri failed, and the bloodshed continued.

Al Qaeda also runs afoul of nationalism. In its propaganda, Al Qaeda plays on anti-foreign sentiment, calling for Muslims to expel the West and other foreigners. But nationalism is a two-edged sword: Al Qaeda capitalizes on the commonly held Islamic notion that all Muslims are part of a single global community (called the *ummah*) in order to mobilize support for its agenda. Al Qaeda wants Muslims to feel an identity as Muslims—their true "nation"—but differences among Algerians, Iraqis, Afghans, and others remain significant.

These national differences, and the extremism of many Al Qaeda members, can prove disastrous. Local leaders may reject the foreign fighters' ideology and claims to leadership, and the population as a whole may turn away from their extreme ideas and brutality on the ground. Some may simply stop backing the rebels, while others may provide intelligence or otherwise assist government security services. Outside the conflict zone, the extremism may lead to broad condemnation that dries up recruits and fundraising. The situation in Somalia is illustrative: Somalis, like all peoples, do not want foreigners dictating their politics, and the presence of foreigners in the senior ranks of the Al Qaeda affiliate in Somalia, Al Shabaab, has been a liability for the group.[24]

The requirements of keeping a global underground organization financially solvent can also prove challenging. In a story too incredible for fiction, when covering the fall of the Taliban in 2001, Alan Cullison, a reporter for the *Wall Street Journal*, lost his laptop computer to a truck accident. He then went to the Kabul bazaar to buy a new one and found a used computer that had previously belonged to Al Qaeda leaders, including Ayman al-Zawahiri. The documents—of which there were almost a thousand, some dating all the way back to 1997—revealed not a fearsome organization made up of legions of evil geniuses and seething zealots, but rather the petty carping that any worker at any flailing business would recognize. For instance, in one exchange, Zawahiri chastises fellow Egyptian jihadists in Yemen: "Please explain the cell-phone invoice amounting to $756 (2,800 riyals) when you have mentioned communication expenses of $300."[25] Repairing a fax machine, disputes about who can stay at the guest house, and other bureaucratic minutiae consume much of his correspondence.

Al Qaeda must keep careful records and establish tight command structures to control the organization: if not, recruits may brutalize the population, middle managers and low-level operatives may steal money, and affiliates may attack targets that are not Al Qaeda priorities. Yet, as scholar Jacob Shapiro contends, by keeping voluminous records, Al Qaeda exposes its operatives to grave danger. When counterterrorism officials capture a financier or the computer of a recruiter, they often gain access to the names, locations, and activities of hundreds of militants whom they promptly arrest or kill.

In the end, Al Qaeda faces a trap from which there is no real escape. In order to remain relevant and advance its global vision, it must continue to recruit new members, spread its ideology, and acquire new affiliates—but in doing so, it generates new bureaucratic hurdles, potentially devastating security risks, and other organizational problems that jeopardize the jihadist movement as a whole. This tension often limits the organization, preventing it from exploiting successes and causing it to experience repeated failures.

What Is the Profile of a Typical Al Qaeda Member?

There is no single or clear path to terrorism or to joining Al Qaeda. Ayman al-Zawahiri is the scion of a prominent Egyptian family; Abu Musab al-Zarqawi, who catapulted to fame as the founder of Al Qaeda in Iraq, was a Jordanian street thug who wrestled with alcoholism before becoming a jihadist. An extensive report by the intelligence arm of the New York Police Department describes the Americans, Europeans, and Australians involved in jihadist terrorism as follows: "The majority of these individuals began as 'unremarkable'—they had 'unremarkable' jobs, had lived 'unremarkable' lives and had little, if any criminal history."[26]

Pakistan's fabled *madrassas* (Islamic religious schools, in this context), many of which are thought to have been funded by Saudi Arabia, have been cited by many as one of the major sources of radicalization in that part of the world. As Vali Nasr, one of the most vocal proponents of this theory, explains, radical interpretations of Islam "are being propagated out of schools that receive organizational and financial funding from Saudi Arabia."[27] However, C. Christine Fair, a highly respected scholar of political and military affairs in South Asia who has done original research on the problem, argues that Pakistan's *madrassas* actually play a much more limited role in the production of Al Qaeda terrorists. While these *madrassas* do certainly produce Islamist militants, few of these militants actually become Al Qaeda operatives.[28]

In the West, the results are also mixed. Peter Bergen and Swati Pandey found that the masterminds of the five worst anti-Western terrorist attacks all had university degrees, and in general, group members were slightly better educated than the average American.[29] Sometimes individuals who had traveled from the Middle East to study in Europe and became radicalized there were often the best and the brightest from their communities, knowing multiple languages and coming from relatively affluent backgrounds. Once they arrived in Europe, however, many of these individuals felt isolated and sought out fellow Muslims, often becoming radicalized in the process.

Yet again, there is a different profile for many jihadist terrorists born in Europe: their fathers were often lower class, and they themselves were often involved in drugs and crime before embracing jihad. Some were radicalized in prison. The failure to integrate many second- and third-generation Muslim immigrants into the fabric of European culture and society has made these immigrants more vulnerable to radicalization. Often, the terrorist cells that form are a mix of individuals with different backgrounds: the group of attackers who bombed commuter trains in Spain in 2004, killing 191 people, included both drug dealers and university students, both individuals who seemed well integrated into Spanish society and others who were outsiders.

How Does Al Qaeda Recruit?

From its inception, Al Qaeda and associated movements have emphasized propaganda. This ranged from encouraging Muslims to fight oppressors in Afghanistan to portraying the United States as bent on brutally dominating the Muslim world and local allied regimes as apostates. In a letter to Taliban leader Mullah Omar in the 1990s, Bin Laden wrote, "90% of the preparation for war is effective use of the media."[30] As technology has changed, so have the efforts of Al Qaeda and like-minded groups: Bin Laden sponsored magazines like *Al Jihad* in the 1980s, then branched out to create videos to be aired on satellite television; the group later produced its own videos to be distributed via Internet forums and uploaded to YouTube, and now embraces social media platforms like Twitter and Facebook to disseminate its message.

Al Qaeda propaganda constantly stresses the oppression of Muslims by non-Muslims, be they Americans in Iraq and Afghanistan, Russians in Chechnya, Indians in Kashmir, or Israelis in Palestine. Some, perhaps even most, of these beliefs are exaggerated and fanciful, but Al Qaeda plays on a form of religious nationalism, and many recruits believe that their community—defined as the world's Muslims—is under constant attack and see themselves as helping defend the faithful. These conflicts also tend to enjoy sympathy from at least some sections of the broader Muslim community, allowing potential recruits to feel like they will be heroes if they join the fight. The atrocities of war and the alleged bravery of the jihadist fighters are ideal recruiting tools for Al Qaeda and similar groups. They play on the narrative that the West and its puppet regimes are engaged in a brutal war on Islam. This sense that the world is standing by while Muslims are being slaughtered inspires young Muslims from around the world to join the fray.

Al Qaeda has used mosques, schools, and boardinghouses to recruit Muslims from around the world—including the United States and Europe. In the early days, these institutions would be set up directly by Al Qaeda, then later, as scrutiny increased, by sympathetic nongovernmental organizations (NGOs) or other like-minded groups. Training camps were also important places for recruitment. Here, Al Qaeda could take those who came to train in order to fight their regimes back home or to liberate Muslim lands from occupiers like Russia and turn them into fighters against the United States.

Personal relationships often play a key role in influencing an individual's decision to join the jihadist movement or in reinforcing radical tendencies. As scholar Marc Sageman contends, "joining the global Islamist terrorism social movement was based to a great degree on friendship and kinship."[31] Family recruits family, and friends recruit friends. Often, these personal relationships form at a mosque, where groups of students and young people gather. Religious leaders and other community leaders often enjoy disproportionate influence in the diaspora, as residents are often away from family and other traditional influences. Most Muslim leaders do not condone extremism, though, and many extremists stop going to the mosque once they become radicalized because the teachings there reject violence and because they believe that community leaders may try to stop them from using violence.

Because Al Qaeda can draw on so many causes and because there is no easy profile of a recruit, stopping radicalization is exceptionally difficult. Individual programs might limit radicalization and prevent recruitment in one neighborhood or in one prison, but the phenomenon is diffuse and context-dependent, preventing one-size-fits-all approaches to the problem from succeeding.

What Is the Role of War?

Without war there would be no Al Qaeda. Terrorism is part and parcel of most civil wars, and until 9/11, a counterterrorism lens was rarely applied to these conflicts. Insurgents of all stripes, including the Viet Cong, the anti-Soviet *mujahedin*, and even clear "good guys" like the French resistance to the Nazis in World War II, have targeted civilians and used terrorism against their enemies. For Al Qaeda, however, the role of war is far more central. Many of its tactics are predicated on civil conflicts, and helping win (and at times create) such wars is a central part of its mission.

Al Qaeda has long seen itself as leading a global insurgency, uniting the Muslim world against foreign invaders and US-backed apostate regimes. Civil wars and rebellions thus neatly fit into its worldview and mission. Some conflicts—repelling the Soviet Union and later the United States from Afghanistan, opposing the United States and the regime it installed in Iraq, fighting India in Kashmir, combating Russia in Chechnya, and so on—are "defensive jihads" that many foreign fighters and traditional clerics in the Muslim world also embrace. However, Al Qaeda also engages in civil wars, assisting Muslims fighting nominally Muslim regimes in Algeria, Egypt, Somalia, Syria, Yemen, and elsewhere. The list is long.

Typically, Al Qaeda enters these wars as an ally of local rebels, but over time it shifts the very nature of the fight. In Chechnya, nationalism drove a rebellion shortly after the Soviet Union collapsed. Syria in 2011 started out with peaceful protests against the Asad regime, and initially the vast bulk of the opposition had little if anything to do with jihadism. In these and other conflicts, Al Qaeda first entered as a friend, bringing funds and skilled fighters to the cause. Indeed, one of Al Qaeda's strengths historically has been its ability to train fighters and provide money to assist its friends. In the combat zone, the jihadists' battlefield performance, and their proselytizing, generated new recruits, while the horrors of war radicalized many formerly moderate fighters. Over time, Al Qaeda-associated forces became stronger than those that did not associate with Al Qaeda.

Wars weaken governments, and weak governments are more susceptible to terrorism. In Pakistan after 9/11 and in Iraq after the US overthrow of Saddam Hussein, terrorist attacks discredited the government and inflamed sectarian passions, leading to more violence and eventually escalating into massive civil wars. These wars, in turn, gave Al Qaeda and like-minded movements greater operational freedom. In some countries these movements established bases and training camps, turning them into mini-Afghanistans.

Becoming a foreign fighter is one way to become a jihadist. Thomas Hegghammer, director of terrorism research at the Norwegian Defence Research Establishment, points out that "the majority of al-Qaida operatives began their militant careers as war volunteers, and most transnational jihadi groups today are by-products of foreign fighter mobilization."[32] Brutal combat seasons the volunteers, making them steady under pressure and giving them a deep sense of loyalty to their comrades in arms. They also gain immediate and practical skills. Clint Watts, a noted scholar and seasoned practitioner of counterterrorism, explains that Iraq and Afghanistan were "training grounds" for foreign fighters, where they learned urban warfare and how to use weapons, including advanced technology.[33] Hegghammer contends that the involvement of a veteran from a foreign jihad in a terrorist plot both increases the chance that the plot will succeed and makes the overall lethality of the attack higher.[34]

But the story is not all guns and roses. Many of these foreign fighters die in the combat zone or end up moving on to fight in other foreign conflicts. Significant percentages simply cannot endure the training or become disillusioned once they come to realize that the harsh realities of waging a bloody jihad are far less glamorous than they seemed from afar. As a New York Police Department report notes, "Individuals reared in a Western urban setting and culture usually lack the physical and mental fortitude and endurance to survive, much less fight in underdeveloped and severe environments such as Afghanistan, Kashmir, Iraq, and Somalia."[35] Language barriers can further compound problems. Many foreign fighters return to their home countries with no intention of conducting terrorist attacks or are arrested and thus disrupted. In the end, roughly one in nine foreign fighters becomes linked with a jihadist terrorist organization: a low percentage, but still significant given the tens of thousands of foreign fighters who have taken part in brutal conflicts over the years.

When foreign fighters return home, the cycle often perpetuates itself: returnees have "street cred" and valuable experience on how to organize for violence, and they may seed new rebel groups or create new terrorist cells. Mohammed Haydar Zammar, for example, had fought in Afghanistan and regularly pressed Muslims in Germany to join the fight: he reportedly took credit for influencing Mohamed Atta and others from Hamburg to become jihadists.[36] Other foreign fighters have had similar sway, and they and their comrades generate new recruits that keep the flames of war burning.

What Is the Role of the Internet?

In the last 20 years, the Internet has radically transformed everything from education to commerce to social relations, so it should be no surprise that the Internet has changed terrorism, too. As Brian Jenkins, one of the leading scholars of terrorism, puts it:

> Terrorists use the Internet to disseminate their ideology, appeal for support, spread fear and alarm among their foes, radicalize and recruit new members, provide instruction in tactics and weapons, gather intelligence about potential targets, clandestinely communicate, and support terrorist operations. The Internet enables terrorist organizations to expand their reach, create virtual communities of like-minded extremists, and capture a larger universe of more-diverse talents and skills.[37]

The Internet, however, also poses risks for Al Qaeda and other terrorist groups and is very much a mixed blessing.

According to a study conducted by the United Nations, the number of websites associated with Al Qaeda increased from 12 in 1998 to approximately 2,600 by 2006.[38] But the shift to the Internet and especially to social media is both an asset and a danger for Al Qaeda.

On the one hand, sympathizers from around the world can add their own content and push Al Qaeda's agenda: the battle against Asad in Syria, against the French in Mali, and against the Kenyans in Somalia are only a few examples of where local groups and sympathizers generate tons of propaganda without Al Qaeda's direct input or oversight. Many jihadists and sympathizers, especially in the West, are skilled users of information technology—indeed, many are better with a computer than with a rifle. Yet this decentralization also allows individuals to promote themes that Al Qaeda does not favor. The current Syrian and both of the recent Iraqi conflicts—three of the most important for the jihadist cause in its modern history—have all been marked by sectarianism, and much of the propaganda designed to recruit and fundraise for these conflicts has stressed intra-Muslim violence and local aims, rather than Al Qaeda's global priorities.

Through the Internet, aspirants can enter a world of global jihad, virtually joining other alienated Muslims and attaching themselves to global causes. Scholar Marc Sageman argues that in the years after 9/11, jihadist networks went from face-to-face contacts to Internet-based ones where they would self-radicalize. Sageman writes that the Internet is a "virtual equivalent of the militant mosques."[39] The result is an echo chamber: those who enter hear their own ideas repeated back to them—even louder—with nary a dissenting voice to move them off the path of radicalization.

Al Qaeda has also made good use of the Internet to bypass Western media and reach key audiences directly. In the past (as today), the media covered terrorist attacks heavily, but the filter was negative from the group's point of view: they were the bad guys, after all. Now, Al Qaeda and other like-minded groups can make videos to disseminate information on the group and its activities in the most favorable light and upload the videos directly to YouTube and other sharing platforms.

At times, this works. In December 2009, five Americans were arrested after allegedly traveling to Pakistan to join a terrorist group—they were reportedly radicalized by watching videos on YouTube.[40] As he radicalized, Major Nidal Hasan, who killed 13 soldiers in a 2009 shooting rampage at Fort Hood, Texas, communicated via e-mail with Anwar al-Awlaki, the influential Yemeni-American preacher and member of Al Qaeda in the Arabian Peninsula who was killed by a US drone strike in Yemen in 2011.[41] *Inspire* magazine, the brainchild of Awlaki and Samir Khan (also killed in the drone strike that killed Awlaki), reportedly helped radicalize the Boston Marathon bombers and assisted them in preparing the pressure-cooker bombs that killed three people.

The Internet is also highly useful for moving and raising money, as individuals around the globe can be alerted to causes and easily donate or support them. Michael Jacobson explains that the Internet has made it easier for everyone, including terrorists, to transfer funds electronically through such services as PayPal.[42]

For operations, however, the Internet has several flaws. Sageman notes that efforts to learn bomb making over the Internet are much more dangerous than if they are combined with direct training.[43] This is an understatement, and this danger may explain the repeated disasters that many untrained Western jihadists have had when hatching terrorism plots. As Peter Bergen points out, "Watching jihadist videos on the Internet may help to radicalize young men, but screening a beheading video in your pj's doesn't turn you into a successful terrorist or insurgent. ... That is achieved by learning on the job in a war zone or at a jihadi training camp."[44] Transferring funds electronically via the Internet also represents a major security risk, as governments have become savvier at tracking and monitoring electronic payments and using this information to identify jihadists and bring down entire terror networks. As one jihadist on an extremist Internet forum warned his comrades, "If your use of the electronic payments has not brought you woes, then that does not mean it is safe."[45]

Even more important, a lack of face-to-face contact is an operational security nightmare. The trust that successful organizations must build to ensure that members work together and do not betray one another is far harder to create through virtual networks than through face-to-face contact. In addition, security services can infiltrate chat rooms and other sites, making it difficult to discuss sensitive details of an operation without the risk of being compromised. Social media sites are even more vulnerable, as the content is public. Indeed, a security service need only monitor the "friends" or "followers" of a suspect on Facebook and Twitter to learn a tremendous amount about a potential network.

Where Does Al Qaeda Get Its Money?

Al Qaeda has been among the best-financed groups in the history of terrorism, and its wealth is one of the sources of its success. In contrast to groups like Hizballah, Al Qaeda does not draw on the resources of a state patron. Rather, Al Qaeda has raised money in innovative ways and, in so doing, has made itself into a durable organization.

In the early days, Al Qaeda's money flowed from Bin Laden's personal wealth. The scion (one of many, admittedly) of one of Saudi Arabia's wealthiest families, Bin Laden drew on his family fortune when he set off for jihad in the 1980s and sprinkled that money liberally on behalf of jihadist causes. However, his personal wealth was often exaggerated: around 9/11, reports that he had a $300 million personal fortune circulated widely.[46] In reality, he received perhaps $1 million a year from the family fortune through 1994.[47] After Saudi Arabia cracked down in the mid-1990s and Bin Laden was expelled from Sudan in 1996, he had even less to his name. Many of his investments in Sudan yielded little or were seized by the Sudanese government.

To replace and supplement his own money, Bin Laden drew on the so-called Golden Chain: wealthy individuals from the Arabian Peninsula, particularly Saudi Arabia, who believed in Bin Laden's mission and supported an array of jihadist causes from Kashmir to Algeria that Al Qaeda also championed. Some religious leaders at mosques were also willing to divert charitable contributions to Al Qaeda. By 9/11, Al Qaeda's yearly budget was roughly $30 million, of which between $10 and $20 million went to the Taliban—its biggest pre–9/11 expense.[48]

Money was often moved by *hawala,* an informal and simple system where money is given to an individual in one country, such as Saudi Arabia, and a relative or other trusted person of that individual living in a different country (say Pakistan) passes the same amount of money (minus a fee) to the intended recipient. The vast majority of *hawala* transfers are legitimate, but Al Qaeda operatives have at times taken advantage of the informal nature of *hawala* transfers to hide their money from hostile governments.[49]

However, because of the small overall amount of money involved compared with legitimate finance and illicit enterprises like illegal narcotics, Al Qaeda was often able to hide money in plain sight. The

9/11 hijackers declared their money when entering the country, put money into US bank accounts, obtained more money through wire transfers, and otherwise followed financial rules, staying below the radar screen the entire time.

Particularly important for Al Qaeda are Islamic charities and NGOs, which Al Qaeda has used to raise and move money both to fund its own operatives and to support like-minded groups. Over the years, Al Qaeda has established its own charities and infiltrated existing legitimate ones. For example, the headquarters and many of the field offices and employees of the Saudi-based charity Al Haramain actively supported Al Qaeda.[50] Following the violence in the mid-1990s, the Central Intelligence Agency estimated that one-third of the Islamic charities in Bosnia were linked to terrorism, giving operatives jobs, salaries, and legitimate covers.[51] Wadih el-Hage, one of the leaders of the 1998 embassy bombings, worked for a charity called "Help Africa People." The alleged 2006 transatlantic bombing plot involved individuals who traveled to Pakistan on behalf of an Islamic medical charity.

Businesses were also part of the network. In 2003, the US Department of Treasury listed 18 individuals and 10 companies believed to link Al Qaeda with Jemaah Islamiyya, an Indonesia-based terrorist group active in Southeast Asia; the initial list had 300 names but was reportedly slashed for political and bureaucratic reasons.[52]

The governments of Saudi Arabia and several other Gulf states did not exercise oversight of many charitable institutions before 9/11 in order to stop the financing of terrorism.[53] Charitable giving is an important part of Islam, and even many of the most culpable charities engaged in legitimate social welfare work as well as supporting violence. The Kingdom's own policy embraced spreading Salafism and helping many of the causes, such as the Chechen struggle against Russia, that Al Qaeda also embraced. However, the 9/11 Commission found "no evidence that the Saudi government as an institution or senior Saudi officials individually funded the organization."[54]

The 9/11 Commission also found that Al Qaeda did not gain significant funding from the drug trade or other criminal enterprises. However, individual Al Qaeda operatives and Al Qaeda affiliates have at times used crime to fund operations, and this has grown in the years after 9/11. Al Qaeda in the Islamic Maghreb uses kidnapping as a business, abducting locals and Europeans for ransom: a *New York Times* investigation found that Al Qaeda and its affiliates brought in at least $125 million from kidnappings since 2008—over half of which was in 2013 alone.[55] Half of Al Qaeda in the Arabian Peninsula's budget comes from ransom payments. Most of that money comes from European governments paying for the return of their citizens. Although such concern is laudable in theory, it makes the citizens of countries like Austria, France, Germany, and Switzerland far more likely to be kidnapped than British or American citizens, whose governments will not pay ransoms (though the latter are thus more likely to be killed). Because of the sums of money involved, leaders in the Al Qaeda core often monitor the individual kidnappings.

How Does Al Qaeda Spend Its Money?

Money is vital for Al Qaeda for many reasons. Terrorist acts themselves are relatively cheap, as Table 5.1 suggests. The 9/11 attacks were perhaps the most expensive in history at $500,000. Most,

Table 5.1 Direct Costs of a Terrorist Attack

Attack	Date	Estimated Cost[a]
London transport system	July 7, 2005	GPB 8,000[b]
Madrid train bombings	March 11, 2004	USD 10,000
Istanbul truck bomb attacks	November 15 and 20, 2003	USD 40,000
Jakarta Marriott hotel bombing	August 5, 2003	USD 30,000
Bali bombings	October 12, 2002	USD 50,000
USS *Cole* attack	October 12, 2000	USD 10,000
East Africa embassy bombings	August 7, 1998	USD 50,000

Entire table taken from "Terrorist Financing," Financial Action Task Force (Groupe d'action financière) / Organisation for Economic Co-operation and Development, February 29, 2008, p. 7, http://www.fatf-gafi.org/media/fatf/documents/reports/FATF%20Terrorist%20 Financing%20Typologies%20Report.pdf.

[a] Unless otherwise noted, all estimates adapted from the August 2004 report of the UN Monitoring Team Report on Al Qaeda and the Taliban.

[b] The United Kingdom Home Office (2006).

however, cost in the hundreds or low thousands of dollars: the Al Qaeda in the Arabian Peninsula attempt to bomb cargo planes in October 2010 cost less than $5,000.[56]

Though terrorist acts are cheap, terrorist organizations are not. To maintain its brand, Al Qaeda has built a sophisticated and wide-reaching propaganda apparatus capable of producing videos and written content for distribution on satellite television and the Internet. Another key component of Al Qaeda's strategy is to provide seed money to fund local revolutions across the Middle East and North Africa and to provide training, weapons, and other financial assistance to jihadist movements facing financial insolvency due to government repression efforts. Money is needed to run training camps, purchase vehicles and arms, acquire and maintain safe houses, and facilitate communication. In some cases, money may also be required to appease the local communities or tribes in the areas in which the group is located; in the case of Sudan, Bin Laden sunk significant funds into establishing businesses and otherwise supporting the local economy in order to gain favor with the leaders in Khartoum.

One particularly important part of running a terrorist organization is taking care of members and their families. Early Al Qaeda documents go into great detail on the salary of members, with married members receiving more. (They also get a great vacation package—one month a year, along with 15 sick days.) Specialized members, particularly military trainers, also receive more money.[57] Some members arrive indebted, while others may need assistance due to family emergencies. And because polygamy (or, more accurately, polygyny) is permitted and often encouraged in some interpretations of Islam, these families can grow quite large and be fairly expensive to maintain. Al Qaeda also provides for the families left behind when a member is killed or imprisoned. This bill too can get quite large, particularly when effective counterterrorism leads to heavy losses.

When the money fails, disaster ensues. When Bin Laden was under financial pressure in the mid-1990s, two key figures—Jamal Ahmed al-Fadl and L'Houssaine Kherchtou—both defected to the United States and became star witnesses against other Al Qaeda members. Both defected for financial reasons: Fadl because he resented receiving less money than other group members and

Kherchtou because Bin Laden could not provide him money when his wife needed an operation.[58]

After 9/11, Al Qaeda's finances bled. Greater US pressure on donors and an aggressive campaign to go after Al Qaeda money hit Al Qaeda's coffers hard and constrained the organization's ability to move money. Al Qaeda attacks in Saudi Arabia, in 2003 in particular, led Riyadh (with US technical support) to undertake an aggressive effort against wealthy Al Qaeda patrons (though many wealthy Saudis still support a range of jihadist groups, including the Taliban, with less government interference).

On the other hand, Al Qaeda's needs also diminished substantially during this period: with the overthrow of the Taliban, Al Qaeda's biggest expense disappeared. In addition, the popularity of jihadist-linked causes such as fighting Americans in Iraq and the Asad regime in Syria has enabled Al Qaeda-supported organizations to gain money on their own, further reducing the financial burden on the Al Qaeda core—in fact, some of this money was actually siphoned off to help the core itself.

Yet the core remains diminished financially. David Cohen, the US Treasury Department's undersecretary for terrorism and financial intelligence, proudly stated that by 2009 and 2010, "we were able to say that al-Qaeda was in its weakest financial condition since 2001."[59] As a result, the core has had to reduce support for members and their families and spend less on training. Complaints over money have increased within the ranks. Western volunteers who came to train at Al Qaeda training camps in Pakistan were charged for their weapons and otherwise exploited rather than welcomed as brothers in arms, leaving them disillusioned. As one French fighter lamented, "What you see in videos on the Net, we realized that was a lie."[60] The core is also less able to use financial support to control affiliates, and its power balance with affiliates today reflects this loss.

Fundraising pressure is a spur for Al Qaeda to act. Though a patient organization, if it is inactive for long periods or if other groups like the Islamic State eclipse it in publicity, the core organization risks losing donors and thus, in the long term, its vitality.

6

FRIENDS AND ENEMIES

How Did the 2003 Iraq War Shape Al Qaeda?

In the years leading up to 9/11, Saddam Hussein and Al Qaeda shared a hatred of the United States, Saudi Arabia, and other common foes, but their visions—that of a secular tyrant with dreams of Arab glory versus that of an organization seeking a pan-Islamic caliphate and the rule of Islamic law—were fundamentally at odds. Al Qaeda officials and Iraqi intelligence officers met in Sudan in late 1994 or early 1995, and they discussed cooperation repeatedly in the years that followed, but little or no actual cooperation occurred. As the 9/11 Commission put it, "we have seen no evidence that these or earlier contacts ever developed into a collaborative operational relationship. Nor have we seen evidence indicating that Iraq cooperated with al Qaeda in developing or carrying out any attacks against the United States."[1]

The US invasion and occupation of Iraq in 2003 came at a time when the Al Qaeda core was on the ropes. Iraq thus came as a godsend for Al Qaeda. The Iraq war validated the Al Qaeda narrative that the United States was bent on subjugating Islam and proved to be a rallying cry that attracted money and young men at a level that dwarfed the anti-Soviet Afghan jihad. Iraq vindicated Bin Laden's argument that the primary enemy of the Muslim world was not local Muslim autocrats, but the "far enemy," the United States. Although mainstream Islamic scholars condemned the 9/11 attacks, these same scholars, many of whom were employed by governments allied with the United States, praised resistance in Iraq. In a statement issued right before the US invasion of Iraq in 2003, scholars at the venerable Al-Azhar University in Cairo declared, "According to Islamic law, if an enemy steps on Muslims' land, jihad becomes a duty on every male and female Muslim." Zawahiri privately described the invasion as a "blessing" that allowed for "jihad in the heart of the Islamic world."[2] As Michael Scheuer, the former head of the CIA's Bin Laden unit, acidly noted, "The war in Iraq—if Osama was a Christian—it's the Christmas present he never would have expected."[3]

The war and subsequent occupation also benefited Al Qaeda on an operational level. Much of the initial fighting did not involve jihadists: former members of Saddam's Baath party, criminals, and nationalists played prominent roles. But Salafi-jihadists gradually became stronger as foreign fighters flocked to Iraq, animated by Al Qaeda propaganda and the broader outrage in the Muslim world. These fighters were zealous, and unlike many Iraqis were fully committed to fighting Americans. The United States chose to divert troops to Iraq rather than consolidate its victory in Afghanistan and increase its chances of hunting down Bin Laden in Pakistan. Yet despite the large numbers of troops present in the country, the failure of the United States to properly secure Iraq after toppling Saddam gave jihadists tremendous operational freedom. While in Iraq, the jihadists developed increasingly sophisticated improvised explosive devices (IEDs) that would prove effective against US forces and would be used in other jihads.

As the insurgency spread, so did the ideology championed by Al Qaeda, which numerous groups in heretofore secular (or at least mainstream Islamist) Iraq began to embrace. At the forefront of the jihadists' rise was Jordanian-born Abu Musab al-Zarqawi. Zarqawi joined the jihadist cause in Jordan in the 1990s and fled to Afghanistan in 1999. The group he established flourished there—he drew almost 3,000 recruits after Al Qaeda gave him seed money and helped him establish a training camp in Herat. Al Qaeda leaders hoped to capitalize on Zarqawi's connections in Jordan, Syria, Lebanon, and the Palestinian territories, where they had fewer followers.[4] After US forces invaded Afghanistan, Zarqawi at first joined with Al Qaeda to fight, but when the Taliban was routed, he fled to Iran. He eventually entered Iraq in 2002 in advance of the US invasion, basing himself in Iraqi Kurdistan, outside Saddam's area of control.

In part due to dramatic videotaped operations such as beheadings of Western captives, Zarqawi quickly became the leading foreign fighter figure in Iraq. Zarqawi at first attacked international organizations like the International Committee of the Red Cross and the United Nations (UN) headquarters in Iraq, as well as the Jordanian embassy in Baghdad, trying to isolate the United States and drive away its helpers.[5] Other Sunni insugents welcomed the violence, seeing these attacks and Zarqawi's subsequent campaign against US-led coalition forces, the Shi'a-dominated Iraqi government, and Shi'ite militias as part of the same broad fight.[6] After several years of negotiations, Zarqawi pledged his loyalty to Bin Laden in 2004, creating the organization that would come to be known as Al Qaeda in Iraq (AQI).

AQI took over parts of Anbar province in western Iraq, including the city of Fallujah, and in general enjoyed considerable power in Sunni areas of Iraq. AQI's prominence and successful recruitment of foreign fighters enabled it to attract and merge with other Salafi-jihadist groups, which fought under its leadership.[7] As it consolidated control over parts of Iraq, it became financially self-sufficient. "Taxation" (often really just extortion) of the locals, oil smuggling, and kidnapping for ransom gave it an annual income of between $70 and $200 million by late 2006.[8] The group was suspicious of foreign funders and sought to be financially independent: a US government study found that, at most, only five percent of the group's money came from foreign sources.[9]

Under Zarqawi, AQI embraced a strategy of deliberately creating a sectarian war, and high-profile and brutal tactics like beheadings helped him achieve this. Zarqawi himself considered the Shi'a to be a "crafty and malicious scorpion" within Islam and declared that "The Muslims will have no victory or superiority over the aggressive infidels such as the Jews and the Christians" until the Shi'a were annihilated.[10] However, he also recognized that attacks on Shi'ite civilian and religious sites would prompt a backlash by the Shi'ite community—and that this, in turn, would rally more Sunni Muslims to AQI's banners. As General Stanley McChrystal, who designed and led much of the day-to-day effort that eventually succeeded in beating back AQI, put it, "Only in the high pitch of an ethnic war would the Sunnis win. In that hell, Al Qaeda would reign."[11]

The United States, many Sunnis believed, deserved to be attacked because it was handing Iraq over to a Shi'a-led government.

The relationship between AQI and the Al Qaeda core was fraught with problems and divisions. Although AQI was attacking Americans, it launched relatively few attacks outside the Iraqi theater and thus did not truly follow Al Qaeda's global agenda. AQI's prominence, which had made it so desirable as an affiliate in the first place, also allowed it to shape the agenda of the broader jihadist movement in ways that Al Qaeda opposed. AQI's attacks on Iraqi Shi'a and its virulent anti-Shi'a propaganda fanned sectarian flames, and sectarianism—not Al Qaeda's anti-US goals—dominated the jihadist discourse.

In addition to shaping the agenda, AQI conducted unpopular attacks that damaged the Al Qaeda brand among ordinary Muslims—much as its successor organization, the Islamic State, would do a decade later. Members of AQI broke the fingers of cigarette smokers and murdered women who refused to wear the *niqab* (the Islamic face covering that leaves only the eyes exposed). These attacks came at a particularly high cost outside the country. Senior Al Qaeda leaders privately warned Zarqawi about the Algerian experience, noting that the militants there destroyed "themselves with their own hands by their alienation of the population with their lack of reason. . . oppression, deviance, and ruthlessness."[12]

Nevertheless, given the popularity of the Iraqi struggle and Zarqawi's own funding stream, it was impossible for Al Qaeda to openly denounce AQI, even as AQI's actions tarnished the Al Qaeda brand. Leading clerics, including many who were formerly sympathetic to Al Qaeda and the anti-US struggle in Iraq, began to denounce Bin Laden. Such condemnations hindered fundraising and recruitment and decreased support from those with looser ties to the movement who are often radicalized indirectly. As Abu Qatada, a leading jihadist ideologue, lamented, "The impact of these retreats on us is worse than 100,000 American soldiers."[13]

Beginning in 2006, AQI sustained a series of heavy blows. US forces hunted Zarqawi ruthlessly, and on June 7, 2006, they finally caught up with him, killing him in an F-16 strike. AQI's heavy-handed role in Iraq had alienated ordinary Iraqis, including Sunni tribal members in the Sunni heartland in western Iraq. Taking advantage of this anger, in 2006 the United States changed its strategy, adopting a more traditional counterinsurgency approach that emphasized protecting the population, sending in more troops as part of a "surge," pushing the Iraqi government to include Sunnis, and supporting local tribes when they stood up to Al Qaeda. Backed by US financial support and firepower, these tribes organized against Al Qaeda, fighting it directly and providing intelligence to US forces. An important, but often less publicized, part of the strategy were the expanded counterterrorism strikes by US special operations forces on AQI that became more and more effective with improved intelligence and popular support.

The effect was overwhelming. The US military claimed that by 2010, 80% of AQI's leaders were dead or captured (17 of the 25 most important Islamic State leaders in 2014 had spent time in US prisons[14]), and internal AQI documents later captured paint a picture of devastation.[15] AQI abandoned large-scale guerrilla war, instead relying on terrorism to keep its cause alive. CIA Director Michael Hayden declared in 2008, "Al Qaeda is on the verge of a strategic defeat in Iraq"—an assessment backed by a plunge in the organization's attacks, a collapse in its ability to hold territory, and widespread criticism of the organization from within the broader Muslim world, including from many former jihadist supporters.[16] The organization, however, proved weakened, but not destroyed. It would come back to Iraq under a new name—the Islamic State.

How Does Al Qaeda View Iran and the Shi'a?

Shared enemies drive Iran and Al Qaeda together, but mutual suspicion keeps the partnership tactical and gives both sides reasons to play it down. Speaking before Congress in 2012, Director of National Intelligence James Clapper aptly described the relationship as a "marriage of convenience."[17]

Tehran's relationship with Al Qaeda has a strategic logic. In the early 1990s, Al Qaeda operatives trained in Iran and with Hizballah in the Bekaa Valley in Lebanon, learning how to use truck bombs and other terrorist tactics.[18] When Al Qaeda went to Afghanistan in 1996, Iran became a route for fighters to travel to and from Al Qaeda camps in Afghanistan, albeit a much less important one than the route through Pakistan. In the months before 9/11, Iranian border inspectors were deliberately told to look the other way and not stamp passports of jihadists going to and from Afghanistan. Keeping such passports "clean" was vital to reducing the risk of discovery and arrest in Saudi Arabia and later in the United States. The 9/11 Commission found that 8 to 10 of the 14 Saudi hijackers who provided "muscle" for the 9/11 operation transited Iran between October 2000 and February 2001.

Iran has at times also functioned as a safe haven for Al Qaeda, particularly after 9/11. When Al Qaeda was forced out of Afghanistan following the fall of the Taliban in 2001, part of the leadership went to Iran. Over the years, Iran would limit or expand this safe haven in part according to the vagaries of the US-Iran relationship. At first, when Iran strongly supported the US war against the hated Taliban, Iran sent many suspected jihadists back to their home countries, where they usually faced arrest. Zawahiri later publicly blasted Tehran for siding with the United States. He stated, "All of a sudden, we discovered Iran collaborating with America" and charged that "Iran stabbed a knife into the back of the Islamic Nation [*ummah*]."[19]

However, starting around January 2002, after President George W. Bush publicly declared Iran part of the "Axis of Evil" in his State of the Union address (a decision motivated in part by Iran's provision of weapons to Palestinian groups engaged in terrorism against Israel), Iran reduced its efforts to control and extradite senior Al Qaeda members in Iran. In the lead-up to the US invasion of Iraq in 2003, when Iran felt threatened by the imminence of the US invasion of its neighbor and talk of regime change against "rogue" regimes in the Middle East, Tehran allowed Sunni jihadists to use the country as a base to prepare resistance to US forces in Iraq. Iran also seeks the return from Iraq of members of the Mujahedin-e Khalq (MEK), an Iranian opposition organization that was long based in Iraq, and when US forces occupied Iraq in 2003, Iran used its hold over Al Qaeda figures as a bargaining chip to press the United States to hand over the MEK. Although the United States for many years designated the MEK a terrorist organization, it granted the MEK's members in Iraq the status of "protected persons" under the Geneva Convention and did not send them to Iran when it controlled Iraq.

Iran's policy toward Al Qaeda since that time has involved a mix of crackdowns and permissiveness. Senior Al Qaeda figure Seif al-Adl claims that because of US demands, Iranian pressure "confused us and foiled 75 percent of our plan [*sic*]" and that there were many arrests—suggesting a positive Iranian role in the fight against Al Qaeda much of the time.[20] Iran claimed that it held several senior Al Qaeda figures in custody, and one US official in 2005 described these Al Qaeda figures as living under "virtual house arrest." However, at times, Iran has eased its restrictions on Al Qaeda members or even allowed some to leave for Pakistan. One Al Qaeda member noted that there were several stages of restrictions and that in the end, it was "not house arrest but rather hospitality."[21] The US Department of Treasury has repeatedly identified and targeted Iran-based Al Qaeda figures who operate there with the regime's knowledge.[22]

In addition to being pawns in the US-Iran relationship, Al Qaeda members living in Iran have been successfully exploited by the Iranian regime to ensure good behavior from the broader Sunni jihadist movement, which is violently hostile toward Iran and the Shi'a. Zawahiri, in internal correspondence with the leader of Al Qaeda in Iraq, urged the leader not to target the Shi'a in Iraq or Iranian assets because Iran was holding over 100 Al Qaeda members in the country and these members were vulnerable to Iranian pressure.[23] Abu Hafs al-Mauritani, a leading Al Qaeda figure who was in Iran for roughly a decade after 9/11, explained that Al Qaeda members agreed not to carry out attacks from within Iran in exchange for maintaining a haven there.[24]

From Al Qaeda's point of view, the logic of maintaining a strategic relationship with Iran and securing Iranian help is even more straightforward. Although Al Qaeda is a formidable terrorist organization, it lacks the resources of a major state like Iran. Having the ability to transit Iran is exceptionally useful for fights in Iraq, Afghanistan, and Pakistan. Some degree of a haven is also vital for Al Qaeda, as it needs respite from US and allied efforts to arrest and kill its members.

However, the hatred of the jihadist movement toward the Shi'a and Iran provides a strong incentive for both Iran and Al Qaeda to keep their relationship quiet. Al Qaeda would suffer considerably if potential recruits and donors learned it had a close relationship with the Iranians. Indeed, in May 2014, the Islamic State slammed Zawahiri for acting "in compliance with Iran's orders"—the ultimate betrayal.[25] For Iran, the incentives for keeping the relationship quiet are different, but no less profound. Many of Al Qaeda's enemies are countries that Iran wants as friends (like Russia) or at least does not want to alienate further (like Europe). In addition, many Iranians abhor the Sunni jihadist community for its anti-Shi'a words and deeds, and as such, any alliance between their government and Sunni jihadists would be unpopular at home.

A study of several of the documents captured in the raid that killed Bin Laden described the relationship between Iran and Al Qaeda as "fraught with difficulties" and "not one of alliance, but of indirect and unpleasant negotiations over the release of detained jihadis and their families."[26] Yet in all likelihood, this strange relationship will endure for the foreseeable future. The two share common enemies and goals, and while both sides will certainly watch their own backs, they will remain bedfellows out of necessity.

Is Saudi Arabia Secretly Supporting Al Qaeda?

In July 2003, 191 members of the US House of Representatives supported a bill to add Saudi Arabia to the official US list of state sponsors of terrorism because of its links to the jihadist cause. Other observers, however, note the deadly enmity between Saudi Arabia's ruling family, the Al Saud, and Osama Bin Laden—as former US Ambassador to Saudi Arabia Charles ("Chas") Freeman declared, "You can be damn sure that any al Qaeda operative is on the Saudi wanted list."[27] Both are right, and both are wrong: Al Qaeda did draw considerable assistance from the people of Saudi Arabia, but Al Qaeda is vehemently opposed to the Saudi regime, and particularly after 2003, the Saudi regime became a bitter foe.

In part as a way to legitimize their leadership and in part because of a genuine belief in Wahhabi teachings, the ruling Al Saud family made religion a centerpiece of their rule. Islamic law is the law of the land in Saudi Arabia, and religious officials have tremendous sway over daily life. Textbooks in Saudi schools denigrate nonbelievers and the West and extol martyrdom. For instance, *Time* magazine reported that "[a]n eighth-grade book states that Allah cursed Jews and Christians and turned some of them into apes and pigs. Ninth-graders learn that Judgment Day will not come 'until the Muslims fight the Jews and kill them.' A chapter for a 10th-grade class warns Muslims against befriending non-Muslims saying, 'It is compulsory for the Muslims to be loyal to each other and to consider the infidels their enemy.' "[28]

Saudi Arabia is linked to a range of jihadist causes. Some of this support has even had the blessing of the United States, such as when the Saudis gave billions to the anti-Soviet *mujahedin* in Afghanistan in the 1980s. The mobilization that arose to support the Afghans contributed to a growing sense of pan-Islamism among Saudis, and subsequent causes in Kashmir, Chechnya, Bosnia, and other theaters of jihad all saw Saudi support and Saudi militants traveling there to fight. Before 9/11, almost 1,000 Saudis were in Afghanistan.[29] Because their legitimacy is linked to their image as champions of Islam, Saudi leaders step gingerly in the world of Islamist politics and have been hesitant to oppose jihadist causes.

However, support for Al Qaeda and like-minded groups comes from the Saudi people, not the Saudi regime. The 9/11 Commission reported that it "found no evidence that the Saudi government as an institution or senior officials within the Saudi government funded al Qaeda."[30] However, before September 11, 2001, the Saudis lacked a financial regulatory system and did not oversee their charities.

David Aufhauser, who led the Bush administration's interagency process on terrorist financing, declared in June 2003 that Saudi Arabia was the "epicenter" for the financing of Al Qaeda,[31] and it remains important today for groups like the Islamic State. Even when money did not go directly into the hands of terrorists, critics blast the Saudis for supporting charities, schools, and religious institutions that endorse the legitimacy of violent jihad and that criticize US policy and Western values. Proselytizing by these organizations enables Al Qaeda and its allies to appeal to recruits already made sympathetic to their worldview.

Al Qaeda itself violently opposes the Al Saud regime, which it considers to be an apostate regime, and seeks its overthrow. But despite its strong anti-regime sentiments, the threat that Al Qaeda actually posed to the royal family seemed quite limited for many years, particularly in the eyes of Saudi leaders. The Al Saud regime's passivity in the face of popular support for extremist causes began to change after the September 11 attacks. As the spotlight turned on Saudi Arabia in the wake of the attacks (in part because 15 of the

19 hijackers were Saudis and Bin Laden was once a Saudi citizen), the Al Saud regime began to move away from many of the causes it had once embraced. However, it still did not aggressively confront its Islamist opponents, and some senior Saudis still denied that the Kingdom had an Al Qaeda problem.

The crackdown on Al Qaeda escalated dramatically after Al Qaeda created a Saudi-based affiliate that launched attacks inside Saudi Arabia itself. On May 12, 2003, Al Qaeda militants launched multiple attacks on compounds housing US security personnel living in the Kingdom, killing 34. Other attacks followed, and Al Qaeda forces conducted numerous gun battles with the regime security forces hunting them.

In response to this marked uptick in terrorist violence within the Kingdom, Saudi Arabia improved its intelligence capabilities and strengthened the paramilitary forces going after Al Qaeda. The Kingdom also created an amnesty program to encourage militants to defect and worked with influential preachers to convince fighters to lay down their arms. The Saudi religious establishment was highly critical of extremists for attacking fellow Muslims, in contrast to past attacks that had primarily targeted Americans. Even former firebrands such as Safar al-Hawali and Salman al-Ouda—sheikhs whom Bin Laden himself had praised in the early 1990s—condemned the May 2003 attacks. The Kingdom also put repentant militants on television, using their stories to discredit the Al Qaeda cause and playing up images of dead children and reports of plots to attack mosques to destroy the heroic image that Al Qaeda fighters tried to cultivate. On the financial front, the Saudis increased their regulation of informal money transfers, stepped up fund-management responsibility, and increased prohibitions on charitable donations outside the Kingdom. By the end of 2005, the low-level insurgency that Al Qaeda had fostered in the Kingdom was crushed.

Unfortunately, Saudi Arabia remains a developing nation where inefficiency is often the rule rather than the exception. Oversight of charitable giving remains incomplete, and many of the Kingdom's new initiatives have not been tested. Nor has Saudi Arabia tackled the knotty issue of fire-breathing preachers and institutions that spread intolerance or aggressively tried to hinder jihadists who do not directly threaten the Kingdom. So while the Saudi government targets Al Qaeda, its citizens still play an important role as recruits and financiers for jihadist organizations.

Why Does Pakistan Support Jihadists?

When Pakistan and India broke apart in 1947, Pakistani leaders stirred up religious fervor and covertly employed militants to prevent the state of Kashmir, disputed between the two new countries (and by Kashmiris who want to be independent from both), from joining the Indian union. Pakistan's attempt backfired, driving the neutral-leaning Maharaja of Kashmir into India's arms. Despite this lesson, Pakistan would repeatedly use militant groups as an instrument of foreign policy over the next 70 years, hoping that the groups would bolster the government's legitimacy at home while granting it deniability abroad.

India dominates the national security thinking of the Pakistani state. Pakistan expert C. Christine Fair contends that "Pakistan's fears about India are historical, neuralgic, and deeply existential."[32] As time has gone on, India has outclassed Pakistan militarily and economically, increasing Pakistan's reliance on militant groups by default. The two enemies have had several wars since 1947, and the latest phase in the rivalry began after unrest broke out in Kashmir in 1989. Pakistan again backed insurgents there and eventually used jihadist groups such as Jaish-e Mohammad, Lashkar-e Taiba, and Harkat-ul-Jihadi-Islami. Civilian and military governments in Pakistan have both supported these militants.

Pakistan-backed groups are responsible for some of the worst attacks on India, notably Lashkar-e Taiba's December 2001 attack on India's parliament and its 2008 attack on hotels that catered to Westerners, a Jewish community center, and other targets in Mumbai that killed over 160 people. In 1999, the Pakistani military worked with militants to seize key passes in the Kargil area on the Indian side of the "Line of Control" (the de facto border between India and Pakistan) in Kashmir. Bruce Riedel, an expert on terrorism and Pakistan, found that the terrorist attacks and the Kargil crisis almost led to a massive Indian military response, which could have escalated into an all-out war—a terrifying possibility, as both countries are nuclear powers.[33] Nor are such attacks a thing of the past: with the support of Pakistani intelligence, Lashkar-e

Taiba regularly conducts attacks on Indian targets, disrupting moves towards peace and seeking to provoke an Indian response.[34] Yet India's relative restraint is not certain, and another attack on Indian facilities abroad or sensitive sites within India could spark a bigger war.

Though Pakistan's military and intelligence services have worked with these groups directly, the level of control often varies. According to scholar and former US official Ashley Tellis, Pakistani intelligence enjoys considerable latitude when planning operations and usually gives its own operatives a high degree of flexibility. Officials at the top of the government set policy, but implementation is often controlled far down the command chain.[35] Pakistani intelligence also outsources some support, including fundraising, recruitment, and even training, to an array of domestic Islamist groups. Powerful domestic organizations like the Jamiat Ulema-e-Islam (JUI) and the Jamaat-e Islami (JI) that seek to Islamicize Pakistan also have their own preferred militant groups. Pakistani leaders also work with explicitly sectarian groups, such as the virulently anti-Shi'a group Sipah-e Sehaba-Pakistan, in exchange for their political support. These groups share Pakistan's antipathy toward India, but they also promulgate jihadist ideas—the need to fight foreign oppressors, the illegitimacy of secular governments, and the duty of young men to embrace jihad—that Al Qaeda shares. (I realize the number of groups involved is confusing, but naming names gives us a sense of the complexity and extent of Pakistan's efforts.)

Pakistan's policies in Afghanistan derive from its fixation with India: it fears that a hostile government in Kabul would team up with India, while a friendly government would help train militants, provide strategic depth in the event of a war, and otherwise assist in operations against India. To this end, Pakistan midwifed the Taliban and helped it conquer Afghanistan before 9/11. Because of Pakistan's deep support of the Taliban—and the Taliban's own support for jihadist causes—as the Taliban gained power, it also supported Pakistani-backed militants fighting in Kashmir.

In the wake of 9/11, Pakistan turned on Al Qaeda and other foreign jihadists and (temporarily) tried to restrict the activities of several other groups in order to avoid America's wrath. At the same time, Pakistan remained close to the Afghan Taliban and to those groups it considers "good jihadists," such as Lashkar-e Taiba, that help it fight India in Kashmir.[36] Some of these relationships are advantageous from Pakistan's point of view: US forces are drawing down significantly in 2015, and the Taliban will play an important role in the country's future—a painful reality recognized by Afghan leaders, including Ashraf Ghani, who became Afghanistan's president in 2014. Pakistani intelligence works with Islamist groups in Pakistan that run religious schools and together raise thousands of recruits, including suicide bombers, to help the Taliban in its fight against the United States and the US-backed government in Kabul.[37]

Putting aside the danger this poses to the United States, the problem for Pakistan is that "good" and "bad" jihadists overlap: some groups that share Pakistan's goals in India and Afghanistan are also seeking an Islamic state in Pakistan itself and support Al Qaeda.[38] Although Lashkar-e Taiba has remained loyal to the Pakistani state, other radicals have turned against it, sowing destruction in Pakistan itself through suicide bombings and attacks on military and government targets (often loosely defined to even include schools where military families are educated). Many Pakistani militants are particularly critical of Pakistan's cooperation with the United States against Al Qaeda and see the government itself as an apostate regime, despite its protestations of being a government of and for Muslims. In 2007, a number of the most rejectionist factions came together formally under the banner of the Pakistani Taliban (not to be confused with the Afghan Taliban), but they remain loosely organized. Some of these anti-state groups attack Pakistani religious minorities such as Shi'ite Muslims, Hindus, Sikhs, Christians, Ahmadis (a Muslim splinter group), and even Barelvis, a Sufi-influenced Sunni movement to which most Pakistanis belong but that hardline jihadists consider apostate. The violence has spread throughout the country, with core areas like the Punjab suffering regular attacks. Hundreds die in these attacks, and in 2014, the Pew Research Center declared Pakistan one of the world's most hostile nations for religious minorities.[39]

The Pakistani government has warred against these anti-state jihadists, but it is losing. Pakistan deployed tens of thousands of troops in dozens of major operations, but though they would at times take territory, they often did not hold it, allowing militants to return and regroup. The army was brutal in its operations—one investigation of an operation in South Waziristan (a region of Pakistan located in the north, near the Afghan border) found that roughly 200,000 locals were displaced; millions were also displaced in operations in the more heavily populated Swat district.[40] These operations furthered the cycle of violence, with suicide bombings and assassinations becoming more and more common as the militants took revenge and sought to further weaken the state. The Pakistani government at times resorted to the humiliating approach of giving militant groups a haven in an area in order to establish a ceasefire, which only served to further reduce the government's credibility. Of great concern to the military, the radicals are also making inroads into the military's ranks and officer corps.[41] In addition, radical groups regularly attack Indian targets, sowing mistrust and torpedoing efforts by Pakistani Prime Minister Nawaz Sharif and others to effect a rapprochement with India.[42]

Since 9/11, over 4,000 Pakistani troops have died fighting militants, almost twice as many as the NATO and US forces who died next door in Afghanistan. In that same time period, Pakistani media claim that Pakistan has lost over 40,000 citizens to jihadist violence—this is almost certainly an exaggeration, but the real figures are certainly quite high.[43] In the end, it is Pakistan, more than any of its enemies, that has paid the highest price for Pakistani support for terrorism.

What Is the Relationship Between Pakistan and Al Qaeda?

Pakistan's relationship with Al Qaeda is complex and contradictory. On the one hand, Pakistan is engaged in a war with Al Qaeda and its allies—a war that has killed thousands of Pakistanis and has helped weaken the Al Qaeda core. On the other hand, Pakistan has indirectly, and at times directly, abetted Al Qaeda, largely by strengthening the broader jihadist movement as part of its rivalry with India. These contradictory policies have enabled Al Qaeda to survive and at times even prosper in Pakistan.

During the fight against the Soviet Union in Afghanistan, it was Pakistan that disbursed US money and otherwise controlled the flow of aid to the *mujahedin*. As Brigadier Mohammad Yousaf, who headed Pakistani intelligence in the mid-1980s, noted, "although they [the Americans] paid the piper they could not call the tune. . . . [A] cardinal rule of Pakistan's policy was that no Americans ever become involved in the distribution of funds or arms once they arrived in the country. No Americans ever trained or had direct contact with the *mujahedin* and no American official ever went inside Afghanistan."[44]

Before 9/11, Pakistan was perhaps as important as Afghanistan to Al Qaeda—it was in the Pakistani city of Peshawar, after all, that Al Qaeda was founded in 1988. Al Qaeda maintained guest houses and training camps in Pakistan. Training camps in Afghanistan under the Taliban, some run by Al Qaeda, often trained Pakistani militants fighting in Kashmir as well, and the various groups saw Al Qaeda fighters as comrades in a broader struggle. The Pakistani government, both civilian and military, thus allowed Al Qaeda and the so-called Afghan Arabs to maintain a presence as the decade went on, though this would rise and fall depending on outside pressure and the Pakistani government's needs of the moment. Pakistan probably knew of Bin Laden's return to Afghanistan in 1996 and perhaps even facilitated it.[45]

In Pakistan, more than any other country, the connections between Al Qaeda and like-minded groups are vital to understand. Al Qaeda was born, grew, and became strong amid a supportive jihadist milieu. Much of this support was carried out via sympathetic domestic Pakistani militant groups and jihadist groups that Pakistan backed in its fight against India, rather than directly by the Pakistani regime. Al Qaeda has never had (and still does not have) a Pakistani affiliate, but as C. Christine Fair contends, it "relies upon a web of information relations with groups based in Pakistan" in order to gain help with operations both inside and outside Pakistan.[46] As scholar Zahid Hussein found, "Pakistani militant groups provided al-Qaeda with logistical support, safe houses, false documentation and, occasionally, manpower."[47]

After the Taliban fell in December 2001, much of the Al Qaeda core fled to Pakistan. Some found their way to Pakistan's main cities. Khalid Sheikh Mohammad (KSM), the 9/11 mastermind, and Omar Sheikh, a British-Pakistani terrorist, both hid out in Karachi, where they kidnapped and murdered the American journalist Daniel Pearl; other militants bombed the Sheraton hotel and killed US defense contractors. Al Qaeda figures settled in cities like Quetta and Rawalpindi—and, of course, Bin Laden ended up in Abbottabad.

Pakistani leaders faced a dilemma after 9/11: how to continue to use jihadist groups to fight India, placate key domestic groups, and shape regional politics, yet cooperate with the United States in the "War on Terror" to gain US goodwill and support (and avoid the wrath of an America in no mood to tolerate open Pakistani opposition). Pakistan tried to square the circle: it maintained support for some militant groups, particularly those focused on India, but allowed the United States to supply US and NATO forces in Afghanistan via Pakistan and gave the United States access and overflight rights—significant assistance. Pakistan also fought against the Arab-dominated Al Qaeda and Uzbek groups, mounting operations that led to the arrest or death of many Al Qaeda figures. Indeed, in the years that immediately followed 9/11, almost every major arrest of an Al Qaeda figure, including KSM, Ramzi bin al-Shibh, and Sharib Ahmad, occurred with the assistance of the Pakistani government.

This steady wave of arrests—over 300 in the first five years after 9/11—led Al Qaeda to migrate to the Federally Administered Tribal Areas (FATA) and other remote parts of Pakistan. The FATA is a remote, semi-autonomous frontier region on the border between Pakistan and Afghanistan with towering mountains, huge gorges, and a sparse population suspicious of government and generally sympathetic to the jihadists. There, Al Qaeda members continued to fight, along with several hundred other Arabs and other nationalities who embraced Al Qaeda's goals and ideology. These fighters in turn collaborated, and often intermarried, with local Pakistani tribes that had their own anti-government and anti-Western agendas.

The Al Qaeda core continued to direct attacks in the West and against targets elsewhere in the world from its relatively safe haven in the FATA. In their study of Al Qaeda's activities in the decade after 9/11, scholars Bruce Hoffman and Fernando Reinares found that the core organization "appeared to have a direct hand in the most important and potentially high-payoff operations."[48] Some of the most important post-9/11 operations, such as the July 7, 2005, attacks in London, emanated from Pakistan, and many involved the Al Qaeda core working with Pakistan-based militant groups. Al Qaeda also engages in limited training and assists the Afghan Taliban in fighting US and Afghan government forces.

When Bin Laden was found and killed in Abbottabad, a tranquil city in Pakistan where he lived in a compound near Pakistan's military academy, many wondered whether Pakistan's intelligence agencies were incompetent, in bed with Al Qaeda, or both. Specific details on Pakistan's role are hard to come by. However, the *New York Times* reported that Bin Laden regularly corresponded from his hideout in Abbottabad with Mullah Omar, the Taliban leader, and Hafiz Muhammad Saeed, the founder of Lashkar-e Taiba, both of whom allegedly work closely with Pakistani intelligence and are thus likely protected—and monitored—carefully by Pakistani intelligence. In addition, Pakistani security reportedly escorted Bin Laden to various meetings with his aides elsewhere in Pakistan. Finally, the report stated that Pakistani intelligence itself even had a special officer assigned to control Bin Laden—and that Pakistan's top military officials knew about it.[49]

Pakistan's attempt to square the circle on Al Qaeda has failed. The array of jihadist groups it reportedly supports against India foster Al Qaeda's ideology, provide it with a haven, assist in training, and otherwise advance the organization, counteracting Islamabad's efforts against it. Indeed, by trying to walk such a careful line, Pakistan has frustrated all sides: jihadist groups are more and more active against the Pakistani state and society, while outside supporters like the United States question the country's commitment to fighting terrorism. As Fair contends, "The biggest hindrances to 'saving Pakistan' are the intentions, interests, and strategic calculation of the Pakistani state itself."[50]

Why Doesn't Pakistan Cooperate More with the United States?

The United States did not focus on the Pakistan problem until late in the game. Pakistan was largely ignored in the 1990s, and in the aftermath of 9/11, Islamabad's initial cooperation against Al Qaeda made it seem like it had turned over a new leaf. Washington slowly realized that Pakistan was still playing both sides, but it did not push Pakistan hard to act against the Afghan Taliban until 2007, even though the Afghan Taliban used Pakistan as a base for attacks on US forces in Afghanistan and the leadership of the Afghan Taliban is based in Pakistan.

The United States has poured billions of dollars into Pakistan's counterterrorism efforts: in fiscal year 2000, the United States gave Pakistan less than $40 million; after 9/11 through fiscal year 2013, the total aid given to Pakistan skyrocketed to almost $30 billion, making Pakistan the second-largest US aid recipient after Afghanistan.[51] This figure excludes covert aid, and the *Los Angeles Times* reported in 2009 that the CIA had given hundreds of millions to Pakistani intelligence, funding a third of its budget.[52] Much of the money went to buy conventional military equipment for the constant struggle with India, and thus did little to help Pakistan fight Al Qaeda or other jihadists. Corrupt officials siphoned off much of the aid, and the money did not significantly improve Pakistan's capacity to fight terrorism.

Yet despite this torrent of cash, Pakistan remains critical of the United States, and the government inculcates a steady drumbeat of anti-Americanism within the country. Pakistan's grievance list is long, and not altogether unjustified: it claims that the United States has repeatedly cut off arms to Pakistan at key moments in the country's history and, in general, has abandoned it when the security concerns of the moment shifted. In addition, the United States has steadily tilted toward India, Pakistan's nemesis, given India's steadily greater economic and political role in the world. After 9/11, the United States also worked with the anti-Taliban Northern Alliance, which Pakistan saw as India's proxy in Afghanistan, and Washington did little to address Pakistan's concerns regarding Kashmir.

The Pakistani security establishment has pushed a steady diet of anti-Americanism, inflating the casualty figures from drone strikes and blaming the United States for many of the country's problems. Pakistanis, in general, have more anger and distrust toward the United States than they do toward Al Qaeda.[53] As a result, the agendas of militant groups like Al Qaeda enjoy more support, and US counterterrorism is deemed illegitimate.

How Important Is Israel?

Al Qaeda has always opposed Israel's existence and at times attacked what it considered Jewish and Israeli targets. Yet the Jewish state has never been an Al Qaeda priority, and it has proven more useful for Al Qaeda as a propaganda foil than as an actual enemy.

Al Qaeda, like most Islamic extremist groups in the Middle East, rejects Israel's very existence and laments the plight of the Palestinians. Its propaganda is often viscerally anti-Semitic and paints the issue in existential terms: Bin Laden declared, "The enmity between us and the Jews goes far back in time and is deeply rooted. There is no question that war between the two of us is inevitable."[54] Al Qaeda considers Israel a dagger stuck into the heart of the Muslim community and little more than "a huge U.S. military base."[55] For Al Qaeda, the existence of the Jewish state is clear proof that the United States and the West want to control Muslim lands.

However, unlike many other well-known Middle Eastern terrorist groups—such as Hizballah and Hamas—Al Qaeda does not consider Israel a priority. Instead, Al Qaeda has merely tried to paint Israel as part of its fight against America: Israel is America's "spoiled child," and conversely, Americans are the slaves of the Jews, helping Israel survive and expand.[56] Back before he was the leader of Al Qaeda, when his exclusive focus was on overthrowing the corrupt regime in Egypt, Ayman al-Zawahiri came under pressure from other Islamists, including the leader of Palestinian Islamic Jihad, to attack Israel; yet despite this substantial pressure, Zawahiri resolutely maintained that Israel should only be fought once there was a true Islamic government in Egypt. This view of Israel as a relatively unimportant target endured even as Zawahiri abandoned the Egyptian project and embraced Bin Laden's more global ambitions. In a 2005 letter to Abu Musab al-Zarqawi in Iraq, Zawahiri contended that the fight against Israel should wait until after America was expelled from Iraq, an Islamic state was established there, and Iraq's neighbors also succumbed.

Israel is most useful to Al Qaeda as a propaganda tool. Bin Laden's 1998 call to jihad was done in the name of the "World Islamic Front for Jihad Against the Jews and Crusaders"—the United States and Israel were linked from the very start. In almost every propaganda statement, Bin Laden and Zawahiri reference the Palestinian cause to stir up anger among Muslims. This is no accident. In his treatise on the successes and failures of the jihadist movement, *Knights Under the Prophet's Banner*, Zawahiri explains that adopting an anti-Israel message is the best way to mobilize the Muslim masses to support the jihadist cause. He states that "the issue of Palestine is the cause that has been firing up the feelings of the Muslim nation from Morocco to Indonesia for the past 50 years. In addition, it is a rallying point for all the Arabs, be they believers or non-believers, good or evil."[57] Israel's continued survival is a painful reminder of the failure of Muslim governments to protect Muslims, and when these governments sign peace deals, agree to ceasefires, or simply ignore the conflict with Israel, it serves as further proof of their continued betrayal.

Proximity also matters. Israel is a small country with well-guarded borders, and it is already on high alert because of its never-ending struggle against Hizballah and Hamas, two formidable terrorist organizations, and because of the long and tragic history of horrendous persecution of the Jewish people. As a result, Al Qaeda's decision not to attack Israel has a lot to do with the fact that it is hard for it to get close enough to do so. In 2002, Al Qaeda-linked militants attacked an Israeli-owned hotel in Kenya, killing 13, and unsuccessfully fired missiles at an Israeli airliner.[58] Also that year, Al Qaeda operatives bombed the historic Ghriba synagogue in Tunisia, killing 19. In 2003, Al Qaeda bombed two synagogues in Istanbul, killing 27. But all of these were targets far from Israel itself.

Perhaps surprisingly, the presence of Hamas and Hizballah on Israel's borders has also made it harder for Al Qaeda to attack Israel directly. Both these organizations violently oppose Israel, but they also are hostile to Al Qaeda and, in any event, want to control any and all violence originating in the territories where they hold sway. Moreover, if you are a young Palestinian who opposes Israel, there is no need to join Al Qaeda—you can simply join Hamas if you want to fight: the organization has warred with Israel on and off for almost 30 years.

However, the Arab Spring and other dramatic events that have taken place in the countries that border Israel are changing the equation. Even if they have few if any links to the Al Qaeda core (at least for now), jihadists with ideologies similar to Al Qaeda's are now active in the Sinai Peninsula and the Gaza Strip, both of which are within a stone's throw of Israel, and the civil war in Syria has brought Al Qaeda-linked jihadists within mortar range of Israel's northern territory. Attacks on Israel are becoming more feasible, and they may become more appealing as the core organization seeks to prove its relevance. The days of Al Qaeda merely giving lip service to the goal of attacking Israel may be coming to an end.

How Do Muslims Perceive Al Qaeda and Why Does It Matter?

Al Qaeda has rarely achieved serious popularity, in part because its fighters have few ties to local communities. Whether in Sudan, Afghanistan, or Pakistan, Al Qaeda and other Arab Afghans were always outsiders, at best admired by, but never part of, the local population. In contrast to Hamas or Hizballah, Al Qaeda does not provide social services and, in general, has sought to be a vanguard organization rather than a mass movement. Al Qaeda affiliates may do better in this regard, as they tend to recruit from and be more grounded in their host communities; a few even provide social services, and thus enjoy support from at least part of the population. Yet many Muslims embrace some of Al Qaeda's ideas and causes and revile many of the foes Al Qaeda fights.

Polling indicates that support for Al Qaeda steadily fell from a high point in 2003, when the United States invaded Iraq and inflamed anti-US sentiment throughout much of the Muslim world. Polls asking Palestinians about "Confidence in Osama bin Laden" indicate a fall from 72% in 2003 to 34% in 2011, when Bin Laden was killed. Egypt, Pakistan, Indonesia, and other Muslim countries saw similar declines. Polls taken in 2014 indicate that Al Qaeda has not recovered its popularity from its abusive behavior in Iraq, and many Muslims scorn it.[59]

Al Qaeda's killing of non-combatants is especially unpopular. In a series of Gallup polls, over 90% of Muslims condemned the killing of civilians.[60] Indeed, after a successful attack, support for Al Qaeda often decreases. Following the 2005 suicide bombings in Amman, Jordan, by Al Qaeda in Iraq, confidence in Bin Laden among Jordanians plummeted from a peak of 61% to 24% the next year.[61]

An important source of the decline in Al Qaeda's legitimacy has been the steady condemnation of the group by Muslim religious scholars and community leaders. (There is a myth out there that moderate Muslims have not stepped up and condemned terrorism, when in fact they have done so openly and repeatedly.[62]) The 9/11 attacks led to condemnations worldwide: to take only one among the most prominent, dozens of leaders of a range of Islamist organizations such as the Muslim Brotherhood in Egypt and Jamaat-e Islami in Pakistan signed a joint statement declaring themselves "horrified" by 9/11 and condemning it "in the strongest terms." Over

100 Muslim leaders and intellectuals in the United States similarly declared, "neither the al-Qaeda organization nor Usama bin Laden represents Islam." After the Al Qaeda attacks in the United Kingdom on July 7, 2005, over 500 British Muslim religious leaders and scholars issued a formal religious decree (*fatwa*) declaring that "Islam strictly, strongly and severely condemns the use of violence and destruction of innocent lives. . . . Suicide bombing, which killed and injured innocent people in London are HARAAM—vehemently prohibited in Islam, and those who committed these barbaric acts in London are criminals, not martyrs."[63]

Yet to say that Muslims condemn Al Qaeda and attacks on innocents is both true and misleading. Al Qaeda stands against many things, and its activities range from terrorist attacks on the United States and Israel to violence against governments throughout the Muslim world, the UN, and Western relief organizations. Other strains of the jihadist movement decry the West's tolerance of homosexuality, treatment of women, and infidel nature. Some Muslims also oppose some of these causes some of the time, and Al Qaeda and its allies draw on this anger.

Al Qaeda and its allies fare better when the image of the United States is doing poorly among Muslim publics or when the issue of the moment is resisting foreigners. When opinion of the United States reached its nadir at the beginning of the 2003 Iraq war, Muslim leaders hesitated to condemn Al Qaeda, fearing they would be painted as US lackeys. Many Muslims also draw a distinction between what they consider legitimate resistance—going after, say, American soldiers in Iraq, whom they view as invaders—and strikes on civilians, which they consider illegitimate. However, the United States tends to label all attacks on Americans by a terrorist group as "terrorism," failing to distinguish between attacks on soldiers during war and strikes on civilians outside a conflict zone.

Finally, even relatively small numbers of supporters can generate a big problem. With over a billion Muslims worldwide, having a 5% approval rating means a base of over 50 million people. And in the Palestinian territories, Indonesia, Egypt, and Pakistan, Al Qaeda has often enjoyed approval from a more significant minority of the population, typically ranging from 10% to one-third, depending on the year and the poll.[64] Even in the West there is some support for the grievances Al Qaeda claims to champion. A poll taken after the July

2005 London bombings found that while an overwhelming majority of British Muslims condemned the attacks, one-fifth had at least some sympathy with the bombers' motives.[65] From these potential supporters, Al Qaeda seeks recruits, money, and silence when its operatives are trying to hide in their midst.

Yet although terrorists can survive with small numbers, public opinion still matters tremendously. If Al Qaeda is widely condemned, then local governments are more likely to cooperate with the United States against the group, as they suffer no political price for doing so. Local populations will provide intelligence and otherwise assist in going after Al Qaeda if its members are considered criminals rather than heroes—information that can prove invaluable in dismantling cells and disrupting terror plots. And even within the more radical community, recruits and donors are less supportive when they do not bask in popular approval.

How Did the Arab Spring Affect Al Qaeda?

At first, many analysts believed that the Arab Spring would turn out to be Al Qaeda's worst nightmare, but it is now proving to have given Al Qaeda a new lease on life. When popular protests led to the fall of the Ben Ali government of Tunisia in January 2011 and the dramatic collapse of the Mubarak regime in Egypt a month later, Al Qaeda was caught flat-footed. Bin Laden initially offered praise for such a "great and glorious event." Zawahiri's comments trickled in to his followers well after the dramatic events occurred, and even then they were more a series of rambles on history than guidance on how to interpret this revolutionary change. Qaddafi's regime in Libya was toppled in August 2011, Ali Abdullah Saleh fell in Yemen in February 2012, and for a while Bashar al-Asad in Syria seemed poised to join the ranks of the defeated. In May 2011, in the midst of these revolutions, US Navy SEALs killed Bin Laden.

Al Qaeda and its mission seemed like yesterday's news. Despite scheming against the Mubarak regime since the 1970s and killing innocent Egyptians in the name of toppling the regime from power, Ayman al-Zawahiri and his cohorts had contributed nothing to the fall of the dictatorship. In contrast, peaceful protest—not violence—was what swept Mubarak from power. The demonstrators in Tahrir Square and elsewhere in the Middle East seemed to offer hope for new politics. As US Secretary of State Hillary Clinton said of Al Qaeda's leaders, "I hope they were watching on television as Egyptian young people proved them wrong."

When dictators such as Mubarak fall due to pressure from pro-democracy protesters, Al Qaeda loses one of its best recruiting pitches: the repression that Arab governments inflict on their citizens. Yet although Al Qaeda opposes regional dictators, it did not rejoice in free elections. Al Qaeda itself strongly opposes democracy. Its leaders, like many Salafis (including those opposed to violence), believe that democratic institutions place man's law above God's—a parliament, after all, could legalize drinking alcohol or otherwise contravene Islamic law. Similarly, Al Qaeda rejects any legal tradition outside a strict application of Islamic law. Zawahiri declared democracy a false religion and charged that supporting it is "tantamount to associating idols with God and falling into unbelief."[66]

Although the rise of the Muslim Brotherhood in Egypt and like-minded Islamists in Libya, Tunisia, and Yemen frightened some in the West who wrongly equate Al Qaeda and Islamism, this was in fact a potential blow for Zawahiri's organization. The Brotherhood's pragmatism and, in most countries, embrace of peaceful politics is anathema to Al Qaeda. In Egypt, Salafi groups also shed their traditional aversion to politics and entered the fray. The engagement of these Islamist movements in politics seemed to show that an Islamic state was best achieved peacefully and gradually, through the political process. One former leading jihadist declared that he and his group entered politics because Islamist rule was being achieved through elections.[67]

Yet even from the start there were cracks in this picture. The authoritarian governments that fell, such as the Mubarak regime in Egypt and the Qaddafi regime in Libya, were staunch, indeed brutal, foes of Al Qaeda. On their own, they imprisoned hundreds of jihadists, along with even more minor players and innocents who were swept up in the massive crackdowns. When these repressive regimes fell, the United States lost intelligence partners that were fully committed to crushing the global jihadist movement.

As dictators fell, prisons opened up. Hundreds of jihadists, some linked to Al Qaeda, were freed in Egypt and Libya, including notable figures such as Muhammad al-Zawahiri, Ayman's brother who was also a prominent jihadist. In general, governments became weak, creating or worsening ungoverned spaces. In some regions of once-strong dictatorships, like the Sinai in Egypt, terrorist groups flourished. Indeed, the Arab Spring was accompanied by civil war in Libya and Syria and significant unrest in Yemen. Jihadist voices and forces in Libya and especially Syria have gone from being marginal players to being core parts of the opposition.

The failure of the Arab Spring to produce stable, democratic governments has proven an even greater boon. Seemingly discredited in 2011, Al Qaeda's long-standing argument that an Islamic state could never be achieved through the ballot box seemed vindicated by the military coup in Egypt. Suppressing the Brotherhood's political aspirations in Egypt and elsewhere risks alienating younger, less patient Islamists. They, in turn, may find Al Qaeda's message attractive, believing that the new governments being formed across the Arab world are inherently un-Islamic and that force is the only currency that matters. Only Tunisia so far can be deemed a democratic success, and its small and peripheral status limits its inspirational power—particularly given the failed transitions elsewhere in the region that bolster the authoritarian regimes' argument that democracy would only bring strife.

The result is that several years after the momentous uprisings of the Arab Spring began, what was initially hailed as the death knell of the jihadist cause now seems to have both reinforced Al Qaeda's ideology and improved its operational position. The counterrevolution in Egypt has discredited peaceful change as a route to an Islamic government. Meanwhile, weak governments and all-out civil war have given Al Qaeda far more freedom of movement and new opportunities to exploit.

7

BEYOND THE AL QAEDA CORE

What Are the Key Al Qaeda Affiliates?

In his May 23, 2013, speech on counterterrorism—perhaps his most important public statement on this issue so far—President Obama contended, "Today, the core of al Qaeda in Afghanistan and Pakistan is on a path to defeat." However, the president then went on to warn that "what we've seen is the emergence of various al Qaeda affiliates. From Yemen to Iraq, from Somalia to North Africa, the threat today is more diffuse, with Al Qaeda's affiliate in the Arabian Peninsula—AQAP—the most active in plotting against our homeland."[1] In 2013, four of the five most lethal terrorist groups (according to the Global Terrorism Database) were directly or indirectly linked to Al Qaeda or the broader global jihadist movement: Al Shabaab, the Islamic State, the Taliban, and the Tehrik-i-Taliban Pakistan.[2] This violence is especially notable, as in 2012 and 2013 the Al Qaeda core itself did not conduct any attacks. Indeed, whether the US-led struggle against Al Qaeda is succeeding may boil down to one issue: the relationship between the Al Qaeda core and its affiliates.

Al Qaeda, like terrorist groups before it, has supported and cooperated with fellow travelers since its inception. Yet, at times, it does more than this, creating formalized relationships whereby a previously independent group takes on the Al Qaeda label and accepts, at least nominally, the authority of Zawahiri (and before that, Bin Laden). This process accelerated after 9/11 as US pressure forced the core to seek out new ways to remain active. Al Qaeda in Iraq was at one time perhaps the most important affiliate, but it had a rocky relationship with the core and its successor organization would eventually reject Zawahiri's leadership in 2014. In 2014, Al Qaeda had four major affiliates: Al Qaeda in the Arabian Peninsula (AQAP), Al Qaeda in the Islamic Maghreb (AQIM), Al Shabaab in Somalia, and Jabhat al-Nusra in Syria. In September 2014, Zawahiri also declared an Al Qaeda affiliate in the Indian subcontinent, which quickly tried—and just as quickly failed—to attack a US Navy vessel (and is not discussed in this volume as it is too soon to determine how serious this group is). Although the key affiliates share many similarities, each has a unique history and distinct objectives.

Al Qaeda in the Arabian Peninsula

Al Qaeda and the broader jihadist movement have long had a presence in both Saudi Arabia and Yemen. Throughout the 1990s, and even today, Saudi Arabia and other Gulf states were an important fundraising source for Al Qaeda and other jihadist causes. Saudi Arabia was Bin Laden's birthplace and the birthplace of Wahhabism. Yemen was the ancestral home of the Bin Laden family and was a logistical hub for operations such as the 1998 US embassy bombings, as well as the location of the 2000 attack on USS *Cole*. In addition, both countries were important sources of Al Qaeda recruits.

The original, Saudi-based organization known as Al Qaeda in the Arabian Peninsula was set up by Bin Laden after 9/11 and instructed in 2002 to prepare for a campaign inside the Kingdom. Many of its fighters were Saudis who had trained in Afghanistan and returned to the Kingdom after the fall of the Taliban, and a significant number had spent time in Saudi prisons where some were brutalized.[3] The top Al Qaeda leadership established parallel networks inside the Kingdom and decided the timing of each branch's campaigns; thus, the Saudi group was the first affiliate organization to make "Al Qaeda" part of its official name.

After a series of attacks on Western and Saudi targets that began in earnest in 2003, the group collapsed, with effective operations ending in 2006. The Saudi government launched a devastating campaign against the group, arresting or killing many of its members, and the Saudi religious establishment and many religious leaders who in the past had seemed favorable to the Salafi-jihadist cause denounced the movement. This, along with the group's killing of Muslim civilians, tarnished its appeal within the Kingdom, and the group fell apart.

Some group members fled to Yemen, where they joined with local jihadists who had rebounded after setbacks earlier in the decade. They quickly rebuilt their organization in 2006–2007 and began a terrorist and insurgent campaign in 2008 under the new name of Al Qaeda Organization of Jihad in the South of the Arabian Peninsula (where Yemen is located). In 2009, that group joined with the remnant of the original Saudi organization and declared itself Al Qaeda in the Arabian Peninsula.

AQAP today is far more linked to the Al Qaeda core, more global in outlook, and more professional than its Yemeni predecessors. AQAP's leader, Nasir al-Wuhayshi, was one of Bin Laden's lieutenants before 9/11, and in 2013 Zawahiri reportedly appointed him as a general manager who would coordinate military and propaganda activities of Al Qaeda, suggesting considerable integration between AQAP and the Al Qaeda core. However, documents found during the raid that killed Bin Laden showed that he saw AQAP as inexperienced, prone to mistakes, and too focused on Yemen.[4]

The bulk of AQAP attacks are against Yemeni government targets. AQAP controls significant territory in remote parts of Yemen, particularly in the south, and is conducting a guerrilla war against Yemen's weak but US-backed regime. When the regime of Ali Abdullah Saleh fell in 2012, AQAP exploited the ensuing power vacuum to expand its operations. AQAP has also struck an number of Western targets in Yemen, such as embassies and foreign tourists. AQAP issues both Arabic- and English-language propaganda, the latter making it more attractive to American and Western recruits. Particularly impressive is *Inspire* magazine, an English-language Internet magazine AQAP produces. *Inspire* has high-end production, speaks in a breezy vernacular designed to appeal to young Westerners, and shows a careful monitoring of the West. It regularly features quotes from US counterterrorism experts and officials as well as takes on the latest news, ranging from drone strikes to former Congressman Anthony Weiner's indecent selfies. Its first issue included an article explaining how to "Make a bomb in the kitchen of your Mom."

Unusual for an affiliate group, AQAP also directly targets the US homeland. On Christmas Day 2009 a Nigerian-born AQAP operative named Umar Farouk Abdulmutallab tried to detonate plastic explosives concealed in his underwear aboard an international flight bound for Detroit. Though he failed (he only succeeded in briefly setting himself on fire), the attack was a near-miss, as the explosives had evaded US security measures. In October 2010, AQAP tried to bomb US-bound cargo planes, and in November of that year, the organization declared it would conduct numerous small-scale attacks against America to weaken the US economy. In 2012, US and allied intelligence agencies foiled an AQAP attempt to smuggle a bomb aboard a US airline. These actions led the United States to step up its counterterrorism cooperation with the government of Yemen and to increase its own drone attacks on AQAP targets inside Yemen.

Al Qaeda in the Islamic Maghreb

The Algerian jihad that raged in the 1990s sowed death and destruction on a scale that made even hardened jihadists blanch. Perhaps 200,000 Algerians died, and both the government and their jihadist opponents regularly tortured and abused civilians. Numerous organizations (and factions within them) emerged, disappeared, or split from established groups. One such group, the Salafist Group for Preaching and Combat (GSPC), formed in the 1990s as a splinter of the brutal Armed Islamic Group (GIA)—a group known for its atrocities.

Beginning in 2003, the GSPC started a process that would eventually make it the core of Al Qaeda in the Islamic Maghreb. This process began when a key commander pledged loyalty to Bin Laden and continued in a desultory way for several years until September 2006, when Zawahiri declared a "blessed union" with the GSPC, emphasizing France as a shared enemy and urging the group to become "a bone in the throat of the American and French crusaders."[5] In January 2007, the GSPC declared it was formally changing its name to Al Qaeda in the Islamic Maghreb (*maghreb* is the Arabic word for "west;" the "Islamic Maghreb" is the traditional term used to designate the lands to the west of Egypt that came under Muslim control in the seventh century—namely, Libya, Algeria, Tunisia, Morocco, Mauritania, and Western Sahara).

Like other Al Qaeda affiliates, AQIM conducts guerrilla warfare against government targets in its home country: Algeria, in this case. After taking on the Al Qaeda name, AQIM expanded its regional operations and attacked Western targets such as embassies in and near Algeria, but it did not strike in Europe or the United States. It sees regional governments as apostates and aids local groups in fighting them—AQIM has attacked or assisted groups in Libya, Mali, Mauritania, and Niger, among other countries. AQIM was instrumental in assisting the 2012 uprising in Mali that, until the 2013 French intervention, led to large portions of the country coming under Islamist control. AQIM also informally works with members of other regional jihadist groups, assisting them with training and logistics. AQIM is particularly fond of kidnapping, which it uses to terrorize the population, scare Westerners away from the region, and, especially, raise money by demanding ransom. AQIM also uses its transnational presence to engage in smuggling.

AQIM is divided into various brigades that operate with a high degree of autonomy. Part of this is to ensure operational freedom in the face of the tough Algerian counterterrorism response, but personal rivalries play an important part as well. General Martin Dempsey, the Chairman of the Joint Chiefs of Staff, described AQIM as "a syndicate of groups who come together episodically. . . . Sometimes their cause is terrorism. Sometimes it's criminal."[6] One notorious commander, Mokhtar Belmokhtar, left AQIM with his followers and attacked the In Amenas gas facility in Algeria, taking over 800 people, many of them Westerners working at the massive facility, hostage for several days. The Algerian military's campaign to free the hostages and capture the militants left at least 23 hostages and 32 militants dead.

Al Shabaab

In February 2012, the Somali-based group known as Al Shabaab (which technically means "the young men" in Arabic but is used more casually here to mean something along the lines of "the guys") formally declared its loyalty to Al Qaeda, a move that capped the transformation of Al Qaeda's on-again, off-again relationship with Somali militants into a more substantial partnership.[7] In the early 1990s, Al Qaeda tried to work in the collapsed Somali state, but often found the violent civil war there overwhelming—so much so that its operatives were unable to make significant inroads, though it was able to use Somalia as part of a regional base for attacks against US and United Nations peacekeepers and strikes in Kenya against US and Israeli targets.[8]

Al Shabaab split off from the Islamic Courts Union, a more moderate Islamist group that had controlled much of Somalia but was ousted from power when Ethiopia invaded in 2006, backing Al Shabaab's opponents—an invasion supported by the United States. Al Shabaab waged an effective insurgency, and in 2009, Ethiopia withdrew its forces. Al Shabaab grew more radical, and in 2008 both Al Qaeda and Al Shabaab used their respective websites to praise each other. In September 2009, Al Shabaab made a public declaration of allegiance to Bin Laden. The love fest continued in the years that followed, with Al Shabaab pledging support for Zawahiri after Bin Laden's death and then in 2012 more formally joining Al Qaeda by declaring that Shabaab members "will march with you as loyal soldiers."[9] Some fighters who had trained in Al Qaeda camps in Afghanistan moved to Somalia to train members of Al Shabaab, and the two groups currently cooperate closely on everything from indoctrination and basic infantry skills to advanced training in explosives and assassination.[10] Al Qaeda members now also reportedly play important roles in Al Shabaab's leadership—many among Al Shabaab's executive council are foreigners,[11] and the organization in turn has embraced more global rhetoric and propaganda.

Al Shabaab has suffered setbacks in recent years: it lost control of Mogadishu in August 2011, and in subsequent years, the Somali government and an African peacekeeping force with significant participation from Burundi, Kenya, and Uganda have further reduced Al Shabaab's sphere of influence. These setbacks have helped contribute to numerous defections from the group. Some Shabaab leaders also rejected the affiliation with Al Qaeda, and infighting has led to clashes between followers of different commanders and purges of senior leaders.

Al Shabaab has so far not attacked the United States or Europe, but it has expanded its regional operations. In particular, Al Shabaab has stepped up attacks against Kenya. On September 21, 2013, Al Shabaab made global headlines when its forces launched a massive, coordinated attack on a shopping mall in Nairobi, Kenya, that lasted four days and left at least 67 people dead and over 200 injured.

Jabhat al-Nusra

Jabhat al-Nusra (JN) is one of the newest Al Qaeda affiliates, and it may prove the most consequential. JN was originally under the control of Al Qaeda in Iraq, though to bolster its credibility it claimed it had no link to AQI or to Al Qaeda. It announced itself in January 2012, well after the fighting in Syria had begun but before it reached the fever pitch that has led to over 200,000 deaths and millions of refugees—tolls that continue to grow every day.

Many JN members are Syrians who were veterans of the fighting against US and allied forces in Iraq—fighting abetted, ironically, by Asad himself in an attempt to undermine the US position next door. As Noman Benotman and Roisin Blake explain,

> Many cadres of JN come from the jihadist network of [Al Qaeda in Iraq leader] Abu Musab al-Zarqawi. . . . Syrians who had been with Al-Zarqawi in Herat, Afghanistan, in 2000 were sent to build branches of his network in Syria and Lebanon, with Al-Zarqawi exercising control from Iraq. These jihadists established "guesthouses" in Syria to channel would-be fighters to Iraq, and the infrastructure flourished. During this period, Syria acted as the main channel for funding for the network. . . .[12]

JN, like other Syrian rebel groups, seeks the overthrow of the Asad regime, but according to a study by the Quilliam Foundation, it also seeks to create an Islamic state in Syria and the broader Levant region. Much of its energy is spent on governing the parts of Syria that it controls—proselytizing, providing social services, and acting as a quasi-state there: an approach distinct from the traditional "vanguard" philosophy of the Al Qaeda core. To spread its ideas, JN operates its own television network and regularly releases videos glorifying its actions. In contrast to many Al Qaeda-linked groups in the past, JN makes a point of working with other Syrian opposition groups to fight the regime and, in relative terms, tries to avoid abuses of civilians in areas under its control. Its philosophy emphasizes influential Salafi-jihadist ideologue Abu Muhammad al-Maqdisi's ideas of creating an Islamic state and proselytizing there, rather than brutally imposing the group's will on the population.

JN seeks to wear down the Syrian regime through steady attacks, following a time-honored strategy of guerrillas throughout history. In rural areas where the regime's control is weak, JN either controls territory directly or operates as a strong guerrilla force; in urban areas, it functions as a clandestine terrorist group. The vast majority of its attacks are against government forces or facilities; it is also behind many suicide bombings, and it frequently targets pro-regime media figures as well as regime leaders. JN is one of the most effective fighting groups currently operating inside Syria. Many of its initial members fought in Iraq against US forces, and it has high standards for its recruits.

Making the story more complex, Jabhat al-Nusra's parent organization, Al Qaeda in Iraq (which would eventually call itself the Islamic State), initially rejected JN's independence, fearing it had gone native and was focusing too much on Syria. AQI wanted to be recognized as the (only) official Al Qaeda affiliate in *both* Iraq and Syria, and in 2013 demanded the subordination of Jabhat al-Nusra; JN resisted and turned to Zawahiri to maintain its independence. Perhaps because Al Qaeda in Iraq was known to be brutal in its treatment of fellow Muslims and its leaders had a history of ignoring the Al Qaeda core, Zawahiri rejected AQI's demand and sided with Jabhat al-Nusra, recognizing JN's primacy in Syria. In 2014, the acrimony led directly to violence, with JN and the Islamic State turning their guns on one another. The infighting has reportedly killed as many as 3,000 people so far.[13]

What about Like-Minded but Unaffiliated Groups?

It is tempting to lump all violent Islamist groups together, but Al Qaeda only affiliates with a select portion of them. Al Qaeda undertakes no serious cooperation with non-Muslim groups and has had at best fitful cooperation with non-Sunni groups like the Shi'ite Hizballah in Lebanon. More frequently, the organization's relationship with the Shi'a is marked by bloody hostility. Even within the Sunni world, Al Qaeda is typically hostile to groups whose ideologies lie outside the Salafi framework, such as the Muslim Brotherhood.

Although all of Al Qaeda's affiliates are Salafi-jihadist groups, not all Salafi-jihadist groups become affiliates: some reject Al Qaeda, while Al Qaeda rejects some candidates. Some groups disagree on priorities, others about ideological issues like the legitimacy of targeting civilians. Personal issues and even personalities play a role. Although some groups may want to affiliate with Al Qaeda, the possibility to do so may be limited because of a lack of personal interaction or due to disputes among leaders.

A number of important groups that cooperate with Al Qaeda are not affiliates. The Taliban, the Haqqani Network, and Lashkar-e Taiba, among other groups active in the Afghanistan-Pakistan area, cooperate with Al Qaeda, share training and logistics facilities, and generally assist in operations. However, these groups do not swear fealty to Zawahiri or take the Al Qaeda name, and their leadership structure remains distinct from that of Al Qaeda. Boko Haram in Nigeria, Ansar Eddine in Mali, and Ansar al-Sharia in Tunisia and Libya share ideological traits with Al Qaeda and perhaps have members engaged in limited training under AQIM's direction and tactical tutelage (thus making them perhaps an "affiliate, once-removed"), but these groups do not take the Al Qaeda name or promise loyalty to Zawahiri's organization. In different ways, Al Qaeda has also worked with elements of the Islamic Movement of Uzbekistan, the Libyan Islamic Fighting Group (LIFG), and various groups active in Chechnya. Some members of these groups joined Al Qaeda, and a few from the LIFG are believed to have become part of Al Qaeda's leadership structure. However, the broader organizations these members represented remained independent and did not take the Al Qaeda name or swear loyalty to Zawahiri. In Southeast Asia, groups such as Jemaah Islamiyya and the Abu Sayyaf Group have had members trained by Al Qaeda and have at times shared operational planning—but again, these groups have not taken on the Al Qaeda name or sworn loyalty to Zawahiri.

Some groups have also tried to take on the Al Qaeda name (probably to gain the legitimacy and perceived financial rewards that may come with the title benefits), but, so far at least, Al Qaeda has not accepted them as formal affiliates. Indeed, Al Qaeda leaders have complained that they collect money or otherwise claim to be Al Qaeda but in reality drag the organization down. "The issue needs to be controlled," one leader lamented.[14]

Not surprisingly, many members of jihadist groups prefer to continue their focus on more local objectives and thus choose to avoid an affiliation with Al Qaeda altogether. In Chechnya, the Arab volunteer leader Khattab corresponded with Bin Laden in the late 1990s primarily about strategy—both were jihadists, but they interpreted their mission differently. Bin Laden focused on the supposed Zionist-Crusader alliance and the "far enemy," whereas Khattab wanted to establish an Islamic government in Chechnya that would then be used as a base for expansion into neighboring countries. In the end, this strategic difference (along with differing opinions over targeting civilians) caused Khattab to limit his relationship with Al Qaeda.[15]

What's in It for Al Qaeda? What's in It for the Affiliates?

Affiliates make Al Qaeda a potent global organization. By conducting attacks in their home countries and regions in Al Qaeda's name, affiliates make it seem as if the Al Qaeda core is shaping events throughout the Muslim world. Affiliates have hundreds or even thousands of fighters, provide ties to local communities, offer knowledge of terrain (both physical and human), and are otherwise better able to fight and operate on their own turf, while the Al Qaeda core by itself might have only a few hundred operatives. As a result, Al Qaeda is able to claim that its banner is flying high in several important theaters where it would otherwise find it difficult to operate.

When a group affiliates, it ostensibly takes on the core's anti-American and anti-Western agenda, often shifting its targeting, particularly within its own theater of operations. For instance, on August 8, 2009, three days after Zawahiri had warned that France would "pay for all her crimes," AQIM executed a suicide bombing of the French embassy in Nouakchott, Mauritania.[16] Some of the most notorious "Al Qaeda" attacks since 9/11 have in fact been carried out by affiliate groups. These include AQI's 2005 hotel attacks in Jordan and AQAP's 2009 Christmas Day attempted airplane bombing over Detroit and 2010 cargo planes plot. Even when they remain focused on targets in their own theater, groups can further Al Qaeda's anti-American and anti-Western goals. AQI's ability to launch attacks in Iraq riveted the attention of the world.

Affiliates may maintain an impressive network outside their country of origin, usually for logistics and fundraising. Often this network involves their respective diaspora communities. Affiliation thus gives the Al Qaeda core potential access to additional resources and networks around the world. Algerian groups operate an extensive logistical network throughout Europe, primarily to raise money through the diaspora and otherwise coordinate with North Africans living there. Al Shabaab is tied to the extensive Somali diaspora, and so on.

Training is part of what attracts affiliates to Al Qaeda and what helps cement the bond. In the 1990s, Al Qaeda operated training camps in Afghanistan, Pakistan, and Sudan that offered classes on bomb making, passport forging, small-arms use, and other valuable skills. In the post-9/11 era, its training capabilities are more limited, but it has still trained operatives in Pakistan—though the aggressive drone campaign has shrunk the amount of time spent in training camps, as recruits cannot stay long without a high risk of detection.[17] In part because of this, Al Qaeda has also encouraged and helped foster the creation of training camps by affiliates and other allied groups. Thus, affiliation with Al Qaeda can help local fighters gain military experience and learn new skills and tactics while allowing the core to give would-be fighters more options for training. Al Qaeda's communications networks relay skills and tactics to all of the various affiliated organizations, sharing best practices. Some of the most important learning occurs at the strategic level: jihadist leaders scrutinize their successes and failures and impart lessons learned to affiliates. Al Qaeda in the Arabian Peninsula has been far more sensitive to local grievances and tribal identities than groups like Al Qaeda in Iraq were in part because Al Qaeda has learned and transmitted lessons about respecting local sensibilities to its affiliates.

Affiliation also provides both the core organization and local groups better propaganda opportunities to reach more potential recruits with existing resources. Al Qaeda has a powerful propaganda apparatus that produces videos and maintains websites, advancing a coherent narrative. Al Qaeda cherry picks from its own and its affiliates' actions, highlighting the most successful and heroic actions (and ignoring or downplaying failures and mistakes). Because of its notoriety, Al Qaeda has a big bullhorn. From Somalia to Iraq, Al Qaeda has used its worldwide recognition to draw attention to local struggles and, in so doing, attract recruits and funds to local fighters.

Al Qaeda offers a distinct brand that has cachet, especially in areas where anti-US and anti-Western sentiment is already strong—in other words, most of the Muslim world. Groups may seek to replace their local brand with that of Al Qaeda, believing the latter to be more compelling for recruits and funders. According to Chris Harnisch, "One of the themes repeatedly echoed throughout al Shabaab's recruiting videos is its shared ideology with al Qaeda. The group goes to great lengths to portray its mission as part of Bin Laden's international effort to defeat the 'Crusaders' worldwide and establish a global Caliphate."[18]

The more global brand also opens up the potential for skilled or otherwise valuable foreign fighters to join the struggle. Jabhat al-Nusra has attracted hundreds of foreign fighters to its banner, a large component of the overall organization; Al Shabaab and AQAP also use foreign fighters, as did AQI. Foreign fighters are often highly motivated and more willing to assume the important role of suicide bomber, often the most lethal method used by these groups.[19]

Yet direct material and operational rewards are not the whole story. For Al Qaeda, shared ideas and identities are important elements of its affiliation strategy. All Al Qaeda affiliates are Salafi-jihadist groups. Having numerous affiliates that bear the Al Qaeda name fulfills its self-image as the leader of the jihadist movement throughout the Muslim world—well beyond the core's traditional base in the Afghanistan-Pakistan area. To uphold its mission, Al Qaeda particularly seeks affiliates in places where it perceives Muslims to be under attack from non-Muslim powers—which for Al Qaeda pretty much means wherever Muslims are to be found. Iraq exemplified this perception; similarly, Al Shabaab's experience defending Somalia from (Christian) Ethiopia, according to one analyst, "was a perfect fit for the al Qaeda meta-narrative."[20] Affiliates help Al Qaeda promote its claim to leadership over the broader jihadist and Salafi universes.

What Are the Limits of Cooperation?

The Salafi-jihadist movement is highly divided, and many of these divisions limit cooperation between Al Qaeda and its affiliates. Leading jihadist thinkers and various important groups may agree about broad goals, but they often disagree as to priorities and how best to allocate resources. While almost all Salafi-jihadists accept the need to fight foreign invaders of Muslim lands, only some focus on fighting so-called apostate regimes. And while the Al Qaeda core emphasizes attacks on the United States and Europe as the first step in toppling these regimes, affiliates are far more local and regional in their emphasis.

Groups join Al Qaeda with their own histories and agendas, and they often retain many of their original goals even after they take on the Al Qaeda label. For the Al Qaeda core, an affiliate's continued focus on local issues is not always a problem—the core too embraces the overthrow of local apostate regimes—but they disagree on how much the affiliate should contribute to the broader global fight. Bin Laden even criticized Al Qaeda in the Arabian Peninsula—the closest of Al Qaeda's affiliates and the one most active in directly targeting the West—for focusing too much on the local struggle and not enough on attacks on the West.[21]

Often this question splits a group, leading some members to break away and affiliate with Al Qaeda while the remaining members either choose to continue pursuing their local agenda or give up the fight altogether. Some members of the GSPC, AQIM's predecessor, opposed the decision to join with Al Qaeda, and many eventually accepted the government's amnesty offer. From the local group's point of view, splintering imposes massive costs: the group loses members (and whatever expertise and resources those members brought to the table) and gains a steady source of criticism and often an immediate rival.

Going global represents an opportunity cost: the more a group focuses on the global struggle, the fewer resources it has to devote to its local struggle. In a rather stunning mistake, the original Saudi AQAP was hurt when the Al Qaeda core and many sympathetic Saudi clerics began prioritizing the anti-US jihad next door in Iraq in 2003. Many of its potential volunteers preferred to go to the more popular and religiously justified fight against US forces than to fight the Saudi regime, and those fighting the Al Saud regime lost money, personnel, and legitimacy.[22] Thus, ironically, Al Qaeda's relentless rhetorical emphasis on fighting global jihad backfired, ultimately thwarting the local ambitions of the Saudi affiliate it had taken great pains to help create.

Groups often try to reconcile these two sometimes conflicting strategies by expanding their attacks to include more Western targets (albeit ones located within their spheres of influence, such as embassies and hotels) and shifting from a strictly national to a wider regional emphasis. AQIM's predecessor organization, the GSPC, focused almost entirely on Algeria in the five years before it took the Al Qaeda name in 2007. Since then, it has continued to focus primarily on Algeria, but it has also carried out a significant number of attacks in Mali, Niger, Mauritania, and other regional states.

Even such limited victories may be few and far between for the Al Qaeda core, as some groups sign on to the Al Qaeda core's agenda—and readily accept the added prestige and resources that come with it—but do little in return to further the core's strategic vision. A study carried out by West Point's Combating Terrorism Center found that affiliates often look to the Al Qaeda core for guidance on strategic issues, like whether to declare an Islamic state, but consult the core much less on operational matters and often blatantly ignore many of the core's directives.[23] To the disappointment of Al Qaeda's core leadership, even after the 2007 name change to Al Qaeda in the Islamic Maghreb, that group's leaders have not tried hard to mobilize supporters in Europe on behalf of global jihad and have not brought the "war" to the Continent.[24] As Jean-Pierre Filiu comments, AQIM "is the branch of the global jihad that has most clearly failed to follow its founding guidelines."[25]

Although rarely mentioned in the rhetorical bursts that accompany such decisions, a group's decision to affiliate with Al Qaeda often comes on the heels of catastrophic failure at home. Devastating setbacks in the struggle against the local regime often force a crisis within the group that leads some to change approaches and join with Al Qaeda. They often seek the new Al Qaeda brand because their own local image has suffered irreversible damage. The core, however, is acquiring damaged goods. Lianne Kennedy Boudali contends that, for some groups, their "decision to join Al Qaeda's global jihad should be understood as an act of desperation."[26]

Many affiliates also advocate a divisive social agenda in opposition to Al Qaeda's preferences—and because they use the Al Qaeda name, this unpopular agenda tarnishes Al Qaeda's image. One of the biggest divides in the Salafi-jihadist community is over who is a "real" Muslim and what jihadists' obligations are to non-Salafis. In both Algeria in the mid- to late-1990s and Iraq during the height of the Sunni insurgency in the mid-2000s, groups embraced an extreme ideology that justified their slaughter of Muslim civilians. In both countries, this violence diminished the groups' popularity, alienating the vast majority of ordinary Muslims at home and abroad.

For Al Qaeda, unpopular affiliate actions can rebound on the cause as a whole, discrediting the core and hijacking its agenda. Although Bin Laden favored attacks on civilian targets like embassies and the World Trade Center, even he worried that regular and indiscriminate attacks on ordinary civilians, like those launched by AQI, could discredit the movement, "distorting the image of the jihadis in the eyes of the umma's [Muslim community's] general public and separating them from their popular bases."[27] Ironically, core members have at times felt that the affiliates were too extreme. However, it is difficult for the Al Qaeda core to disavow an affiliate.

For the affiliate organization, taking on the Al Qaeda brand brings a host of downsides, not least the wrath of the United States and other foes of Zawahiri's organization. The 9/11 attacks were a disaster for locally-focused jihadist groups that maintained even limited organizational ties to Al Qaeda, as the United States came down on them in full force. As the jihadist strategist Abu Musab al-Suri lamented, the 9/11 attacks cast "jihadists into a fiery furnace. . . . A hellfire which consumed most of their leaders, fighters, and bases."[28] So for the affiliate as well as the core, taking on the Al Qaeda name is at best a mixed blessing.

Does the Al Qaeda Core Control the Salafi-Jihadist Movement Anymore?

Al Qaeda often finds it difficult to control its affiliates, let alone broader parts of the Salafi-jihadist movement. Though it sees itself as a vanguard organization, before 9/11 jihadist insurgencies in Algeria, Chechnya, and Kashmir all flourished with little Al Qaeda role, while important terrorist operators like Ramzi Yousef, who masterminded the 1993 bombing of the World Trade Center, acted independently. As Al Qaeda gained in stature—and as its fundraising prowess and network of training camps grew—it attracted more fighters to its banner, but Bin Laden only controlled a fraction of the overall movement.

Al Qaeda often used money to influence and shape the causes of potential allies. For much of its history, Al Qaeda has been flush with cash by the standards of jihadist groups, and it used this capital to support like-minded fighters, assist the overall cause, and forge alliances with different groups. In addition to its own reserves, Al Qaeda had access to an extended network of donors, primarily Arabs from the Persian Gulf states, who funded a variety of jihadist causes. An endorsement from Al Qaeda served to help other groups attract funding from this important set of benefactors.

Not surprisingly, cooperation motivated by money can diminish when the money dries up. US and allied pressure on Al Qaeda's finances has reduced the organization's ability to dispense largesse, often to the point where it has had to seek financial help from affiliates, charge potential recruits for training, or otherwise reverse its historic role as a relatively wealthy organization that provides resources to other groups. European jihadists now complain that they were charged over $1,000 for AK-47s and other supplies while training in Pakistan.[29] Some causes, such as Iraq after 2003 and Syria after 2011, are highly attractive to donors, while other groups, such as Al Qaeda in the Islamic Maghreb, often raise money through their own activities, like kidnapping for ransom or smuggling.

Part of the problem stems simply from the nature of running a global clandestine organization whose component parts are often thousands of miles away. Al Qaeda must communicate with affiliates and it uses cell phones, the Internet, and even fax machines to do so, but these communications can be intercepted by US or allied intelligence services, exposing operations and putting operatives at risk of drone strikes or arrest. On the other hand, if Al Qaeda leaders hunker down, they are ineffective commanders. Clandestine methods of communication, such as the use of couriers, reduce this risk, but they are also far less effective. For example, when Bin Laden tried to reach out to AQIM's predecessor organization in 2002, Algerian security forces killed his emissary.[30]

Perhaps Al Qaeda's most effective means of control lies in its efforts to shape the preferences of the local groups via propaganda and training and by raising its own profile. The secure base that Al Qaeda enjoyed in Afghanistan under the Taliban—and more sporadically in Iraq and Pakistan—was instrumental in maximizing the influence of such programs. The lack of a secure base from which to operate, the overwhelming technological surveillance capabilities of US and allied intelligence services, and the rise of sectarian-based conflicts like the ones in Syria and Iraq that focus attention away from the United States have all hindered Al Qaeda's ability to dominate the movement.

In the end, Al Qaeda has moved affiliates closer to its anti-Western agenda, but the affiliates' own agendas and passions still consume their energies. Al Qaeda has not made affiliates into local clones, and the broader movement remains chaotic and divided.

So What Do We Talk about When We Talk about Al Qaeda?

Most terrorist groups can be defined by an identifiable structure, hierarchy, set of goals, and body of committed members, but Al Qaeda's essence is more varied and has changed over time. It has core members, affiliates, like-minded groups, and sympathizers—much to the confusion of observers of all stripes. To help us think through what Al Qaeda means, it is useful to break it down into several over-lapping but nevertheless distinct components.

The essence of Al Qaeda is the small core of followers around Ayman al-Zawahiri. Probably numbering only in the hundreds, Al Qaeda has a group of dedicated and (mostly) skilled operatives who swore loyalty to Bin Laden and, upon Bin Laden's death, to Zawahiri. They see themselves as a vanguard: an elite cadre of fighters that understands the Muslim community's true interests and serves as the point of the spear for the revolution. This group often focuses on high-profile terrorist attacks, such as the 9/11 attacks.

But Al Qaeda is more than just this small core. Al Qaeda has run training camps in Afghanistan, Pakistan, Sudan, and elsewhere since the late 1980s. The 9/11 Commission reports that before 9/11 as many as 20,000 fighters trained in Bin Laden-supported camps;[31] other reports place the number much higher. Most of the individuals who have trained at Al Qaeda camps are known to Al Qaeda, both bureau-cratically and individually, and many are sympathetic to at least some aspects of the movement. But while Al Qaeda has occasionally worked with these individuals, they are not necessarily under the operational control of the Al Qaeda core. Ahmed Ressam, who was convicted in 2001 of planning to blow up the Los Angeles airport, appears to have trained in an Al Qaeda-linked camp in Afghanistan and to have had some contact with Bin Laden himself. Al Qaeda operatives apparently gave him $12,000 as seed money, and Ressam claimed that he and others were told to commit crimes such as bank robberies to fund an operation in the United States. However, his bombing attempt was not under Al Qaeda's direct control, nor was it orchestrated by senior Al Qaeda leaders.

Though individuals like Ressam act on their own, another aspect of Al Qaeda is its mission to support other jihadist groups. As scholars Peter Bergen and Bruce Hoffman contend, "The danger of al-Qaeda comes not only from its central leadership in Pakistan, but through its cooperation with other like-minded groups."[32] In addition to its formal affiliates like Al Qaeda in the Arabian Peninsula, Al Qaeda has supported such groups as the Islamic Army of Aden-Abyan in Yemen, the Islamic Army of Iraq, the Islamic Movement of Uzbekistan, Jemaah Islamiyya in Indonesia, Lashkar-e Taiba in Pakistan, and the Taliban in Afghanistan and Pakistan.

Other groups have some sympathy for Al Qaeda and links with some individual fighters, some of whom may even cooperate with Al Qaeda on terrorism operations from time to time, but a command relationship is lacking. Some of the fighters for these groups may have trained in Al Qaeda-run camps in Afghanistan; others may have fought with Al Qaeda members (current or future) in places like Bosnia, Chechnya, and of course Afghanistan; still others may have family or community ties to Al Qaeda core members. The density of the links to Al Qaeda, the command relationship, and other important factors vary by group and historical period. Many of the ties are personal as well as organizational.

At times, groups attack targets that Al Qaeda would attack, use tactics that Al Qaeda uses, and involve individuals who espouse an ideology akin to that of Zawahiri and Bin Laden, yet have few if any direct ties to Al Qaeda. Ansar al-Sharia, whose members were prominent among those who perpetrated the attack on the US embassy in Benghazi on September 11, 2012, appears at first glance like Al Qaeda, but the organization and its members are independent from the Al Qaeda core and have received little or no direct assistance. As Dana Milbank comments, "That this group killed the

U.S. ambassador and three others in Benghazi makes it monstrous and dangerous. But calling it al-Qaeda doesn't make it so any more than calling it Chick-fil-A will make it serve tasty nuggets."[33]

Al Qaeda can also be thought of as encompassing those individuals—particularly those living in Western countries—who embrace Al Qaeda's ideology and take up its call to act but who have not gone to Afghanistan or Pakistan to train or perhaps even met a member of the Al Qaeda core. These "homegrown" jihadists do not pose the strategic threat that the Al Qaeda core does, but they have at times proven deadly. Dzhokhar and Tamerlan Tsarnaev, the Boston Marathon bombers, planned and executed their attacks with no direct supervision from the Al Qaeda core. According to the indictment of Dzhokhar, the boys learned to make bombs from *Inspire* magazine, the English-language publication of Al Qaeda in the Arabian Peninsula available on the Internet. Nevertheless, because the tactics and core ideology of the bombers appear similar to what Zawahiri endorses and because they learned from propaganda provided by an Al Qaeda affiliate, the Al Qaeda label is at times used.

In this context, Al Qaeda might also be described as an ideology: a call for violent resistance against the United States, Western countries in general, Israel, and perceived apostate Muslim regimes. A young Muslim might listen to a Zawahiri lecture on the Internet, read a tract by Abu Muhammad al-Maqdisi, hear a local preacher praise Muslims who go to fight in Syria, or otherwise be exposed to Al Qaeda's message and become radicalized. Indeed, one of Bin Laden's successes was to take ideas such as jihad against the West and against apostate regimes and move them from the extremist fringe to a more mainstream position.

However, to label these individuals "Al Qaeda" overstates the organization's specific appeal and ability to conduct attacks. Because Al Qaeda's cause is vast, it is easy to exaggerate the number of sympathizers. Polls indicate that many Muslims, particularly in the Middle East, reject the legitimacy of Israel, believe violent resistance to American forces in Iraq was justified, and admire fighters opposing the Asad regime in Syria. In a 2009 poll, over three-quarters of Egyptians and Palestinians and a strong majority of Jordanians approved of attacks on US troops based in Muslim countries.[34] But this does not mean that these people condone attacks on innocent civilians or wish to see blood run in the streets of American cities. Very few are violent themselves, and even fewer are tied in any way to an Al Qaeda-linked group or Al Qaeda itself. In addition, even within the world of zealots and bombers, differences between the Al Qaeda core and others are often sharp and at times lead to violence.

Exact numbers are elusive. The Al Qaeda core probably numbers in the hundreds, but the number increases exponentially when those trained by Al Qaeda and affiliated insurgencies are included: then the figure is well above 100,000 active jihadists, and possibly far more, though for the overwhelming majority of these individuals any operational relationship is latent at most, and few have any interest in global terrorism. The number—and the distance from actual Al Qaeda operations—grows even more if Al Qaeda is classified as an ideology and those who accept substantial parts of it are counted. Here the figures probably reach the millions, but at this point "Al Qaeda" really means "Islamic extremist causes" rather than an organized terrorist group, and the danger these individuals pose, especially to the West, is often small or nonexistent. And with an estimated 1.6 billion Muslims in the world, even a few million violent jihadists is only a small percentage of the total. Still, as we saw on 9/11, even a handful of committed extremists can wreak devastation.

Although these categories are analytically discrete, in practice they overlap considerably. Some individuals may go back and forth between local groups and Al Qaeda, cooperating due to personal connections forged in training camps or ideological sympathy. A local jihadist may begin by cheering on fighters opposing the US military presence overseas, and then join a jihadist-linked insurgency or travel to Pakistan for training at the hands of Al Qaeda (or both). While in Pakistan, or perhaps even in his own country, he may meet a member of Al Qaeda and receive some instruction. Mohamed Atta, the leader of the 9/11 plot, is a prime example of this phenomenon: he was first motivated to use violence by Russian atrocities against Chechen Muslims and traveled to Afghanistan in order to enter the fray in Chechnya; while training in an Al Qaeda camp, he was recognized for his determination and ability to operate in the West and was selected to join Al Qaeda and lead the 9/11 operation. Thus, at different points, he was part of all the various Al Qaeda components.

So what do we talk about when we talk about Al Qaeda? It varies by person and by context, and applying the broad label "Al Qaeda" to every category is more confusing than enlightening. Jihadists in Libya differ from Al Qaeda in Pakistan, and both of these are different from Al Qaeda-trained terrorists in Europe and Al Qaeda wannabes in the United States. As a result, counterterrorism efforts must vary dramatically depending on who the targets are and what the end goal of the counterterrorism effort is. The best strategy for defeating a local Al Qaeda-affiliated insurgency in North Africa may not necessarily be the best strategy for combating the broader Al Qaeda ideology. At times, an instrument that helps with one aspect of Al Qaeda may actually be detrimental when fighting another.

8

THE ISLAMIC STATE

The Islamic State is Al Qaeda's most important progeny and its greatest nemesis. The Islamic State grew out of Al Qaeda in Iraq, and both groups' objectives, enemies, and tactics are all part of the broader jihadist movement that Al Qaeda so long sought to unify and lead. At the same time, the Islamic State and its leader Abu Bakr al-Baghdadi violently broke with Al Qaeda in late 2013, challenging it for leadership of the jihadist cause and pursuing tactics that may backfire on the movement as a whole.

What Should We Call This Group?

Making a confusing group even more confusing, the Islamic State has repeatedly changed names throughout its history. When establishing itself in Afghanistan, Abu Musab al-Zarqawi's group Jund al-Sham existed only a few months before Zarqawi renamed it Jamaat al-Tawhid wal Jihad (Group of Monotheism and Jihad). Following 9/11 and the dispersion of jihadists when the Taliban fell, Zarqawi and like-minded jihadists moved to northern Iraq and quickly began fighting American forces after Saddam's regime fell. After negotiations and Zarqawi's decision to accept Bin Laden's leadership, the group became Al Qaeda in the Land of the Two Rivers, usually referred to as Al Qaeda in Iraq (AQI), in 2004. In 2006, it merged with several small groups and changed its name briefly to the Majlis Shura al-Mujahedin, and then quickly again merged with several other small groups, assuming the name the Islamic State of Iraq (ISI), though it was often just referred to as AQI.

ISI kept that name until 2013, when its large presence in Syria led it to add "al-Sham" (the Arabic term for Greater Syria), thus making it the Islamic State of Iraq and al-Sham, or alternately, the Islamic State of Iraq and Syria, often simply referred to by its acronym, ISIS. Some news outlets and the US government translate "al-Sham" as "the Levant," referring to the eastern Mediterranean area that includes Syria, Jordan, Israel, and Lebanon, which is where the acronym ISIL comes from. And then, in 2014, the group changed its name *yet again*, simplifying it to the "Islamic State" to signify that its ambitions and sovereignty were not limited to the boundaries of Iraq and Syria and that it rejects the borders imposed on the Muslim world by the colonial powers.

Some of the Islamic State's enemies derisively refer to it as *Daesh*, drawing on the Arabic acronym for the Islamic State of Iraq and Greater Syria (al-Dawla al-Eslamiyya al-Iraq al-Sham). In Arabic, *Daesh* sounds similar to *daes* (someone who crushes something under his feet) and *dahes* (someone who sows discord). Both are accurate, and disparaging, descriptions of the Islamic State.

So that is nine possible names. I will mostly refer to it as AQI for the pre-2011 period and the Islamic State for more recent years in the hopes of making this less confusing.

Who Is Abu Bakr al-Baghdadi?

In contrast to Bin Laden or Zawahiri, very little is known about Abu Bakr al-Baghdadi, the Islamic State's leader who now styles himself "Caliph Ibrahim." Born Ibrahim Awad Ibrahim al-Badri in 1971 and a skilled soccer player as a youth—one former team-mate referred to him as "the Messi of our team," comparing him to the famous Argentinian striker Lionel Messi—little would suggest that this shy and pious boy would grow up to become one of the world's most wanted men.[1] Like Bin Laden and Zawahiri, Baghdadi is well educated. In fact, he has more serious religious credentials than Al Qaeda's leaders, having received his PhD from the Islamic University in Baghdad.

Baghdadi joined the jihadist resistance to US forces in Iraq in 2004, if not earlier. US forces detained him for most of that year, but he was ultimately deemed not to be a particularly dangerous threat—indeed, according to some accounts, he got along well with camp officials—and was released.[2] In 2006, his group joined the umbrella organization for Iraqi jihadists, known as the Islamic State of Iraq (ISI). (I and others often use ISI interchangeably with Al Qaeda in Iraq [AQI], which dominated the organization, though technically it was not the only group.) Baghdadi became a member of the group's senior leadership council. For several years, Baghdadi controlled forces in the western Iraqi town of Qaim, where the Pentagon claims he "was connected to the intimidation, torture and murder of local civilians."[3]

Baghdadi became the leader of AQI in 2010, just before the group began moving into Syria. As the leader, Baghdadi oversaw AQI terrorism against Iraqi security forces, various Shi'ite groups, the Iraqi government, and the Sunni leaders who worked with it. He helped AQI rebuild after the devastation it suffered during the US-led "surge" that began in 2006. Baghdadi appointed a number of former military and intelligence officers who had served under Saddam to senior positions in AQI. Under Baghdadi, AQI also launched the "Breaking the Walls" campaign, which freed hundreds of AQI members from Iraqi prisons and sent Baghdadi's prestige soaring within the organization. He cleverly exploited the Syrian civil war to further rebuild his organization, using the fighting there to develop a haven and attract new recruits and support.

Baghdadi tried to take AQI to a new level when, on the first night of Ramadan in 2014, he proclaimed the return of the caliphate, with himself as leader. As caliph, he would be the "commander of the faithful," and thus—at least in theory—Muslims everywhere would owe him obedience. However, Middle Eastern regimes, Sunni religious leaders, and even most jihadist groups reject Baghdadi's leadership—not to mention the tens of millions of Muslims around the world who find his proclamation absurd. The prominent theologian Yusuf al-Qaradawi declared that Baghdadi's declaration "is void under sharia."

Where Did the Islamic State Come From?

The Islamic State began as an Iraqi organization. Jihadist groups proliferated in Iraq after the 2003 US invasion, and many eventually coalesced around Jordanian jihadist Abu Musab al-Zarqawi. Bin Laden gave Zarqawi seed money to start his organization, but Zarqawi at first refused to swear loyalty to Bin Laden, as he shared only some of Bin Laden's goals and wanted to remain independent. After months of negotiations, however, Zarqawi swore an oath of loyalty, and in 2004, his group took on the name Al Qaeda in Iraq to signify this connection. Bin Laden got an affiliate in the most important theater of jihad at a time when the Al Qaeda core was on the ropes, and Zarqawi got Al Qaeda's prestige and contacts to bolster his legitimacy.

Yet, even in its early days, Zarqawi's group bickered with the Al Qaeda leadership. Zawahiri and Bin Laden pushed for a focus on US targets, while Zarqawi (and those who took his place after his death in 2006 from a US air strike) emphasized sectarian war and attacks on Sunni Muslims they deemed apostates, such as those who collaborated with the Shi'a-led Iraqi regime. Zawahiri criticized this in private correspondence captured by US forces: he asked Zarqawi, "why kill ordinary Shia considering that they are forgiven because of their ignorance?" and noted that this was a distraction from targeting the Americans.[4] Zarqawi and his followers also acted with incredible brutality, making their name with videotaped beheadings—a tactic that its successor organization would also use to shock and generate publicity. Despite Zawahiri's misgivings, Zarqawi's strategy seemed to work well, as Al Qaeda in Iraq mounted a broad insurgency and for several years controlled some of the Sunni-populated parts of Iraq.

Eventually, though, AQI's indiscriminate violence against Iraqi Sunnis led them to resent and fear the group, leading to a backlash that, when combined with the US troop surge in Iraq that began in 2006, hit AQI hard. When the Syrian conflict broke out in 2011, Zawahiri, among others, urged Iraqi jihadists to take part in that conflict, and Baghdadi initially sent small numbers of fighters into Syria to build an organization there. One of these fighters was Abu Mohammed al-Joulani, who would go on to establish Jabhat al-Nusra, a group that started out as Baghdadi's stalking horse but ended up turning against him.

Syria was in chaos, and the Iraqi jihadists established secure bases of operations there, raising money and winning new recruits to their cause. Establishing a presence was easy, as the Syrian government had allowed jihadists to transit, and at times base themselves, on Syrian territory as a way to support the anti-US insurgency in Iraq in the previous decade: indeed, during the 2003 Iraq war, Syria was probably the most important transit point for foreign fighters entering Iraq. The jihadists' ambitions grew along with their organization, expanding to include Syria as well as Iraq. AQI forces, now calling themselves the Islamic State of Iraq and Syria, also faced less pressure in Iraq with the departure of US forces at the end of 2011. At the same time, Iraqi Prime Minister Nouri al-Maliki put in place a series of disastrous policies to bolster support among his Shi'ite base, employing extreme sectarian rhetoric and systematically excluding Iraqi Sunnis from power. Many Sunnis protested, which led to a violent government crackdown that further alienated the Sunni community. Thus, Baghdadi's organization steadily shored up popular support, regained its legitimacy in Iraq, and replenished its ranks. It also increased its attacks on government targets and security forces, stepping up assassinations in particular, and launched several high-profile prison breaks that humiliated the Iraqi government and freed many of the group's most experienced cadre. At the beginning of 2014, the group sent forces into Iraq claiming it was defending local Sunnis and restored its presence in cities like Fallujah. In Syria, the group took over large sections of territory, benefiting as the Syrian regime focused on targeting more moderate groups while the Syrian opposition as a whole remained fractious.

The group changed its name again in the summer of 2014 to the Islamic State and, supported by other disenfranchised Sunnis, swept across Iraq. Exploiting their mobility and high morale, they shocked Iraqi government forces, capturing broad swaths of territory in Sunni-dominated areas of the country; killing large numbers of Iraqi soldiers, police, and others associated with the government; and capturing equipment the United States had provided to the Iraqi military. Over 20,000 Iraqis were killed in the first eight months of 2014, and almost two million were displaced.[5]

Why Did the Islamic State Fight with Al Qaeda?

Although the Syrian conflict revived the Islamic State, it also eventually led it to split with the Al Qaeda leadership. Zawahiri had encouraged AQI to move into Syria, but he also wanted to have a separate group under separate command operating in Syria, with Syrians in the lead to give it a local face. Zawahiri probably also wanted to have a separate Syrian group because of his past doubts concerning AQI's loyalty and wisdom. Thus, Jabhat al-Nusra (JN) was established as a Syrian spinoff of AQI.

Soon, however, AQI began to fear that JN had "gone native," focusing too much on Syria, acting independently, and ignoring the AQI leadership, and on April 9, 2013, Baghdadi declared JN to be part of (i.e., subordinate to) AQI in order to rein it in. Nusra leaders balked, pledging a direct oath to Zawahiri as a way of retaining their independence. Zawahiri found this lack of unity frustrating; in an attempt to settle the matter, he proclaimed Jabhat al-Nusra to be the official Al Qaeda affiliate in Syria and Baghdadi's group to be the official Al Qaeda affiliate in Iraq. He ordered Baghdadi to accept this decision and to focus on Iraq. Baghdadi refused, once again declaring Jabhat al-Nusra to be subordinate to him. This precipitated a violent clash in which perhaps 3,000 fighters from both groups died. In February 2014, Zawahiri formally declared that Baghdadi's organization, now calling itself the Islamic State of Iraq and Syria, "is not a branch of the al-Qaeda group. . . does not have an organizational relationship with it and [al-Qaeda] is not the group responsible for their actions."[6]

Al Qaeda and the Islamic State differ on both tactics and strategy—and on who should lead the overall jihadist movement. This tension was present when AQI was created in 2004, and it never went away. Although Bin Laden and Zawahiri supported AQI publicly, in private they did not approve of its declaration of an Islamic state in Iraq and had poor relations with the group's leaders. In particular, Zawahiri feared that AQI was putting the cart before the horse: you needed to have full control over territory and popular support before proclaiming an Islamic state, not the other way around.[7] Jihadists also suspected that AQI leaders were trying to usurp overall leadership from Bin Laden. In addition, Zawahiri chastised the Iraqi jihadists for their brutality, believing that such behavior would alienate the broader Muslim community. Indeed, in private, Al Qaeda spokesman Adam Gadahn recommended to Bin Laden that Al Qaeda publicly "sever its ties with the Islamic State of Iraq" because of the group's sectarian violence.

The Islamic State (and its various predecessors) believe that leading on the battlefield—rather than from remote bases in Afghanistan or Pakistan—is what counts. And although the Islamic State focuses on fighting local regimes, it also devotes significant energy to fighting rival groups, including other Salafi fighters; by contrast, a core part of Al Qaeda's mission has always been to unify the jihadist movement under its global objectives. Like his predecessors, Baghdadi sees purifying the Islamic community by attacking the Shi'a and other religious minorities and enforcing "correct" Islamic beliefs and practices to be a top priority and largely ignores the Al Qaeda credo of hitting the "far enemy" (the United States) in order to topple the regimes in the Middle East it supposedly props up.[8] Most important, Baghdadi believes his organization should be in charge of jihadist operations in Iraq, Syria, Lebanon, and Jordan—at the very least.

Jabhat al-Nusra may have grown out of the same Iraqi jihadist movement that produced the Islamic State, but the two groups differ in significant ways. Unlike Baghdadi's organization, JN's forces work with other Syrian fighters against the Asad regime and, by the low standards of the Syrian civil war, are relatively restrained in attacks on civilians—in fact, at the same time the Islamic State was making headlines for beheading captured Americans, Jabhat al-Nusra made headlines for releasing the United Nations peacekeepers it had captured. Having learned from AQI's disaster in Iraq when the population turned against it, Jabhat al-Nusra proselytizes rather than terrorizes to convince rather than compel Muslims living in the territories it controls to embrace "true" Islam.

The Islamic State and Al Qaeda are competing to be the dominant organization within the modern jihadist movement. Al Qaeda has the support of many traditional jihadist ideologues, including the extremely influential Abu Muhammad al-Maqdisi. Maqdisi mentored Zarqawi when the two were together in Jordan but later rejected his brutality against the Shi'a and other abuses; Maqdisi has called the Islamic State, the successor organization to Zarqawi's group, "deviant."[9] Al Qaeda's affiliates also offer it a strong position in the global movement, but many of them have ties to Iraqi jihadists from their own time fighting in Iraq, and in any event their grassroots find the Islamic State compelling. Already, small groups and individual local fighters have pledged fealty to the Islamic State in places as diverse as Gaza, the Sinai, Algeria, Libya, and Pakistan. Baghdadi claims he is leading the fight against the apostates—a popular cause given the wave of sectarianism sweeping the region. The Islamic State's recent success and its massive presence on social media have enabled it to recruit huge numbers of foreign fighters to Syria and Iraq, giving it tremendous power. Meanwhile, Al Qaeda's core organization is hounded by drones, and its leaders are aging. With Bin Laden's death, Baghdadi now claims that it is Zawahiri, not himself, who has fallen away from the founder's vision. To many young aspiring jihadists, it is Zawahiri, not the Islamic State, who seems weak and out of touch.

This struggle within the jihadist movement may dominate Al Qaeda's focus in the years to come, and both organizations may be tempted to use high-profile terrorist acts to grab international attention and demonstrate to potential followers that they are the rightful leaders of the cause.

What Does the Islamic State Want?

The Islamic State seeks to build, well, an Islamic state—but on its own terms. As such, it has gone beyond terrorism and even insurgency, establishing an army and state-like structures in the vast territory it controls. In contrast to Al Qaeda, the Islamic State does not see itself as a vanguard fighting to rouse the Muslim world and force the West to withdraw from the Middle East. Rather, it wants to build a state, purify it, and then expand it: it proclaims *baqiya wa tatamadad* ("lasting and expanding") as its motto.[10] Fighting its immediate enemies, such as the 'Alawite regime in Syria, the Shi'ite regime in Iraq, and supposed enemies within its own territory (such as religious minorities and disloyal Sunnis), is its most important goal.

The Islamic State wants to consolidate control over territory in Sunni parts of Iraq and Syria and expand from there. This includes not only conquering more territory within these two countries, but also undertaking operations in Jordan, Lebanon, and Saudi Arabia—countries where it has recruited fighters and at times launched terrorist attacks. Though the Islamic State terrorizes its enemies, calling it a terrorist group, as the United States and many other Western countries do, is both true and misleading. As Jessica Lewis of the Institute for the Study of War points out, the Islamic State's strategy "fundamentally relies on military superiority."[11] They seek to conquer.

Sectarianism is important to the Islamic State's success. Just as Zarqawi built a movement by fomenting sectarian war in Iraq, his successor Baghdadi has exploited and exacerbated sectarianism in Iraq and Syria to build support. The Islamic State regards the Shi'a and other Muslim "deviants" like the Yazidis (whom it considers polytheists) as worse than infidels and believes that the fight against non-Muslims should wait until religious minorities are purged from the Muslim body. When the Islamic State broke from Al Qaeda, it did so in the name of sectarianism, with one leader declaring that "no one will stop us from fighting the 'Alawis and waging jihad in Syria!... Car bombs will strike the Shi'a, from Diyala to Beirut."[12] Even a fellow Islamist group like Hamas is considered deviant, as it follows Muslim Brotherhood, not Salafi, teachings and thus must be fought. Not surprisingly, minorities of all sorts and even many Sunnis flee when Islamic State forces approach.

The group's flag—black with the Islamic profession of faith written on it in white Arabic calligraphy—is an attempt to recreate the Prophet Muhammad's flag.[13] Not surprisingly, given this sectarian orientation, the Islamic State draws heavily on Wahhabi teachings. The group uses Wahhabi texts from Saudi Arabia in its schools, destroys shrines to Christian prophets and non-Sunni places of worship, and, like Saudi Arabia, has religious police to enforce attendance at prayers. Princeton scholar Bernard Haykel has declared them "untamed Wahhabis."[14]

The Islamic State also draws on a millenarian strand within Islam. Recruiters play on a discourse that the apocalypse is underway and that the conflict in Syria is the battle between the forces of God and His enemies. This motivates only a minority of those going to fight, but it reflects the view that Syria is at the heart of the Arab and Muslim worlds, both historically and symbolically. Syria quickly fell as Muslim armies spread out from the Arabian Peninsula after the birth of Islam, and it was the heart of one of Islam's most important dynasties, the Umayyads—"the first great Muslim dynasty to rule the empire of the Caliphate (661–750 CE)."[15] As such, Syria's suffering and its ultimate fate are at the core of Muslim identity for millions of people. The *hadith* (reports of the sayings of the Prophet Muhammad) emphasize the importance of Syria as the scene of the last battles. As Islam expert William McCants explains:

> Syria is very important to this narrative. In the early Islamic prophecies about the end of days, few regions matter more than Syria. The prophet recommends during the last battles to go fight in Syria if you can; if you can't, go to Yemen. The prophet also talks about a group of believers—the true believers—who are going to persevere until the end and fight in the last battles. They will gather in Syria—in Damascus—and around Jerusalem, where they will fight for God until the final hour.[16]

For now, the Islamic State is not focused on a direct clash with the United States and the West. Its punishment for American airstrikes is to kill American journalists, aid workers, and others who might come across its path. But it believes that the path to victory lies in consolidating and expanding its territorial control, not terrorism against the United States.

However, in its propaganda the Islamic State tries to encourage so-called "Lone Wolves" to carry out attacks on their own in their home countries. As the Islamic State's propaganda and deeds are attractive to a small but real set of young Muslims in the West, we can expect attacks to be done in its name on a regular basis. In addition, it tries to take credit for inspiring attacks in the West, as it did in May 2015 when two American Muslims allegedly attacked a Prophet Muhammad cartoon contest in Garland, Texas, sponsored by the organization of Pamela Geller, an Islamophobe activist. The Islamic State offered no evidence that it had coordinated the attack in any direct way, but it does want to convey the image that it is active against the United States and other supposed enemies of Islam.[17]

How Strong Is the Islamic State?

By capitalizing on the growing sectarianism in the Syrian civil war as well as the weakness and venality of the Iraqi government, the Islamic

State has steadily increased its strength. In the two and a half years before its dramatic seizure of Mosul in June 2014, it claimed almost 20,000 attacks in Iraq.[18] This pace accelerated as it rolled through Iraq. It is now a "winner" and the most prominent group fighting the regimes in Iraq and Syria. Its victories have produced a tremendous surge in recruits: the Central Intelligence Agency estimates that as of September 2014, the Islamic State has perhaps 31,000 fighters.[19] In February 2015, the head of the National Counterterrorism Center testified that over 20,000 foreign fighters from at least 90 countries had gone to Iraq and Syria, including 3,400 from the United States and Western Europe, and that the majority of them are fighting for the Islamic State.[20] The Islamic State also seized massive quantities of arms and equipment when it captured territory from the Syrian and Iraqi armies, including US weaponry provided to Iraqi forces, and it now has surface-to-air missiles, anti-tank weapons, Humvees, and even tanks. They also apparently have (unarmed) surveillance drones, though it is unclear exactly how many they have or how technologically sophisticated these drones are.[21]

Foreign funding helps sustain the Islamic State. Wealthy donors in Persian Gulf states such as Kuwait, Qatar, and Saudi Arabia have historically funded an array of Sunni militants, including Salafi-jihadists, out of sectarian solidarity, to fight Iran, or because they shared other elements of the militants' goals. Their governments often turned a blind eye to this backing.[22] Far more important, however, is the money the Islamic State gains because it controls territory. The Islamic State oversees some of Syria and Iraq's most lucrative oil resources, controlling perhaps 50,000 barrels a day in production, and uses long-standing smuggling routes to sell oil and refined petroleum products on the black market. Oil smuggling netted the Islamic State $2 million a day in September 2014 (note that Al Qaeda's total budget around 9/11 was only $30 million a year), though this is likely to decrease due to US attacks on Islamic State-linked smugglers and the plunge in the price of oil that began in late 2014. The Islamic State, like its predecessor Al Qaeda in Iraq, also gets tens of millions each year from ransoms. Finally, the group also gets money from taxing local populations and looting. Some estimates put its overall income at $2 billion a year.[23] The Islamic State uses this money to pay its fighters, even giving them apartments and bonuses when they marry and have children, as well as to recruit new fighters and facilitate their travel to the battlefield.[24]

The Islamic State's territory waxes and wanes with its military fortunes, but as of late 2014, it controlled a territory that at its peak was roughly the size of Britain—though much of the area is sparsely inhabited. It is strong in the Syrian provinces of Raqqa, Idlib, Deir al-Zour, and Aleppo, as well as parts of western Iraq, including large cities like Mosul. By having a presence in both Syria and Iraq, it can shift its bases and leadership as necessary, taking advantage of the weakness of its various opponents and making it difficult for the United States and others to locate and target important leaders.

The Islamic State has proven more militarily effective than its local enemies for several reasons. The group's fighters are highly committed, making them more willing to take risks, including undertaking suicide attacks, than their rivals—daring that pays off on the battlefield, though at enormous cost. The organization has also drawn heavily on former Iraqi military officials, and many of its leaders were seasoned during the years of fighting against US and allied forces in Iraq, in contrast to other groups that sprang up only in 2011. Like Al Qaeda, the Islamic State is also well organized. Baghdadi is its leader, but he has two deputy leaders (one for Iraq and one for Syria). There are governors for the provinces the group controls in Iraq and Syria as well as other officials who in total form a large set of commanders. Under each governor are local councils that handle finance, military matters, personnel, intelligence, the media, and so on. Another council ensures that the local decisions comply with Islamic law (as the group interprets it).[25] The group also has a Minister for Foreign Fighters and Suicide Bombers: that is one minister in charge of both—after all, the functions overlap in the same portfolio.[26] New recruits who come in are inducted in a thorough, bureaucratized manner, with their personal information logged and passports copied or taken before they are given weapons or training.[27]

However, much of the Islamic State's military success has to do with the weakness of its enemies. Although the United States provided billions in aid and training to the Iraqi forces, former Iraqi Prime Minister Nouri al-Maliki appointed political loyalists, not competent leaders, as senior officers. In addition, the regime's discrimination against Iraq's Sunnis undermined morale among Sunni soldiers who understandably had little interest in fighting for a government they despised (and that despised them). This resulted in an Iraqi military that was well armed and equipped but that collapsed when confronted on the battlefield by Islamic State fighters. Even the better-motivated Iraqi Kurdish military forces (called the *peshmerga*), which for many years held off Saddam's forces, had become less formidable, as years of relative peace in Iraqi Kurdistan had dulled their fighting edge. In Syria, the Islamic State often fights against other militant groups that are divided and less experienced. It would have a hard time standing up to large numbers of skilled military forces, but for now it does not face this danger.

The Islamic State uses a mix of tactics. Its fighters try to assassinate leaders and intimidate security forces. It also engages in more conventional operations, using a mix of traditional tactics as well as suicide bombings to frighten and defeat enemy forces. The Islamic State's military skill has improved as it systematically incorporated former security officers from Saddam's regime into its leadership. Both of Baghdadi's deputies held senior positions in Iraq's military. The Islamic State also tries to bribe tribal leaders to gain their support.[28] As the United States and its allies have stepped up air strikes, the Islamic State has adjusted its tactics, dispersing its forces, operating more at night, and otherwise trying to avoid US attacks.

In areas it controls, the Islamic State tries to govern in its own brutal way. The Islamic State offers a medieval form of law and order which, for many Sunni citizens living in a war zone or fearing discrimination from the Shi'ite government in Baghdad or the 'Alawite regime in Damascus, may be appealing (for now, at least). Its personnel police local communities, both to stop crime and to ensure adherence to the Islamic State's draconian rules. In addition to imposing severe punishments like amputation for theft and stoning to death for adultery, they force women to completely cover themselves (and go so far as to cover up female-looking mannequins in store windows). At the same time, the Islamic State runs schools, subsidizes staples like bread, and provides rudimentary services, ensuring electricity and gas supplies, repairing roads, and restoring infrastructure. It even operates a consumer protection office.[29] But despite its aspirations to be a real state, it is unclear how well the organization is actually doing at providing basic services or whether it can sustain such activities over the long term: there are already reports of severe water and electricity shortages and other service deficiencies in areas the Islamic State controls. Baghdadi has called for doctors, engineers, judges (religious ones), and other specialists to come join the Islamic State.[30]

The Islamic State is a brutal conqueror, frequently executing captured soldiers. When the Islamic State swept through Iraq, hundreds of thousands of Iraqis (especially Shi'a living in the newly-acquired territories and religious minorities such as the Yazidis) fled their homes. Many of the women and girls captured were forced to convert and marry fighters or become sex slaves (essentially the same thing). Christians in Islamic State territory must convert, pay a religious tax, or be killed. Sunni Muslims who worked with the Syrian or Iraqi regimes in any way are also viciously targeted. The UN High Commissioner for Human Rights declared that the Islamic State was creating a "house of blood," committing abuses and killings on an "unimaginable" scale.[31]

Acts of senseless violence and unspeakable brutality can be found in almost every armed conflict. Such is the nature of war. However, for the Islamic State, brutality is deliberate, not a byproduct of war, and is wielded for specific strategic purposes. Zarqawi made his mark by personally beheading those he captured in Iraq, including in 2004 the captured American technician Nicholas Berg. The beheadings were widely condemned—even Zawahiri criticized them—but they electrified a segment of young Muslim men who rushed to follow the bold and bloody Zarqawi: they were the key to his prominence as a leader. As Iraq descended into civil war, cruelty became a daily feature, with both Shi'ite and Sunni extremists torturing captives, beheading foes, and circulating videos of it all to frighten their enemies. Today, Abu Bakr al-Baghdadi carries on this ghastly tradition, embracing beheadings and other horrific means of terrorizing his enemies. Muslims worldwide have condemned the Islamic State, calling its actions "heinous war crimes"[32] and starting social media campaigns like #NotInMyName. Al Qaeda even appealed to the Islamic State not to behead the British hostage Alan Henning because he was an innocent aid worker helping Muslims (and thus killing him would repel rather than attract followers)—a strong argument that the Islamic State ignored.

Videos showing the beheadings of captured US and UK citizens in particular are designed to send a message to the American and British people: stay out of our business. Each time a Western hostage is beheaded, the group tries to link the killing to some action taken by the US or UK government to intervene in the conflict. The Islamic State believes that the people in these countries are reluctant to become entangled in yet another war in the Middle East and that savagely murdering an American or British citizen each time the US or UK government starts to get involved will make them even more so. They share Al Qaeda's view that the United States does not have the stomach for a tough fight and will pull out of a conflict as soon as Americans start getting killed. However, what the Islamic State may not fully understand—but Bin Laden certainly did—is that this only goes so far: Americans in particular do not take kindly to being threatened and can get pretty hawkish pretty fast when innocent Americans start being slaughtered. Indeed, opinion polls suggest that American public support for US airstrikes in Iraq and Syria increased significantly following the beheadings of American journalists Steven Sotloff and James Foley.[33]

How Does the Islamic State Publicize Its Cause?

The Islamic State and its predecessors inherited Al Qaeda's emphasis on proselytizing and propaganda. Zarqawi, as head of Al Qaeda in Iraq, disseminated martyrdom and beheading videos to catapult himself to jihadist stardom. Today, Islamic State fighters share flashy videos on social media (complete with CGI flames and Michael Bay-worthy explosions) and engage in sophisticated public relations campaigns—even hijacking seemingly benign hashtags like #WorldCup2014 and others related to the Scottish independence campaign to propagate their message. Content ranges from a child holding a severed head, to images of Islamic State fighters distributing food, to (many) tweets about cats—as a dog owner, I think this speaks for itself.

Although some of this content is spread from the top ranks of the Islamic State, the jihadists have thousands of followers who retweet messages, use apps that allow the Islamic State to assume control of their Twitter handles, and generate their own content, enabling the group to effectively crowdsource jihad. Many of its Western supporters are particularly active. To attract foreigners, it publishes content in multiple languages, including English and Russian, as well as Arabic. The English-language *Dabiq* magazine has impressive production values and spouts an array of compelling vitriol. The Islamic State also issues "cool" videos like *Flames of War*, which has relatively high-end production values and integrates the latest news with images of Islamic State operations and fighters. Despite its barbaric tactics, the Islamic State's use of video and social media is sophisticated and technically proficient.

In 2014, the Islamic State recorded the executions of two American journalists and other Western captives, justifying these killings as a response to the US bombing campaign against Islamic State forces. They dressed the hostages in orange jumpsuits—the same outfits given to jihadist detainees in American custody, and with the British captive issued a series of riveting videos justifying their actions. Similarly, the Islamic State uses social media as a weapon in combat, showing itself victorious and at times brutally treating its foes to spread the word that it will give no quarter and thus panic its enemies.

This campaign has earned grudging respect from a range of commentators in the West who, though they obviously abhor the content of the messages, acknowledge the level of sophistication of the group's social media strategy. Such tactics do help the Islamic State to fundraise, recruit, and proselytize more effectively than traditional insurgent groups. Although such death videos nauseate most of the world, they make the Islamic State look "cool" to a key demographic: angry young Muslim men in search of adventure. Throw in videos that offer a bit of sectarian hatred and a touch of promise about Islamic government (and plenty of explosions and big guns), and the mix helps keep the Islamic State well supplied with impressionable foreign fighters and foolhardy suicide-bomber fodder.

Yet this approach has many costs and risks. Zawahiri himself once warned Baghdadi's predecessor, Zarqawi, not to "be deceived by the praises of some of the zealous young men and their description of you as the sheikh of the slaughters." Instead, he called for Zarqawi to recognize the importance of "the general view" in Iraq and correctly warned that alienating the population as a whole through brutality would backfire.[34]

Social media is also a counterintelligence nightmare for Islamic State militants, especially foreign fighters. Although tweets and Facebook postings inspire them to fight and help them get to Syria and Iraq, these technologies are easily monitored. As former Federal Bureau of Investigation official Clint Watts points out, social media offers "a window into what's going on in Iraq and Syria right now." The same bragging the group did in Syria to inspire others can be turned against it: intelligence services can determine the identities of supporters and potential recruits, flagging individuals not previously on the government's radar; they can also identify when foreign fighters may be trying to come back home and then track their movements. With data analysis, governments can use social media to trace entire networks of contacts. Intelligence officers can communicate with actual and potential terrorists, feeding information—and misinformation—to their networks.

What Are the Islamic State's Relations with the Syrian Government?

The Asad regime declares itself to be at war against "terrorists," and the Islamic State portrays itself as the defender of Sunni Muslims in Syria against "apostate" regimes like Asad's. So they should be enemies, right?

Yes and no. This is the Middle East, where strange bedfellows are the norm. If there were no Islamic State, Asad would have to create it—and, in fact, he kind of did. When the unrest in Syria began, the struggle was widely (and accurately) portrayed as a mass revolt of people fed up with brutality and injustice. When peaceful unrest broke out in 2011, the Syrian regime deliberately released hardened jihadists from jail in order to turn the protests violent and paint the opposition as extremists. Asad portrayed it as a sectarian fight against "terrorists," playing on the fears of his own 'Alawite community as well as Syria's Christians, Druze, and other minorities.

The Asad regime has at times refrained from military operations in some Islamic State-controlled areas, used its air force to bomb the moderate opposition forces fighting the Islamic State, and bought oil from the Islamic State. Asad and the Islamic State loathe each other, but both also oppose the moderate opposition, and by weakening the moderates Asad undermines the greatest long-term threat to his rule. Izzat Shahbandar, a close ally of the Asad regime, claimed that Asad was (successfully) trying to get the Islamic State to destroy the more secular groups supported by the West and, in doing so, to force the world to choose between his regime and the worst of the extremists. Indeed, Shahbandar admitted that at times the Syrian military "gives them a safe path to allow the Islamic State to attack the FSA [Free Syrian Army, which the US backs] and seize their weapons."[35]

Over time the Asad regime's rhetoric and tactics created a backlash among Sunni Muslims that transformed the conflict into a sectarian one, with groups like the Islamic State rising as moderate forces decline. The Syrian people are increasingly left with the miserable choice of either the Asad regime or hardline Islamists. Indeed, the Obama administration has hesitated to arm the Syrian opposition in part because it fears the weapons could end up in the hands of groups like the Islamic State.

With the Islamic State's advances in Iraq and the US entry into the war, Asad has stepped up air strikes against areas under Baghdadi's control. The Iraqi regime is Asad's ally, and losing strategic border crossings to the Islamic State prevents the flow of supplies and fighters from reaching Syrian government forces via Iraq. Such strikes also put the United States and Syria on the same side, helping Asad make the claim that he represents the forces of civilization.

What Is the Khorasan Group?

The Khorasan Group[36], which the United States also bombed in September 2014 when it struck Islamic State forces in Syria, is linked to Al Qaeda and its Syrian affiliate Jabhat al-Nusra, not the Islamic State. The name "Khorasan" refers to a historical region that encompassed parts of Iran, Turkmenistan, Afghanistan, and Pakistan,[37] and it draws on Islamic prophecies that call on Muslims to "join the army" when they "see the black banners coming from Khorasan." However, though there have been reports of some groups in Pakistan adopting the Khorasan name, it does not appear that the group currently operating in Syria that the US government calls "the Khorasan Group" actually refers to itself by that name.[38] An analyst with the SITE Intelligence Group notes that the Afghanistan/Pakistan region "has housed such senior operatives as late Al Qaeda leader Osama bin Laden and current leader Ayman al-Zawahiri. Thus, to differentiate between the various Al Qaeda branches and locations, jihadists often refer to Al Qaeda leadership as 'The Khurasan leadership' or 'the brothers in Khurasan,' rather than using the name 'al-Qaeda central.'"[39] Details are few, but the roughly 50 operatives in this organization come from Afghanistan, Pakistan, South Asia, and the Middle East and appear to report to Al Qaeda's central leadership in Pakistan.[40] Yet the fighters are also integrated with Jabhat al-Nusra in Syria. As far as analysts can tell, it appears that the Khorasan Group uses the areas that Jabhat al-Nusra controls for its own activities, advises the group, and tries to coordinate with other Al Qaeda groups elsewhere in the region. US officials contend that the group is there to use the war in Syria as a sanctuary from which it can plan attacks on the West, recruit Westerners, and develop new tactics and explosives.[41] The US strikes on the Khorasan Group angered Syrians who contend that Jabhat al-Nusra, unlike the Islamic State, is a staunch enemy of the Asad regime.

Is the Islamic State a Terrorist Threat to the American Homeland?

Satellite television and social media bring images of sorrow and slaughter in Syria into the homes of Western Muslims every day. As the Syrian conflict became more sectarian, many Western Muslims went to fight in a struggle they saw as genocidal against Sunni Muslims, and several thousand are now fighting under the Islamic State's banner.

US and European security officials are paying attention. Secretary of Defense Chuck Hagel declared the Islamic State an "imminent threat to every interest we have,"[42] and FBI Director James Comey warned in May 2014 that "there's going to be a diaspora out of Syria at some point and we are determined not to let lines be drawn from Syria today to a future 9/11."[43] These officials look back at the flow of foreign fighters who went to Afghanistan in the 1980s and their connection to the 9/11 attacks and understandably worry that Westerners might go to Syria and Iraq to fight local dictators but come back as radicalized and battle-hardened tools of jihadist groups eager to bring the war home to the West. Many other officials and analysts share their views, and this consensus has influenced US decisions to intervene against the Islamic State.

This risk is real. The foreign fighter problem in Iraq and Syria is simply bigger than past cases—more than all recent jihads combined, in fact. Recent reports estimate that between 2,500 and 3,000 foreign fighters from Western countries have traveled to Syria and Iraq as of August 2014, including over 100 Americans; France,

Britain, Belgium, and Germany have the largest numbers of citizens in the fight. As the wars continue, the flow is likely to increase.

But a closer look demonstrates that while the threat of foreign fighters is real, it has been exaggerated and it probably can be managed—though not eliminated—through effective policy. Similar fears about foreign fighters were raised concerning many earlier conflicts, especially after the 2003 US invasion of Iraq, yet for the most part, these conflicts did not produce a surge in terrorism in Europe or the United States.

The vast majority of foreign fighters will never present a serious problem back home. Many of the most radical die, blowing themselves up in suicide attacks or perishing in firefights with opposing forces. Many never return home but continue fighting in the conflict zone or at the next battle for jihad. Some of those who go to Syria and Iraq quickly become disillusioned, and even those who return often are not violent. Security services arrest or disrupt others, particularly if returnees group together to attempt large-scale attacks. Indeed, becoming a foreign fighter—particularly with today's heavy use of social media—makes a terrorist far more likely to come to the attention of security services than if he had never left home. Security service leaders are paid to worry, but they ignore their own remarkable record of success: they regularly detect jihadists and disrupt their plots, in locales ranging from Kosovo to Australia.

So far the Islamic State's agenda is first and foremost local and regional: killing 'Alawi and Shi'a, toppling the governments in Iraq and Syria, and so on. Even the US bombing of Islamic State forces that began in 2014 does not necessarily change this. The Islamic State beheaded American journalists but did not try to attack outside the region, and though its predecessor jihadist organization in Iraq fought American forces for years after the 2003 US invasion, it did not attack the US homeland or carry out a significant attack in Europe. In contrast to Al Qaeda, which calls on Muslims to attack in the West, Islamic State propaganda urges Muslims to come join it in Iraq and Syria. However, the Islamic State's propaganda increasingly is encouraging Muslims to act in general, and some isolated individuals in the West are heeding the call. So attacks by Islamic State-inspired Lone Wolves seem likely, and it is possible that the Islamic State itself might dedicate more assets to attacking the West.

Still this potential terrorism threat does require a response. US and European governments need to identify opportunities to encourage potentially dangerous individuals to take more peaceful paths and to determine which individuals deserve arrest, visa denial, preventive detention, or other forms of disruption. Steps include increasing community engagement efforts to dissuade potential fighters from going to Syria or Iraq, working more with Turkey to disrupt transit routes, improving de-radicalization programs to "turn" returning fighters into intelligence sources or make them less likely to engage in violence, and avoiding blanket prosecution efforts when fighters return. Most important, security services must be properly resourced and organized to handle the potential danger. Taken together, these measures will reduce the likelihood that any one individual will either want to move or succeed in moving all the way down the path from concerned observer to foreign fighter to terrorist.

But almost inevitably, there will be some terrorist attacks carried out by returnees from Syria or Iraq, some of whom may be affiliated with the Islamic State. There is a Russian roulette character to the threat: through a combination of skill and luck, security services might stop all plots from becoming serious, but they could also make one mistake that proves fatal, even though the number of overall threats is low. Terrorism has unfortunately become a feature of modern life, and the fallout of the civil wars in Syria and Iraq will make that problem more difficult. Lone Wolf attacks are particularly likely, as the "coolness" of the Islamic State is inspiring Muslims around the world. But these are not likely to be attacks on the scale of 9/11 or carried out in a sustained way. Both the United States and Europe have dealt with this problem before and already have effective measures in place to greatly reduce the threat of terrorism from jihadist returnees.

Why Did the United States Go to War with the Islamic State?

The Obama administration was eager for US forces to leave Iraq in 2011 and hesitant to become involved in the Syrian civil war, believing, with good reason, that US attempts to "fix" the Middle East have often failed or have had significant costs. This hesitation continued even as violence and discrimination increased in Iraq and the role of jihadist groups in the Syrian civil war grew tremendously. In both cases, potential allies—the Iraqi regime and the

Syrian opposition—were flawed, the threat seemed distant, and the risks of greater involvement were too great.

Perhaps more important for the administration, the American public was not clamoring for any sort of intervention—on the contrary: polls showed that the public was firmly against another Middle Eastern war, and Congress, except for a few vocal senators, remained resolutely opposed.[44] Rather than fearing that President Obama would be seen as weak on foreign policy, the Obama team felt insulated by the successful overthrow of the Qaddafi regime in Libya in 2011 and the killing of Bin Laden earlier that same year. Polls showed that, for the first time in many years, Democrats were seen as more effective on foreign policy than Republicans.[45] Syria and Iraq were not issues in the 2012 election.

Since the beginning of Obama's second term, however, all of this has changed. The series of international crises since Obama's second inaugural in Syria, Iraq, Ukraine, Nigeria, and the South China Sea—and his measured, seemingly tepid responses to them—collectively created the sense that the American-led international order was coming undone and eroded the American public's confidence in the administration's foreign policy. The president's 2012 announcement of a "red line" regarding Syrian chemical weapons use—and then his 2013 decision to accept a deal with the Asad regime and refrain from bombing when Asad used chemical weapons to kill almost 1,500 civilians, including over 400 children—was attacked as feckless. Comedian Jon Stewart compared the president to a helpless parent unsuccessfully threatening a teenager with being grounded and compared the red line to a "dick-measuring ribbon."[46] Republican leaders contended that Obama was allowing a humanitarian crisis to grow, facilitating a victory by Iran and its allies, and twiddling his thumbs while an Al Qaeda-like terrorism presence grew—and that all this was typical of his broader weakness on foreign policy. Perhaps even more politically damning, former Obama administration officials such as Secretary of Defense Robert Gates and Secretary of State (and current Democratic presidential candidate) Hillary Clinton also made clear that they, unlike the president, favored more US involvement in Syria. With this steady drumbeat of criticism, polls showed that while Americans had little appetite for military involvement in Syria, they also felt the president was handling the crisis, and foreign policy overall, poorly.[47]

The Islamic State's invasion of Iraq and seizure of Mosul changed the strategic and political picture, essentially compelling the president to act. By expanding the war to Iraq, the Islamic State threatened to visibly destroy the massive US investment of blood and treasure in Iraq. On withdrawing US forces from Iraq in December 2011, Obama had made the case that that investment was protected. Now, administration officials feared that Baghdad might fall and the entire Iraqi state might collapse, causing an even more massive humanitarian crisis in the region, which would be seen as the fault of the administration's inaction.

The administration began right after the fall of Mosul to lay the groundwork for intervention by insisting on a new government in Baghdad. But before that process could be completed, the immediate humanitarian threat to the Yazidis compelled sudden action. The Yazidis are a Muslim minority, and the Islamic State regards them as apostates. It openly promised to kill Yazidi men and enslave Yazidi women, among other atrocities. Thousands of Yazidis were trapped on Mount Sinjar, and the president declared that in the face of a massacre, "the United States of America cannot turn a blind eye."[48]

The Yazidi crisis may have forced the administration's hand, but the US government would not have committed itself to bombing in order to save a minority that it had never heard of before without several broader strategic concerns. Administration officials feared that the Islamic State's targeting of minorities would continue and the humanitarian horrors would multiply. In addition, the Islamic State fighters were driving on Baghdad and Erbil, and though on paper the military balance favored Iraqi and Kurdish forces, their collapse in Mosul and elsewhere meant that the possibility of the Islamic State continuing to seize large swaths of territory was quite real. Implicit in the administration's rhetoric was that the Islamic State represented a broader threat. Security officials worried that the large number of Western volunteers in its ranks made the Islamic State well suited to attack the US homeland. The threat was even clearer to US interests in the Middle East, where the Islamic State was emerging as the dominant force in a critical region. "If you threaten America," declared Obama in his speech defending the intervention, "you will find no safe haven."[49] Action seemed essential. "If left unchecked, these terrorists could pose a growing threat beyond that region, including to the United States."[50]

What began as a limited intervention to help the Yazidis and other embattled minorities quickly grew. In response to the US and allied bombing campaign, the Islamic State publicly beheaded two Americans and a British citizen who had fallen into their clutches—horrors that outraged the public and increased support for intervention. In addition, it was deemed to be impossible to defeat the Islamic State as long as it enjoyed a haven in Syria, so political outrage combined with strategic logic led to a broadening of the campaign to include targets in Syria.

The military campaign against the Islamic State, however, has many limits. The intervention was popular when it began, but this could easily change—especially if, as is likely, it does not produce dramatic results quickly. Because American public support for intervention is fragile, the administration has also pledged to avoid a "boots on the ground" role for US forces: they can advise and train but not fight directly. This fits with an American public that wants to do something about the Islamic State but is wary of another Middle East quagmire: polls taken in September 2014 show 70% support airstrikes, but only 38% support sending ground troops in for combat. Thus, local forces will have to be the ones who act on the ground.

Nor does the United States want to work with or even indirectly help many of the Islamic State's other enemies. The half-hearted campaign in Syria seems to reflect a continuing administration view that there are no acceptable and effective partners to support and no American solution to the instability there. So even though Bashar al-Asad's regime, Iran, and the Lebanese Hizballah—whose proficient forces have acted as Asad's shock troops in several important battles—are fighting against the Islamic State, the United States wants nothing to do with them. However, by taking on the Islamic State, one of the Syrian regime's enemies, the United States frees up regime troops to go after other foes.

US strategy is still in flux. The intervention that began in haste in August 2014 is being reexamined now that the immediate crisis is over. Whether and how much to take on the Asad regime in Syria, the role of US ground forces, and how to reshape Iraq's political dynamics are all issues on the table that are likely to evolve as the intervention continues.

9

COUNTERTERRORISM

The United States uses a wide range of national security instruments to fight terrorism in general and Al Qaeda in particular. Each instrument has its strengths and weaknesses, and they cannot all be used in every circumstance. Together, however, they offer a powerful counterterrorism package that has devastated the Al Qaeda core since 9/11. Yet Al Qaeda endures: it is weaker than it was at its peak, but its allies and ideology remain influential, particularly in the Middle East. The Islamic State poses a new, and distinct, challenge. Countering the Islamic State is less about the counterterrorism techniques that have worked well against Al Qaeda and more about traditional military and foreign internal defense methods.

Isn't Diplomacy Worthless When It Comes to Fighting Terror?

Diplomacy in the context of counterterrorism seems foolish, if not bizarre. Issuing a diplomatic demarche to Ayman al-Zawahiri or Abu Bakr al-Baghdadi would be laughable. Nor does it seem any more sensible at the global level: for years, the United Nations (UN) refused to condemn terrorism due to sympathy for national liberation movements that used terrorism as a tactic, such as the Palestine Liberation Organization. The UN still does not have a workable definition of terrorism, and many resolutions to stop terrorism funding and support remain squishy. Hostile governments can easily ignore diplomatic demarches and UN resolutions: in October 1999, the UN Security Council passed a resolution demanding that the Taliban turn over Bin Laden. They ignored it.

However, as terrorism expert and former senior Central Intelligence Agency official Paul Pillar contends, "Diplomacy is linked with all the elements of counterterrorism."[1] Intelligence cooperation, extradition, military basing and access, and efforts to monitor and seize terrorist assets all occur in the context of bilateral and multilateral relations between governments, which diplomats create, maintain, and nourish. It is through diplomacy that foreign countries give the United States access for military bases, agree to shut down a financial center linked to terrorism, or facilitate a particularly tricky extradition.

The UN, with heavy US prodding, has also made progress since 9/11, passing resolutions that ban support for designated terrorist groups, and many countries now rely on the UN list of designated terrorist organizations to regulate fundraising and recruitment and otherwise frame their own counterterrorism efforts. UN resolutions and other agreements on terrorism also strengthen international norms, making terrorism an increasingly illegitimate tactic. And while UN resolutions by themselves may do little, they create a framework in which governments can make demands on other states to stop terrorism in the name of the international order, thereby enabling leaders to take steps at home to confront terrorism without being seen as lackeys of US imperialism or puppets controlled by some other powerful state.

What Role Does the Legal System Play?

Given the immorality of terrorists and the horrors they perpetrate, it seems feckless to give them rights in a court of law. Former Vice President Richard ("Dick") Cheney declared in 2009, "When we get people who are more concerned about reading the rights to an Al Qaeda terrorist than they are with protecting the United States against people who are absolutely committed to do anything they can to kill Americans, then I worry."[2] Yet like diplomacy, trials and the criminal justice system are vital for counterterrorism. The world may not be completely safe now that Ramzi Yousef, the skilled bomb maker and mastermind of the 1993 World Trade Center bombing, is behind bars in a Colorado supermax prison, but it is *safer*. Convicting Yousef and other terrorists takes them off the streets. According to a 2014 report by Human Rights First, almost 500 people have been convicted of charges related to terrorism in U.S. federal courts since 9/11.[3]

The pre-trial investigations also can be intelligence bonanzas, leading to new leads and information that often result in more arrests and more plots disrupted. Large terrorist organizations like Al Qaeda are mini-bureaucracies: they keep personnel records, pay stubs, files on potential attack sites, and so on. All of this is a gold mine for counterterrorism officials when suspected terrorists are arrested or brought in for questioning. Trials also have legitimacy because there is an accepted and high bar for conviction, with the accused presumed innocent until proven guilty. Allies are more likely to cooperate if they know a suspect will be given full rights and due process in a traditional US civilian court. Also, the threat of prosecution can be used to compel cooperation from a suspect: a low-level terrorist might cooperate in exchange for a reduced sentence, leading to valuable information on a more dangerous terrorist and the group in general.

Many terrorist groups are also involved in criminal activities such as fraud and kidnapping, and going after these activities can bring unknown terrorists to the attention of police. Travel facilitation, including forgery of documents, has always been an important part of Al Qaeda's activities. Al Qaeda has long found it hard to find operatives who are comfortable speaking English or otherwise operating in the West, and it also has few operatives who have legitimate passports from Western countries: reducing forgery makes it harder for Al Qaeda to operate.

Terrorist groups fear that an arrested member will confess and reveal what he knows to security forces (even Zawahiri gave up names while in prison in Egypt), so each capture pushes the group to change its passwords, find new safe houses, and otherwise assure itself that its secrets are still secret. These countermeasures are time-consuming and costly, disrupting the group's effectiveness.

Still, using the legal system as a counterterrorism tool has many limits. Though planning a terrorist attack is a crime, the legal system often kicks in only after an attack has occurred. So it helps prevent terrorists from striking again but is less effective in stopping attacks from occurring in the first place. The very legitimacy of the legal system comes from the high bar for conviction. In some cases, the evidence against the suspected terrorist may be strong enough to convince counterterrorism officials that the suspect needs to be taken off the streets, but not strong enough to meet the rigorous legal standards required to secure a conviction in a US criminal trial. In some instances, such evidence may exist, but in order to present it in court, prosecutors would have to reveal classified information that jeopardizes key sources or intelligence collection systems. The legal system often catches those at the bottom of the chain—the low-level operators who actually carry out the attacks—rather than the skilled individuals who run the logistics and direct Al Qaeda. In the 1998 East Africa embassy bombings, for example, the United States successfully prosecuted several of the individuals involved in the attack, but Bin Laden, Zawahiri, and many others who mattered most avoided justice. Finally, the threat of jail time is unlikely to deter most terrorists: some were already hardened criminals to begin with, others are idealistic and willing to sacrifice not just their freedom but their lives for the cause, and many come from war zones or chaotic areas where the US legal system seems far away (or not all that bad) compared to their everyday reality of civil strife and drones passing overhead.

Because Al Qaeda is based abroad and operates globally, the use of the criminal justice system as a tool of counterterrorism relies heavily on foreign government support, as their domestic security services and law enforcement personnel are usually the ones who have to arrest and extradite the suspect, assist investigators, and collect critical evidence. In the 1998 embassy bombing cases, Kenyan officials helped Federal Bureau of Investigation officers conduct interviews and searches and send suspects and evidence to America. At times, foreign governments are politically unwilling to act or incapable of acting because they are too weak to arrest the terrorist. Other times they are simply sloppy and not very well trained, and key evidence is destroyed or goes missing. Foreign governments may also be reluctant to have their role revealed in public, especially if it involves disclosing sensitive intelligence methods.[4]

Extraditing a suspect to the United States for trial can also prove difficult. This process can be time-consuming: in 2004, the United States requested that its close ally, Britain, extradite the preacher Abu Hamza for his involvement in Al Qaeda-linked terrorism in Yemen and for trying to set up a training camp in Oregon. This request was granted—eight years later.[5] The European Court of Human Rights blocked the extradition of Hamza's aide, Haron Aswat, on the grounds that being confined to an American high-security prison would constitute "inhuman or degrading treatment."[6] In developing countries, the legal bar is usually lower, but the political bar is higher: because of the deep unpopularity of the United States in the Muslim world (in 2014, the United States had an "unfavorable" rating of 85% in Egypt and Jordan and 59% in Pakistan), governments and judicial officials often fear open cooperation with the United States because of the political consequences of being tarred with the brush of America.[7] In some cases, the offense with which the suspect has been charged in the United States, such as support for a foreign terrorist group, may not be illegal in the country in question, as it does not directly threaten that country's nationals. In some countries, such as Pakistan, officials also worry that the powerful jihadist groups active in that country will retaliate against anyone who cooperates.

What about Military Tribunals, Guantanamo, and Other Post-9/11 Legal Measures?

Because of the criminal justice system's many limits, and because it is derided as "soft" on terrorists, after 9/11 the Bush White House authorized the creation of military commissions to try terrorist suspects, arguing that applying the standard rules of evidence and principles of law used in civilian criminal cases to terrorism cases "is not practicable" given the nature of terrorism.[8] Congress later codified and amended military tribunals in a series of Military Commissions Acts. Military commissions became the only legal option other than indefinite detention for Guantanamo detainees, as Congress also passed a law preventing the president from transferring detainees to the United States for trial, thus excluding the traditional civilian criminal justice system.

In theory, the commissions were meant to be expeditious, getting around the delays and high bar of the traditional legal system to ensure that terrorists spent time in jail. In practice, this largely failed. Although procedure in military commissions differs in several ways from federal civilian courts, the accused still enjoy considerable rights, most of which are codified in the legislation Congress passed. Defense lawyers also proved to be highly aggressive on behalf of their clients—as one detainee's defense lawyer put it, "there is very much the viewpoint that we're paid by the government to challenge the government"[9]—and civil libertarians' fears that "military justice" was an oxymoron proved unfounded. Indeed, though comparing cases between the systems is difficult, the military commissions have convicted far fewer people than the civilian system, which has a nearly 90% conviction rate.[10]

In addition to military tribunals, after 9/11 the United States relied on secret detention sites abroad as well as detention facilities at Guantanamo, Bagram, and elsewhere to hold and interrogate individuals. However, the US withdrawal from Iraq and drawdown from Afghanistan, the tempest that erupted over the Guantanamo facility, and, more broadly, the question of the appropriate procedures for foreign detainees have led the Obama administration to move away from detention as a counterterrorism tool—though not, of course, to end it completely.

Continuing a detention program is contentious at home and abroad: even close allies in Europe are critical of indefinite detention in Guantanamo. The lack of a detention program, however, means that the United States must either release potentially dangerous individuals—exact figures are hotly disputed, but perhaps 100 of the current Guantanamo detainees could notionally be tried for terrorism-related crimes or are deemed too dangerous to release[11]—or rely on its liaison partners to act for it. In addition, the United States cannot itself take suspected terrorists off the streets of foreign countries. As a result, it must either leave them to continue plotting attacks or have allied police or intelligence services remove them, something that allies at times may not be willing or able to do. The latter approach can also lead to other human rights abuses.

What Is Rendition and Why Is It So Controversial?

Because extradition can be difficult or politically impossible, the United States has at times resorted to renditions: the extra-legal transfer of a suspected terrorist from one foreign country to another foreign country (such as grabbing someone off the street in Pakistan, bundling them onto a plane, and sending them for trial in Egypt). Exact numbers are elusive, but former Director of Central Intelligence George Tenet testified that there were over 80 renditions before 9/11, and a Human Rights Watch report in 2005 claimed that there were between 100 and 150 in the three years after 9/11.[12] This figure includes both renditions where an individual is transferred to the United States for trial and those where an individual is transferred to a foreign country, where he is often tried but where the judicial system is far more suspect (often, but not consistently, referred to as "extraordinary renditions").

Rendition proponents contend that if used sparingly, this tactic can fill an important gap by maintaining some semblance of the rule of law for suspects in countries with broken judicial systems like Pakistan while still getting them off the streets and gaining intelligence on their activities (usually from so-called "pocket litter"— information from a cell phone, handwritten notes, or other material a suspect may have with him upon arrest).[13] Ramzi Yousef, the mastermind of the 1993 World Trade Center bombing who also plotted several more ambitious attacks, was discovered in Pakistan and was arrested by Pakistani officials, along with an American State Department official. The FBI and the US Secret Service transported Yousef to the United States, where he was tried and convicted and is now in prison for life.[14] The first "extraordinary rendition," where the suspect was sent from one country to another foreign country, was Abu Talal al-Qasimi, who in 1995 was transferred from Croatia to Egypt, where he was executed.[15]

Critics, however, see renditions as criminally wrong because of their extrajudicial nature. One common misconception about renditions is that they are done secretly from the host government. (This misconception arises when, after a rendition is leaked, the host government pleads ignorance and offers pro forma protests.) In fact, according to former CIA officer Michael Scheuer, every rendition in Europe and elsewhere he knew of involved the support of the host nation.[16] The Open Society Justice Initiative reports that over 50 foreign governments were involved in the extraordinary rendition program.[17]

A more serious criticism involves torture and other human rights abuses: many rendered suspects have reportedly been sent to Egypt, Libya, and even Syria, countries whose human rights records range from bad to horrific. Some suspects are held incommunicado in secret locations, effectively "disappeared." Part of the purpose of renditions is to take suspects off the streets, but by sending them to countries like Egypt, where the judicial system does not respect the rights of defendants, innocent people are more likely to be subjected to torture and false imprisonment. Khaled al-Masri, a German citizen, claims that on New Year's Eve 2003 he was kidnapped while traveling in Macedonia, imprisoned, interrogated, and tortured while in CIA custody in Afghanistan. When his interrogators realized he was not a terrorist, just a car salesman from Bavaria, and had little to say, he was unceremoniously deposited in Albania's mountains.[18] From the American government's point of view, however, getting a suspected terrorist off the street and the associated intelligence benefits make renditions to countries with suspected human rights records worthwhile despite the greater risk of mistakes.

How Do We Go After Al Qaeda's Money?

Before 9/11, America's capacity for, and interest in, disrupting terrorist financing was minimal. Since 9/11, the US Treasury Department has led an aggressive effort against Al Qaeda's money.[19] To judge the effectiveness of this campaign, it is important to note that while committing a terrorist act is often cheap, maintaining a terrorist group can be quite expensive. As such, successfully targeting financing may have little or no impact on any single operation, but overall, it can reduce the number of attacks, make them less deadly, and weaken the terrorist group in myriad ways.

After 9/11, the United States sought to target the front companies, charities, and major donors of Al Qaeda. It also sought to disrupt Al Qaeda's financial network, preventing it from using banks, couriers, and other means of transferring funds. On September 28, 2001, just days after the 9/11 attacks, the UN Security Council adopted Resolution 1373, requiring countries to freeze the assets "of persons who commit, or attempt to commit, terrorist acts" and otherwise assist in financially targeting Al Qaeda and the Taliban as well as other terrorist groups.[20] A new executive order, EO13224, gave the Treasury Department new powers to freeze assets, while the USA PATRIOT Act extended anti-money-laundering powers, required banks to report more information on assets and transfers, and otherwise gave Treasury a new set of financial tools. The 9/11 aftermath also saw important advances by the Financial Action Task Force, the World Bank, the International Monetary Fund, and other institutions to combat terrorism financing.

Tracking terrorist financing also aids intelligence: by finding out whom Al Qaeda pays, you find out who is in Al Qaeda. The discovery of receipts, bank transaction reports, or even entire ledgers can help intelligence officers find addresses, names, and other information—what Juan Zarate, who led Treasury's efforts against terrorism financing after 9/11, described as "a gold mine of information."[21] Information showing financial links between the Al Qaeda core and Riduan Isamuddin (better known by his nom de guerre, Hambali), who led Jemaah Islamiyya in Southeast Asia and was responsible for the 2002 attacks on nightclubs in Bali that killed over 200 people, helped lead to his arrest.

As groups become short of money, they turn more to crime: a dangerous move on their part. Kidnapping, extortion, robbery, and "taxation" of areas under their control make them less popular among their constituents and make it harder for the terrorists to portray themselves as Robin Hoods. Crime also attracts the attention of law enforcement. Intelligence services hunting terrorists might miss operatives, only to have police investigating credit card fraud stumble upon them because of their financial crimes. Gregory Vernon Patterson and several friends robbed a gas station to fund a spate of terrorist attacks they were planning to carry out in the Los Angeles area. Patterson dropped his cell phone at the robbery scene, however, leading police to search his apartment and, in so doing, discover various jihadist documents that they eventually linked to a terrorism plot.

But going after the money is difficult. Even large terrorist groups like Al Qaeda are relatively small in a financial sense. Al Qaeda's budget at its peak was around $30 million; by comparison, around the same time period, illicit narcotics had a $400 billion share of the global economy.[22] So terrorist money is often only a drop in a sea of illegitimate funds. Also, when disrupting donors, there are disagreements as to how much intent matters: after 9/11, the United States pushed to have any suspicious financing stopped, while US allies wanted to be sure that only those who intended to support terrorism were punished.

Some money is also transferred outside the standard financial system. In remote areas where banks have little presence (but where terrorist groups are often active), *hawala* networks are present. These are informal money-transferring networks that often involve family members who arrange for money deposited in one country to be paid out by another family member in a second country. Such networks are vital to diaspora communities who need to send remittances back home to places like Somalia that lack banks, but they can also be used to illicitly transfer money. *Hawala* networks do not involve extensive paperwork, and they often are unregulated and outside government control, making them attractive for terrorists.

Vital to stopping funding is targeting the legitimacy of terrorism itself. If individuals believe the terrorists are heroes, they are more likely to give money. Some governments, notably Saudi Arabia, have tolerated public support for an array of causes that Al Qaeda also champions, such as helping rebels in Chechnya and Kashmir, while Gulf state citizens motivated by sectarianism have funded the Islamic State. Especially in the years before 9/11, the Saudi government was lax on monitoring aid to jihadist-linked causes, enabling terrorists to raise money and exploit charities without the government knowing. To stop this financing, the United States needed to persuade Saudi Arabia to confront important domestic interest groups that favored these causes and saw US efforts to halt fundraising as a veiled attempt to stop Muslims from fulfilling their religious obligation to give to charity. A key change occurred in 2003, when Al Qaeda attacked Saudi Arabia directly. This soured many Saudis on the group and led even many anti-American clerics to condemn it, reducing its overall legitimacy. Yet even today, many citizens in Gulf countries support what they feel are legitimate struggles, such as the anti-Asad fight in Syria or the Taliban's fight against the Afghan government and its US backer, even though the groups they support may have links to Al Qaeda or the Islamic State.

The cumulative impact of anti-fundraising efforts has been considerable. Some donors were prevented from paying through arrest or the disruption of the payment network, while others were deterred for fear of penalty. Al Qaeda found it harder to pay the families of its operatives, crucial for maintaining morale and ensuring their loyalty, as more and more operatives died or were imprisoned while the overall budget went down.[23] People looking for training must pay their own way, a barrier for many Muslims from developing countries and poor families in the West. The documents discovered in Bin Laden's compound in Abbottabad suggest that the

Al Qaeda core is now relying on affiliates for funding, rather than the other way around. Affiliates, in turn, often engage in crime, such as kidnapping or theft, to gain money, making them less popular and exposing them to disruption by law enforcement. Like other counterterrorism instruments, going after the money by itself does not stop terrorism. But even with its many limits, it provides valuable information on Al Qaeda members and makes the group more vulnerable to disruption. For the Islamic State, however, this effort has just begun. And because the Islamic State relies heavily on taxation and exploiting resources in areas it controls, success will require changes on the ground, not just going after donors.

What Is the Role of US Military Force?

The role of "kinetic" military operations (the military's jargon for operations that kill people or destroy things) in counterterrorism against Al Qaeda and its allies involves three methods: drones and other airstrikes, conventional military operations, and raids by special operations forces, like the one that led to the killing of Osama Bin Laden. Against the Islamic State, more traditional conventional military force is also valuable.

Military forces can deny terrorist groups a haven. The US invasion that toppled the Taliban denied Al Qaeda a secure base, and though the organization has made limited inroads in Pakistan and elsewhere, these are a poor second to the freedom it enjoyed in Afghanistan. Al Qaeda can no longer train thousands and plot with impunity as it did before 9/11. The Islamic State has a haven in part because it has resisted attacks from the Iraqi and Syrian governments (and more recently, the US and other coalition partners) and various tribes and opposition groups.

When military forces occupy territory, they can devastate a terrorist group that has embedded itself within a community. A secure population is more likely to work with government forces and inform on terrorists and otherwise work against them. Military forces can also coerce locals or enable government officials to use their power—to grant travel permits, business licenses, permission to go to a hospital or attend a university, and so on—to compel cooperation. In western Iraq, as US forces gained the trust of the population in 2006 and 2007, they worked with local tribes against Al

Qaeda in Iraq and helped the government consolidate its authority. These efforts devastated Al Qaeda in Iraq (AQI), at least temporarily. But succeeding as an occupying force is difficult. Some militaries lack, and make little effort to learn, critical information about who in a particular neighborhood is a terrorist, instead arresting young men in general and killing innocent people. Such blanket approaches usually backfire, alienating communities. Terrorists play up their role in defying a foreign military, making their actions more legitimate and gaining popular support. Foreign occupation feeds into Al Qaeda's narrative that Muslim lands are under attack and serves as a magnet for foreign fighters. It also is costly. In peacetime, deploying a military unit is expensive, but in wartime, it is staggering. In fiscal year 2008, deploying one brigade combat team—about 4,000 soldiers—in Afghanistan cost US taxpayers over $8 billion.[24] And this cost says nothing about the human toll as suicide bombings, improvised explosive devices, and other attacks steadily inflict casualties.

Because conventional forces are such a blunt instrument, a more common American tool is the use of special operations forces to kill or capture suspected terrorists. In 2004, Secretary of Defense Donald Rumsfeld issued a secret order authorizing special operations forces to carry out strikes in Syria, Yemen, and Pakistan,[25] and such raids became common in war zones in Iraq and Afghanistan. The Council on Foreign Relations reports that there were 2,200 such missions in 2011, the vast majority of which were capture operations that did not involve shots being fired.[26] Such raids depend on excellent intelligence: the wrong information can lead to innocent deaths and jeopardize the safety of the team members. When intelligence is strong, however, such raids offer the chance to kill or detain individual terrorists and to capture massive tranches of documents that may reveal the names, locations, and roles of other terrorists, enabling further raids and arrests. If done at a constant pace, such operations can dig deep into the bench of Al Qaeda and associated movements.

Military force can also be attractive because it proves the country's leadership is acting strongly in the face of terrorism. This may help bolster national morale. It may also boost the poll ratings of a president or prime minister—though failure, of course, carries the risk of political disaster.

However, deploying conventional military force comes with a host of downsides that often make it prohibitive. Terrorists themselves typically have few physical assets: their training camps are rudimentary, and simply destroying their facilities often barely sets them back. In addition, terrorists are difficult to deter: they are highly motivated and live in dangerous environments already, so the threat of US force may mean little to them. In much of the world, the use of military force would be a gross and unnecessary violation of sovereignty: if terrorists are active in Germany, Malaysia, or Jordan, the easiest thing to do is ask the government to use its own security forces. Even in areas where governments are hostile or exercise at most limited sovereignty, the use of force is also considered less legitimate even by many US allies, generating ill will toward American counterterrorism and American foreign policy in general. As discussed below, however, military force is vital when confronting the Islamic State, because unlike Al Qaeda, the Islamic State controls vast stretches of territory and engages in conventional military conflict.

What about Drones and Other Air Strikes?

Perhaps no current US counterterrorism instrument is as misunderstood as the drone program. During most of the Bush administration, the United States conducted only a handful of drone strikes, almost all of which were in Pakistan, but when President Obama took office in 2009, drones became America's weapon of choice. Drone strikes in Pakistan went from a just a few in 2007 to over 120 in 2010.[27] They have diminished since then, but the administration has also used drones in other theaters, particularly Yemen.

The drone campaign removes key figures from the Al Qaeda lineup at no risk to the Americans involved. Drones have killed over 3,000 Al Qaeda, Taliban, and other jihadists, including over 100 senior figures.[28] Al Qaeda's bench is deeper than most, but it is not infinite. When new leaders step up to the plate, they often lack the experience and skill of their predecessors. In a letter found in the raid on Bin Laden's compound, Bin Laden explained to a key lieutenant (who was later killed in a drone strike) that the death of experienced leaders leads "to the rise of lower leaders who are not as experienced as the former leaders" and warned that "this would lead to the repeat of mistakes."[29] The correlation is only rough, but as the number of drone strikes grew from 2008 to 2012, the number of attacks linked to the Al Qaeda core plummeted, as did the overall lethality of attacks: from 2005 to 2008, the START database of terrorist attacks shows four attacks per year linked to the core, which killed a total of 165 people. In the four years that followed, there were only two attacks, killing a total of just two people, suggesting that the increase in drone strikes correlated with the plunge.[30] A broader study of the counterterrorism tactic known as leadership decapitation (i.e., killing or capturing top leaders) finds that terrorist groups that suffer the loss of their top leaders are far more likely to collapse than groups that do not.[31]

Perhaps the biggest impact of drones, however, does not involve the deaths of militants, but rather how Al Qaeda must adjust in order to protect its personnel. A tip sheet found among jihadists in Mali advised militants to avoid drones by maintaining "complete silence of all wireless contacts," to "avoid gathering in open areas," and to take strenuous measures to root out spies, among other suggestions. The guidelines also recommended that top leaders "should not use communications equipment," suggesting that the terrorists themselves may be aware of the debilitating effect the loss of top leaders can have on an organization.[32] All of these are sensible tips, but the implications for group effectiveness are staggering. In essence, group leaders cannot lead, as they must hide or remain incommunicado. Training on a large scale is hard if not impossible, as large gatherings can be lethal. In combat, they cannot mass or bring in significant reinforcements.

From a counterterrorism perspective, drones are a vast improvement over past forms of air strikes. The United States launched cruise missiles against Sudan and Afghanistan after the 1998 embassy bombings in order to strike what it saw as Al Qaeda-related targets. Because cruise missiles do not provide the kind of real-time intelligence that drones do and take hours to arrive on target, it was difficult to make sure those strikes hit the right targets at the right times. The individuals who were actually hit were probably low-level trainees, and the organization went on high alert and became harder to strike.[33] These strikes also allowed Al Qaeda to emerge as heroes, claiming that they successfully defied the United States. They were emboldened, not deterred.

Critics remain skeptical, though. A common criticism of drones is that they kill innocents. And they do. However, the question becomes more complex upon closer examination. Administration officials claim that drones kill almost no civilians. In June 2011, John Brennan, the president's counterterrorism advisor at the time, even claimed that a year of strikes had resulted in zero non-combatant deaths.[34] The Bureau of Investigative Journalism, in contrast, claims that as of January 2015, as many as 959 civilians, including as many as 204 children, were killed by drone strikes in Pakistan alone between 2004 and the end of 2014, with dozens also killed in Yemen and Somalia.[35]

What explains the vast disparities? First, many strikes kill young men, about whom little is known. Administration officials arrived at their low civilian death toll by counting all military-age males in the blast area as combatants unless intelligence after the fact explicitly proved them to be innocent—and follow-on intelligence was usually not sought on that question. Others take the opposite approach, assuming that all dead who are not confirmed militants are innocents, even if they are young men carrying weapons and associating with known terrorists. Making this more complex, the overwhelming majority of strikes in Pakistan occur in tribal areas where militants and the Pakistani government prevent journalists and human rights workers from treading, leading both of these sources, for different reasons, to often inflate the number of civilian drone casualties.[36]

Audrey Kurth Cronin, a terrorism expert, critiques the reliance on drones, noting that drone strikes, because they kill innocents, make it difficult for the United States to retain the moral high ground: How can Americans criticize Al Qaeda for killing innocent people when the United States does so as well? US allies also disapprove of drones, and some terrorists cite drone strikes as a reason for attacking the United States.

Allied regimes, particularly leaders in Pakistan, denounce the drone program. Yet as with most aspects of US policy toward Pakistan, the reality is more complex and confusing. Pakistani army chief Ashfaq Parvez Kayani privately told US military leaders that the Pakistani military wanted "continuous Predator coverage" in areas where it was fighting militants.[37] In both Pakistan and Yemen, drones kill militants who are fighting the local government, such as the Pakistani Taliban and Al Qaeda in the Arabian Peninsula: in effect, America acts as its allies' counterinsurgency air force. Pakistan wants to benefit from the drone program while avoiding any responsibility, and thus its leaders publicly play a double game: Pakistan's prime minister in 2008 told the US ambassador, "We'll protest in the National Assembly and then ignore it."[38]

While governments may be two-faced, their people's anger is more genuine. Civilian casualties, even small numbers, are an affront, especially when these casualties come at the hands of a foreign government, and can inflame nationalism. Add to that the staggering unpopularity of the United States and you have a recipe for decreasing government legitimacy. Some critics also worry that these attacks serve as recruiting devices for insurgents. Yemen expert Gregory Johnsen points out that drone strikes in Yemen that kill locals often anger their entire tribe, increasing support for anti-US activities.

At times, however, this local anger can be overstated. Some studies have relied on interviews arranged by anti-drone organizations, biasing their sample. Indeed, many reports based on the surveys that show drones' unpopularity miss the fact that many Pakistanis know little about the program and do not realize that it is killing many of the militants who have wreaked havoc on Pakistan itself.[39] Perhaps most important, the Pakistani, Somali, and Yemeni governments are unpopular with their own citizens for many reasons, and drones are at best a small part of the overall equation.

As useful as drone strikes can be, they are inferior to arrests. As Cronin points out, "Drones do not capture hard drives, organizational charts, strategic plans or secret correspondence."[40] If there are jihadists active in Europe or an orderly Middle Eastern country like Jordan, the United States can, and does, ask the government to arrest them. In theory, the United States could marshal a US Navy SEAL team to capture every suspect in Pakistan and Yemen, but in practice, this would be incredibly risky, if not impossible. Sympathetic government officials might tip off the jihadists to the US raiders, and their very presence on the ground would be a much bigger affront to local sovereignty than drones. And, of course, some of the jihadists (or their supporters) would inevitably fight back, leading to far more US casualties and perhaps even the deaths of the suspects and innocent civilians.

The biggest argument for drones is that the alternatives are worse. No US president, Democrat *or* Republican, would allow Al Qaeda to enjoy a safe haven. There are other means of going after havens, but most of them are too dangerous or unrealistic. Using fixed-wing aircraft or cruise missiles is far more likely to kill innocents, as these use larger bombs and lack the ability to monitor a target in real time to ensure that civilians are not in the blast zone. In theory, Pakistan and Yemen could try to capture or kill suspected terrorists on their own soil themselves, with more legitimacy and little controversy; however, even if they had the will and capacity to do so (which they do not), both countries' militaries have a brutal track record and often indiscriminately bomb civilian areas or use scorched-earth tactics.

The most sensible alternative to drone strikes is really inaction. In some cases, individual terrorists abroad may actually pose little direct threat to the United States. In other cases, the risk of inflicting civilian casualties, further delegitimizing allies, or creating dangerous precedents may be too high. But at times there are real threats, and drones are the best way to take them out.

Do Drones and Other Controversial Tools Result in "Blowback"?

That counterterrorism instruments often fail is no surprise—terrorists are tough targets, after all. At times, however, these instruments can actually backfire. Such "blowback" can take many forms and is difficult to measure and identify.

In today's context, the term "blowback" is most commonly used to refer to the nasty consequences that result from the use of certain counterterrorism tools: angering masses of people and thus creating more sympathy for the terrorists and, presumably, increasing their fundraising and recruitment capabilities and making it easier for them to operate. The US invasion of Iraq, for example, led to a surge in anger among Muslims around the world and was cited as a reason for conducting terrorist attacks. Attempted Times Square bomber Faisal Shahzad, radical American-Yemeni cleric Anwar al-Awlaki, and the Tsarnaev brothers, who carried out the Boston Marathon bombing, all cited the US war in Iraq as one of the motivations for their actions against the United States.

US drone strikes, especially those reported in Pakistan, are criticized for outraging local populations and creating more sympathy for the terrorists. Retired US Marine Corps General James E. Cartwright, former vice chairman of the Joint Chiefs of Staff and a former adviser to President Obama, has argued, "We're seeing that blowback. . . . If you're trying to kill your way to a solution, no matter how precise you are, you're going to upset people even if they're not targeted."[41] Following a particularly high-profile US drone strike targeting Pakistani Taliban leader Hakimullah Mehsud, one newspaper reported that "[f]ormer cricket star Imran Khan, chairman of the Pakistan Tehreek-e-Insaf party, has built a massive following in denouncing the ongoing U.S. drone campaign in his native country."[42] Such US actions that outrage the population allow the terrorists to portray themselves as Robin Hoods and make the people more willing to overlook their brutality, extreme ideology, and repeated attacks on fellow Muslims.

More subtly, attacking Al Qaeda might lead to an increase in attacks on the United States. Al Qaeda has many enemies, and if the United States hits it hard, it might decide to shift its resources away from those other enemies and toward the United States. As the Al Qaeda core is already strongly anti-US, this argument has little resonance when it comes to Zawahiri and his closest followers, but it does apply to Al Qaeda's affiliates and to groups that have similar ideologies but no operational relationship with Al Qaeda, like Ansar al-Sharia in Libya. On the one hand, counterterrorism officials do not want to stand idly by as these groups grow stronger and then suddenly find themselves confronted with a major threat. On the other hand, although these groups share Al Qaeda's hatred of the United States, their energies are focused locally and regionally. Even Al Qaeda in the Arabian Peninsula (AQAP), the only Al Qaeda affiliate so far to have directly targeted the US homeland, devotes the overwhelming amount of its resources to carrying out attacks in Yemen. This debate is particularly germane to the issue of US attacks on the Islamic State: US officials fear that this group might eventually focus on attacking the US homeland, but they also worry that US attacks on the group make this focus more likely.

Human rights activists and legal scholars contend that torture, extrajudicial killings, and indefinite detention subvert the US image as a champion of the rule of law. In December 2014, the Senate Select Committee on Intelligence released a massive report detailing numerous abuses that were part of the CIA's rendition, detention, and intelligence programs, offering harrowing details on the use of torture and the secret detention of suspects later deemed not to be master terrorists. With less legitimacy, the United States could lose the international cooperation that is so vital for disrupting Al Qaeda. However, this is unlikely: Al Qaeda opposes many regimes, and even those not on its enemies list usually oppose terrorism. A bigger challenge is that a decline in legitimacy makes it harder for allies to openly cooperate with the United States. High-profile actions like the Abu Ghraib torture scandal and reports of a US drone strike mistakenly targeting a wedding party in Yemen[43] make cooperation more politically costly for US allies.

The damage to the United States may be greater outside the counterterrorism realm. Former President Jimmy Carter wrote in a 2012 op-ed in the *New York Times* that because of the drone campaign, "our country can no longer speak with moral authority" on human rights issues.[44] To the extent that US leverage on human rights issues comes from perceptions that the United States adheres to international standards of behavior in its foreign policy, many counterterrorism programs undermine US ability to pressure other states to curb human rights abuses.

It is easy to argue by anecdote one way or another, but assessments of broader trends usually suffer from a lack of data. Terrorism scholars lack a general theory of recruitment—and if we do not really know why people become terrorists in general (remember, there is no single profile), it is hard to judge how a controversial counterterrorism instrument affects radicalization and recruitment.

We can and do look at the individual statements of terrorists for why they join. Many cite a familiar litany of grievances, such as US support for Israel or the US military presence in the Muslim world. The problem is that the list is long, and it is hard to tell if one grievance would simply be replaced by another in the mind of an angry, idealistic, and excitable young volunteer. Instead of hating America or the West for ten reasons, they now hate the West for nine. This problem is particularly acute because conspiracy theories run amok in the Muslim world. In no Muslim country do more than 30% of the people think that Arabs carried out the 9/11 attacks.[45] Many Muslims believe 9/11 was an inside job, either orchestrated by Jews to cement US support for Israel against Muslims or by the Bush administration to justify the Iraq war (and another personal favorite from former Iranian President Mahmoud Ahmadinejad: that the West is destroying Iran's rain clouds).[46] With such a conspiratorial mindset, even benign US moves are seen as suspect. The US-led intervention in Kosovo, which liberated many Muslims from the brutal Serb regime in Belgrade, was perceived by many to be a deliberate US plan to allow the Serbs to kill Muslims and, only when the butchery was done, to pretend to act.

Nor are all terrorists created equal. Part of the logic of the drone program is that if leaders are removed or are forced to stay on the run, the followers will be unable to function. So even if the death of a leader inspires five more people to join the group in outrage, the group may remain weaker, as the skilled individual is not easily replaced.

Although blowback is difficult to determine and measure, that does not mean it does not exist—and some things like torture are inherently wrong, even if blowback is minimal. The United States and its allies should be on the lookout for signs of blowback, watching the discourse among jihadists from their testimonials, as well as social media sites like Twitter, to see which actions are especially hated. Particularly important is judging how counterterrorism efforts will affect the actions of different terrorist groups. Killing one Al Shabaab leader by drone, for example, would be counterproductive if it were to convince the group as a whole to shift its focus and begin aggressively targeting the United States. Such prudence is at the heart of thinking strategically about counterterrorism: the United States needs to both ensure that the terrorist narrative is discredited and defeat the individual terrorists.

How Do We Collect Intelligence on Al Qaeda?

Much of the day-to-day work of counterterrorism is done through the coordinated action of intelligence and police services. Counterterrorism intelligence has grown by leaps and bounds within the US government since 9/11—in 2010, the US government put the total cost of funding the US intelligence community that year alone at just over $80 billion.[47] When a terrorist cell is identified, security services monitor it and arrest the individuals. The US role is often to provide information and help coordinate across national borders.

As with standard intelligence collection, a variety of methods—so-called "INTs"—are used to gather intelligence on terrorism. This might range from human spies (HUMINT), to intercepting phone calls, e-mail, and other signals (SIGINT), to imagery on terrorist activities (IMINT). Spies are millennia old (spying is often referred to as the "second-oldest profession"),[48] while SIGINT and IMINT were regularly used in the Cold War against non-terrorist targets.

Penetrating Al Qaeda with spies is difficult. The core organization tries to vet potential members carefully, and Western intelligence services have had little luck getting their operatives close to Al Qaeda. However, one of the most important sources of information on terrorism comes from the interrogation of terrorists and their supporters, and US intelligence has reportedly even turned some Guantanamo Bay prisoners into double agents.[49] This issue has (understandably) become conflated with the question of torture in the wake of various accounts that the CIA waterboarded and otherwise abused suspected Al Qaeda members. Yet interrogation without torture has yielded tremendous information on terrorists, and many would say that gentler means were more effective than torture in any event.

Signals intelligence (SIGINT) is particularly important for counterterrorism. Some argue that SIGINT was far more important to counterterrorism than HUMINT in the pre-9/11 era: SIGINT helped US intelligence determine Bin Laden's responsibility for a bombing that killed five US contractors in Saudi Arabia and the 1998 bombings of two US embassies in Africa that killed 224 people. Beyond determining responsibility for actions, SIGINT can help uncover volumes of data on financial support networks and the identities of supporters. SIGINT is also used in locating individuals, enabling them to be arrested. Khalid Sheikh Mohammad, the 9/11 mastermind, and key jihadist facilitator Abu Zubaydah both were located in part due to SIGINT intercepts. Perhaps most important, SIGINT can provide information on a planned attack, allowing for it to be disrupted. In 1998, information from SIGINT helped foil Al Qaeda attacks on a US airbase in Saudi Arabia, among other targets.[50] SIGINT often provides reach when HUMINT cannot: given that the Al Qaeda core hides out in remote parts of Pakistan, this reach is vital.

In the post-9/11 era, SIGINT has become even more important. As the use of drones to kill Al Qaeda members has grown in importance, so too has the role of SIGINT. While drones can offer a picture of local activities, supplementing this with SIGINT is vital. SIGINT can help locate the individuals in the first place and confirm that the individuals in the drone's sights are the right ones.[51] Even more important, the total volume of communication has increased with the spread of information technology: intelligence collected on the Internet and associated features and applications, ranging from e-mail to the latest form of social media, are all forms of SIGINT. Although these technologies offer terrorists many new means to communicate, fundraise, and disseminate attack plans, they also offer counterterrorism officials innumerable chances to detect and disrupt the terrorists. Edward Snowden, a contractor with the National Security Agency (NSA), revealed considerable information about American SIGINT capabilities, but Al Qaeda and other terrorists do not appear to have increased their security in response.[52]

SIGINT, of course, can be maddeningly incomplete or imprecise. Before 9/11, US intelligence picked up a surge in "chatter," and in late 2000, one Al Qaeda operative told another of a planned "Hiroshima" against the United States.[53] In hindsight, the intelligence community was criticized for ignoring these harbingers. However, the reality is that such activity merely told officials what they already knew—that Bin Laden's organization was actively planning strikes—but did not tell them where, when, or how the attack would be carried out.

The growth in intelligence collection since 9/11 has raised concerns about both wasteful spending and civil liberties violations. The post-9/11 FBI has tried to prevent terrorist attacks rather than just investigating them after the bombs have gone off, but that has led to a far more aggressive effort to recruit spies in the American Muslim community. Civil libertarians are concerned about the heavy use of FBI informants, some of whom egged on potential perpetrators by proposing a plot, providing (fake) explosives, and encouraging the target to take an oath to Al Qaeda, leading to criticisms that they created a plot where none existed (FBI officials counter that the suspects are given multiple chances to back out).[54]

Civil libertarians also decry the singling out of Muslim communities and mosques for surveillance, as well as the overall surveillance of Americans. For example, the New York Police Department, working with the CIA, built databases on where Muslims lived, worked, and worshipped; infiltrated student groups; monitored sermons; and spied on mosques—an aggressive approach that failed to generate a lead, much less a terrorism conviction.[55] The trove of NSA documents leaked by Edward Snowden revealed the vast amount of information the US government has been collecting since 9/11 on individuals both at home and abroad in the name of counterterrorism. The collection of "metadata"—information about who called whom and when but not the content of a conversation—without a warrant has received particular criticism.

Finally, some of the money dumped into counterterrorism is simply wasted. A bipartisan Senate report on Department of Homeland Security "fusion centers," over 70 of which were created since 2003, found that the intelligence gathered was "oftentimes shoddy, rarely timely, sometimes endangering citizens' civil liberties and Privacy Act protections. . . and more often than not unrelated to terrorism."[56]

How Do Tools Change When Fighting Affiliated Movements?

The standard counterterrorism toolkit changes, or should change, when fighting Al Qaeda affiliates. Affiliates differ from the Al Qaeda core in several important ways from a counterterrorism perspective. Affiliates are usually insurgents who have hundreds or even thousands of men under arms, in contrast to the far smaller Al Qaeda core. Nor do affiliates prioritize attacks on the United States and Europe, confining their anti-Western activities to their local or regional theater.

Because of the size of affiliated movements, using drones or other "kinetic" means to target affiliated organizations is less effective. They simply have too many members and potential leaders: the drone campaign would have to be far more extensive to have an effect similar to the results of drone attacks on the Al Qaeda core. The United States has targeted leaders of Al Qaeda in the Arabian Peninsula (AQAP) and Al Shabaab in Somalia, but these efforts have been more limited and far less effective than the effort against the core in Pakistan. Indeed, the danger of a more kinetic approach is that it could result in the worst of all worlds: barely reducing the group's capabilities while making the group prioritize attacking the United States.[57]

Because the affiliates' focus is more local and regional, the threat differs as well. From an American point of view, the threat that affiliates pose is more to US interests in the Middle East, where affiliate violence threatens regional stability. The US response should involve helping local governments govern and fight more effectively—in that order. The United States has extensive programs to train and equip military forces, and Washington can also provide assistance with intelligence, building police forces, and other basics of counterterrorism and counterinsurgency.

Although these measures seem simple on paper, in practice they are exceptionally difficult. The presence or absence of an Al Qaeda-linked insurgency is not random, and fixing it involves more than flooding an ally with money and other forms of support. The regimes in these countries, even if democratically elected, are usually considered to be illegitimate by at least one segment of the population. Some social groups get to feast at the government trough, enjoying educational opportunities, lucrative government contracts, and other rewards, while other groups are excluded. Regimes use corruption to reward supporters and at the same time ensure their loyalty by compromising them. Part of the reason that jihadists returned to power in Sunni-populated parts of Iraq in the summer of 2014 is because the Maliki government systematically excluded and persecuted the country's Sunni population.

These political and social problems undermine military effectiveness. The biggest threat to many leaders is not the insurgents, but rather a coup from within their own ranks. In Egypt, Mali, Pakistan, Yemen, and other countries dealing with jihadists, military officers have seized power from civilian governments at various times. To guard against this, civilian leaders make sure the military is run by loyalists: in Saudi Arabia, for example, many senior military officers are members of the royal family, while others have close ties by marriage and other relationships. Rivalry, not cooperation, among military leaders is encouraged, making it unlikely that military units can coordinate their operations. This may be a terrific strategy for preventing a military coup, but it is not exactly the best way to create a military capable of defeating an insurgency.

Attempts by external actors like the United States to reform the system flounder on such problems. By encouraging democracy, we threaten the power of a leader and his supporters. By encouraging minority rights, we threaten the privileges and biases of the dominant community. By calling for an end to corruption and for transparency in government, we threaten the leader's ability to control his power base. And by pushing military reform, we risk making the military the only functioning institution in a weak country, making a coup more likely. However, if the ally fails to reform, the insurgency is likely to continue and the United States is tarred with the ally's brush, seen—correctly, if unfairly—as supporting a dictator. So we should accept that we are often choosing between fighting bad guys and helping a bad government.

How Do We Win the War of Ideas?

The devastation wrought by the 9/11 attacks shocked most Americans, but as the rubble was cleared, what continued to astound many was the deep unpopularity of the United States among Muslims around the world, particularly in the Middle East. The United States tried to improve its image in several ways, often under labels such as "public diplomacy" and "winning the war of ideas." One effort, the "Shared Values Initiative," involved commercials featuring American Muslims freely worshipping, showing their prosperity, and attesting to their happiness about living in the United States. Others involved American diplomats trying to defend American policies and counterterrorism efforts to publics around the world. With the rise of social media, the United States began to develop new ways of engaging the wider world: for example, the US State Department created the "Think Again Turn Away" campaign to discourage would-be foreign fighters from going to Syria or Iraq.

These efforts largely failed. Even as government propaganda presented images of a happy American Muslim community, the more complex reality was also widely reported. Not surprisingly, news images of the second Palestinian *intifada* and the war in Iraq drowned out the occasional commercial. After 9/11, there was a surge in anti-Muslim violence and vitriol in the United States. Before 9/11 there were 28 reported anti-Islamic incidents; this spiked to almost 500 in 2001 and then declined to the mid-100s in the years that followed, a lower figure than in 2001 but far higher than in the pre-9/11 era. (Most hate crimes are not reported, so the real numbers are probably far higher.)[58]

None of these attacks turned the American Muslim community against their government—indeed, poll after poll suggests little radicalization among American Muslims—but the associated images and rhetoric did not square with the rosy picture being presented by government efforts. Moreover, by design the American system has multiple voices. So even as President George W. Bush stressed how welcome American Muslims are, many other American politicians and leading voices portrayed American Muslims as a fifth column who want to impose Islamic law in the United States and support Bin Laden. In 2010, Muslims planned to build a community center and mosque two blocks from the World Trade Center complex, which led to tremendous vitriol. Former Speaker of the House Newt Gingrich compared the mosque organizers to the Nazis.[59] This regular hostility and cacophony of voices made it hard for any single public relations line to sink in.

The deeper problem, however, is that much of the unhappiness with the United States is linked to US policies in the Muslim world. Bin Laden's charge that the United States backs Israel and supports oppressive Arab regimes is true. When the United States invaded Iraq in 2003—a move that bolstered anti-American sentiment to new heights in the Muslim world—it also bolstered Bin Laden's claim that the United States was an oppressive imperialist power bent on subjugating the Muslim world and robbing its resources. This unpopularity does not mean that US policy is wrong: most Americans are proud of their country's support for Israel, and administration after administration has accepted the reality that they must do business with repressive regimes like the Al Saud. But unpopularity at a popular level is a byproduct of these policies.

A more successful approach would focus on Al Qaeda, its ideology, and its many mistakes. Al Qaeda strongly opposes democracy, which most Arabs and Muslims favor.[60] Al Qaeda and its affiliates also have killed many Muslims—far, far more than the number of Christian and Jewish Westerners they've killed. Moreover, the tendency of the broader movement as a whole, including new groups like the Islamic State, to declare other Muslims unbelievers is deeply unpopular. These actions helped generate the backlash in Islamist circles against the group and led to a decline in support for Al Qaeda and other jihadists. In other words, make the debate about how bad the jihadists are, not how wonderful America is.

To help this process along, the United States should work with allies in the Muslim world to elevate Islamist critics of Al Qaeda. These individuals and groups, both in the mainstream and among the more radical elements, carry far more credibility than would any official US statement. Playing up their critiques in the media puts Al Qaeda and the Islamic State on the defensive: the more the debate is about them rather than us, the better we do. Left to themselves, the jihadists discredit themselves.

Al Qaeda and other jihadist groups also draw strength from the difficult and oppressive conditions common in many Muslim countries. Whether it is corruption and venal politics in Pakistan or military dictatorship in places like Algeria and Egypt, jihadists are able to channel anger at the illegitimacy (and often incompetence and stagnation) of the regimes they oppose. The United States has a poor track record of fostering political change in the Middle East, and the collapse of the Arab Spring makes this hope seem even more elusive. Nevertheless, the United States should encourage political reform when possible and remember that while dictators can be convenient allies in the short term, long-term counterterrorism depends on effective and legitimate governance.

Much of the Islamic State's appeal rests on its successes in Syria and Iraq. By scoring victories against the Iraqi government and supposed apostates like the Shi'a and 'Alawi, the Islamic State has emerged as a champion of the Sunni Muslim community. Many supporters admire its prowess more than its teachings. Beating it back and inflicting losses on the battlefield would thus be a propaganda victory as well as a military one. The group has also tied its prestige to being an Islamic state: if it loses its control over territory, this claim would ring hollow.

What is the Role of Allied Governments Threatened by Terrorists?

Since 9/11, the entire world has been the battlefield against Al Qaeda. The struggle is not confined to the Arab heartland from whence most Al Qaeda leaders emerged. Al Qaeda or its allies have attacked in Indonesia and the Philippines, in Western Europe, and increasingly in Africa, as well as the Middle East and the United States. Jihadists of around 70 different nationalities have been captured in approximately 100 countries.[61]

Foreign partnerships are vital for counterterrorism and, not surprisingly, the State Department, Department of Defense, CIA, and Justice Department all have programs designed to improve the capacity of foreign partners in counterterrorism.[62] In 2005, a senior CIA official testified that virtually every capture or killing of a suspected terrorist outside Iraq was at least in part the result of assistance from foreign intelligence services—a staggering claim.[63] Foreign governments usually police their own territory. Often the local jihadist group is active primarily against the ally and only secondarily against the United States—this is particularly the case for the Islamic State. Allies can take advantage of the law in their efforts to disrupt terrorism and recruit sources on their own soil. Being a member of a terrorist group is almost uniformly illegal, and states can simply arrest and question those they believe are linked to terrorism. In addition, they can identify and go after, or at least intimidate, major financiers of terrorism. These seemingly basic functions are something the United States cannot readily do outside its own borders.

Size is another local advantage. Local governments can draw on police and domestic intelligence services to gather information—a huge number of personnel compared to the small number of CIA and other US intelligence officials that might focus on a single country. Allied intelligence services also have a huge advantage given their knowledge of local languages. US intelligence is regularly criticized for having few speakers of Arabic, Punjabi, or other languages that many Al Qaeda members speak.[64]

Liaison services may also have better access to a terrorist hotbed due to geography or historic ties. Sanctuaries are vital for Al Qaeda and other terrorist movements, and it is often difficult for the United States to gain access to them—indeed, if America could, they might not be sanctuaries. It is not surprising that Pakistani intelligence knows Afghanistan, its backyard, quite well. According to press reporting, the United States has worked with Ethiopia's intelligence service against Al Qaeda in Africa.[65] The *Wall Street Journal* reports that the United States has "relied on a Saudi intelligence network that stretches deep within Yemen's tribal areas."[66] Indeed, the United States at times even cooperates with quasi-states given the importance of liaison—in Somalia, for example, US intelligence has collaborated with Puntland and Somaliland, even though these are not recognized states.[67]

Given these advantages, it is not surprising that allies have often had more success in infiltrating Al Qaeda and associated movements, often using their own nationals as assets. Egypt, Jordan, Morocco, Syria, and Pakistan all have reportedly penetrated Al Qaeda with human assets.[68] Local services have two key advantages over the United States in this undertaking. First, they have superior cultural knowledge—they are more likely to know what makes the individual tick and, just as important, how to turn him from being a terrorist into being a source. Second, they are able to use the power of the state to coerce the individual to reveal information. This can range from threats of imprisonment to pressure on families—withholding or granting a business permit or the right to attend a university—that can lead an individual to reveal information.

When the local country is on board, dramatic and mass-scale counterterrorism actions can be taken. After terrorism surged in Saudi Arabia in 2003, the Saudi government arrested almost 10,000 suspects. Going after terrorist recruiting and fundraising is particularly difficult to do without host nation support given the vast nature of logistical activities. Saudi efforts to go after terrorist fundraising, passport production, and recruitment inside the Kingdom played an important role in reducing Al Qaeda's ability to travel abroad.[69]

US intelligence often acts as a conductor of global liaison services. For example, the arrest of the Al Qaeda operative and key Jemaah Islamiyya leader known as Hambali involved US coordination of information and action from Indonesia, Malaysia, the Philippines, Singapore, and Thailand.[70] US intelligence has established joint operation centers in over two dozen countries to track and capture terrorists in cooperation with foreign governments, and the United States trains foreign partners to improve their collection and analysis capabilities.[71]

However, liaison services, particularly in the developing world, are often involved in corruption and repression. The same security services that disrupt terrorists are the ones that spy on peaceful opposition and put down demonstrations. For example, the *Washington Post* reports that the CIA worked closely with Uzbekistan despite its poor record on human rights.[72] In 2005, the Bush administration reportedly hosted the head of Sudanese intelligence, despite the brutality of Sudan's intelligence services in Darfur, because of his assistance with efforts against Al Qaeda.[73] US cooperation with these services, and US funding of their activities, thus indirectly backs the most repressive parts of these repressive regimes.

Counterterrorism can also conflict with the political sensitivities of a friendly regime. In the 1990s, the Saudi regime was reluctant to provide detailed counterterrorism information to the United States. Many US officials believed that this was because the information would implicate important members of Saudi society, perhaps including royal family members, in supporting the jihadist cause.

Allies, in turn, have many complaints about the United States. Frequent leaks of sensitive information are often cited as a reason the United States cannot be trusted. Given the unpopularity of the United States in places like Yemen and Pakistan, leaks that these governments are supporting the drone program and other US counterterrorism efforts are embarrassing for the government. Classification of sensitive material inevitably plays a role in limiting information sharing. SIGINT in particular is often highly classified, making it harder to pass to foreign governments (not to mention lower-tier regional and local officials), even though they are often key actors on the ground.

Foreign governments are so important that the biggest US counterterrorism problems can be categorized based on how well this relationship is working. In hostile countries like Iran, there is no liaison. Almost as bad are countries like Pakistan and Yemen, where the government often tolerates terrorists for its own purposes, or Somalia, where there is no functioning government. Nevertheless, intelligence cooperation generally functions quite well, and in most of the countries where Al Qaeda is active, the United States has a friend willing and able to help.

How Does Al Qaeda Adapt?

Al Qaeda has proven remarkably resilient. As scholars Bruce Hoffman and Fernando Reinares note, "the core al-Qaeda organization has astonishingly withstood arguably the greatest international onslaught directed against a terrorist organization in history."[74] Part of what has made Al Qaeda so formidable is that it is tenacious and creative in its response to US-led pressure.

Al Qaeda's adaptation is most visible in its operations. As anyone who has been to an airport since 9/11 knows, airport security is extensive and intrusive. Yet Al Qaeda still targets civil aviation, and in so doing it has devised ways to evade Western security measures. In December 2001, Richard Reid, the infamous "shoe bomber," succeeded in smuggling explosives onto a flight from Paris to Miami: he failed to detonate the bomb because alert passengers and crew members subdued him. In 2009, on a flight from Amsterdam to Detroit, Umar Farouk Abdulmutallab, supported by AQAP, smuggled explosives onto the flight in his underwear: he too failed to detonate the explosives, again hindered by alert passengers. In 2006, Al Qaeda operatives devised a way to disguise explosives by smuggling them in water bottles to get them past security—their goal was to blow up perhaps 10 flights from the United Kingdom to the United States and Canada. British and US intelligence foiled the plot (and now we can't take liquids past security checkpoints at airports), but again Al Qaeda showed its creativity. It is a testament to Al Qaeda's skill that despite enormous attention to aviation security, it repeatedly came up with new ways to destroy airplanes, and had it had a bit more luck it would have succeeded.

Because the core organization was under heavy pressure, Bin Laden and Zawahiri devoted much of their post-9/11 efforts to supporting other groups in both formal and informal arrangements—and trying to make these groups more aligned with their own goals. This required toleration. Al Qaeda worked with individuals like Abu Musab al-Zarqawi, the founder of Al Qaeda in Iraq, even though he embraced an anti-Shi'a and anti-Iran agenda that did not mesh with Al Qaeda's priorities. Within the core organization, Al Qaeda relaxed its emphasis on hierarchy: as Bin Laden and Zawahiri were hunted, lieutenants and allies were given more freedom of operation, enabling them to attack with less central direction.

Al Qaeda is also constantly trotting out new critiques of the West and other enemies while also emphasizing tried-and-true themes like America's malign intentions in the Muslim world and the apostasy of regional governments. After 9/11, Bin Laden and Zawahiri even blasted the United States for having "destroyed nature" and for not signing the Kyoto Protocol (an international agreement aimed at reducing greenhouse gas emissions), claimed credit for the "astronomical" US deficit, and called for Muslims to boycott Denmark and other countries for printing cartoons that mocked the Prophet Muhammad.[75] Much of this rhetoric failed to inspire or did not stick, but it shows Al Qaeda's willingness to recast its propaganda as necessary.

Yet to say that Al Qaeda adapts to US pressure is both true and misleading: many of its adaptations are limited, costly, and make the organization less dangerous. The organization can and does replace lost leaders, but though its bench is deep for a terrorist group, it is not infinite. Thus, lesser leaders come to the fore, making the overall organization weaker. Al Qaeda can survive without an Afghanistan-like base, but even though it has some sanctuary in Pakistan it is less able to plan, train, control the overall movement, and organize the mini-army it built before 9/11. It expands its ideological critique to include a host of other issues, but in so doing the movement risks losing its coherence—particularly given its more diffuse leadership. So Al Qaeda can and does adapt and survive in the face of US pressure, but it is often a lesser threat as a result.

How Do You Counter Radicalization?

In the years after 9/11, a range of programs sprang up with the goal of "countering violent extremism" (known, in true government style, as CVE): trying to discourage radicalization and recruitment. According to the State Department's counterterrorism coordinator at the time, Daniel Benjamin, the aim of CVE is to "make environments non-permissive for terrorists seeking to exploit them."[76] CVE efforts may try to stop people from hearing or seeing terrorist group propaganda (increasingly difficult in this information age), discredit the terrorists and their message, promote positive feelings about the United States or other potential victim countries, and address problems like discrimination that foster anger.[77] Successful CVE can turn potential recruits away from terrorism, thus preventing the problem in the first place, while at the same time making communities hostile to terrorism and allowing security forces to quickly identify and disrupt any threat.

CVE programs vary widely. Many try to bring in the local community, believing (correctly) that religious leaders, workers at community centers, and other local leaders have more ties to and credibility with the community and can better spread a message of nonviolence than would out-of-town FBI officers or aid workers. Similarly, local police are often more plugged in to the community and can identify at-risk recruits for either monitoring or a tough talking to, depending on their judgment. Other programs emphasize combating jihadism online, preventing radicalization in prisons, and working with particular groups (youth, women, and so on). The London-based Radical Middle Way holds public events with clerics from Egypt's prestigious Al-Azhar seminary to undermine support for activities like suicide bombing. Online activists in the Middle East are challenging conspiracy theories there. Some programs are designed to take existing extremists and deprogram them, moving them away from violence.

CVE efforts are difficult because there is no consistent path to radicalization. Some recruits are motivated by the killing of Muslims in wars, while others recoil at discrimination. Some are socially alienated, while others simply seek the thrill of blowing stuff up and killing people. As William McCants and Clint Watts point out, "Anyone can potentially sympathize with a terrorist organization if the conditions are right."[78]

No matter how good the argument, it will not convince if the messenger is not credible.[79] However, some of the most credible messengers are also the most troubling. Britain has used former jihadists to explain how radical groups duped them and has worked with the Muslim Brotherhood to debate Al Qaeda's local champions.[80] Some of these voices, however, are only moderate by comparison with Al Qaeda: they may also be anti-Semitic and anti-Israel, oppose Western policies in the Middle East, oppose women's rights, and so on. So giving them legitimacy and even money to spread an anti-Al Qaeda message can harm other goals, to say nothing of the political difficulty of such efforts.

Countering an ideology is also difficult in a free country. In America, and in most Western countries, free speech is a core value. This offers considerable scope for propagandists of all stripes—neo-Nazi as well as jihadist—to disseminate hateful ideas. The Internet and social media make it even easier. Community policing may do little if radicals primarily interact online and are in small groups that operate apart from their neighbors. In addition, terrorism is a small-group phenomenon, so even if Al Qaeda's popularity falls (as it has since 9/11) and America's grows, recruiting may still increase as the general trend may not affect the small group of individuals who are recruited.

Finally, increasing scrutiny of a particular community can create the very problem you want to avoid. Seemingly coercive measures can create "suspect communities" where radicalization is more likely and where community members are less likely to work with the police and government in general.[81] If young Muslims are consistently told they are different and dangerous, they may become different and dangerous. McCants and Watts point out that the British "Prevent" program, a widely-cited CVE effort, initially angered many British Muslims, making normal citizens feel like they were seen as a security threat, and the British government had to revise the program.

What Threat Does Al Qaeda Pose Today to the United States and Europe?

Because the Al Qaeda core has proven resilient, it is always difficult to count it out. Again and again, officials have written its obituary, but over 25 years after its creation it endures.

Yet enduring is not the same as prospering. The Al Qaeda core has conducted relatively few attacks post-9/11 given its overall notoriety and the counterterrorism focus on it. As of February 2014, the core had conducted fewer than 80 attacks in its history: an average of roughly three per year. In 2012 and 2013, the Al Qaeda core did not conduct any terrorist attacks. The core is hurting.

Al Qaeda's ability to strike the US homeland has been greatly diminished since 9/11. Constant pressure on the leadership, the disruption of cells around the world, and more aggressive efforts to deter and disrupt terrorism at home all make it harder to stage a repeat of 9/11. In the years immediately before and after 9/11, the Al Qaeda core assumed direct control over plots against the United States. Repeated failures after 9/11 changed the picture. Now the most immediate threat is from independent, and far less capable, homegrown radicals. Yet the core's interest in attacking the United States remains strong. In 2009, Najibullah Zazi was arrested for trying to attack the New York subway; Zazi had trained at an Al Qaeda camp in Pakistan, and his effort was overseen by several senior Al Qaeda leaders. In 2010, Faisal Shahzad came close to detonating a car bomb in Times Square in New York. Shahzad too had trained in Pakistan, and he was recruited by Al Qaeda's ally, the

Pakistani Taliban.[82] Al Qaeda and its Yemeni affiliate also repeatedly targeted US aviation, smuggling bombs aboard airplanes and almost destroying the crafts. Yet even if several of these near-misses had succeeded, the devastation would have been far less than what was anticipated after 9/11, when US officials feared that Al Qaeda would wage a campaign of terrorism spectaculars.

It is worth doing a thought experiment about whether another 9/11 could be plotted and successfully executed today. First, there is no convenient and safe place like the Taliban's Afghanistan where different recruits could go for training: recruits coming from Germany, like Mohamed Atta did, would be more likely to be identified and arrested before even departing. Pakistan fulfills this role on a lesser scale, but even if recruits traveled there, training would be harder as any large group of foreigners would face a greater risk of detection and targeting in Pakistan itself. Assuming that the recruits survived, follow-on meetings in places like Malaysia and Spain and getting money from donors in the Gulf would be far harder, as security services in all these countries are now on alert. Entering the United States and operating undetected for months, as the 9/11 hijackers did, would also be difficult, particularly if they needed to maintain contact with the core organization and had to communicate by phone or Internet. No single component of the 9/11 plot would be impossible to duplicate, but each one is far harder—and taken together, the chances of executing a similar plot today would be much lower.

Although dozens of Americans have been prosecuted for terrorism-related offenses, few were terrorist masterminds. Some had a history of mental illness, and few made it past the planning stage. Many made stupid mistakes, ranging from taking a jihadist video to a shop to be duplicated to using Facebook to seek comrades for jihad.[83] Indeed, until the Boston Marathon bombing in 2012, terrorists did not even prove able to detonate a primitive bomb—a sharp contrast to the 1970s, when there were dozens of bombings every year.[84] The most dangerous and those who came closest to success, such as the "shoe bomber" and the "underwear bomber," had foreign help.

The danger is greater to Europe. In contrast to the low levels of radicalization among American Muslims, European Muslim communities are less integrated and resentment is higher. Europe is also closer to where Al Qaeda is based and cheaper to enter. Al Qaeda has proven adept at working with affiliate groups and Pakistani allies to enlist local operatives. The Pakistan nexus is particularly acute in Britain, where over one million ethnic Pakistanis live: three of the four July 7, 2005, bombers of London's public transportation system were of Pakistani origin, and the Al Qaeda core in Pakistan helped orchestrate the attack. As Hoffman and Reinares contend, "The fusion of local, homegrown radicals with the directing hand of an al-Qaeda affiliate connecting to the core in Pakistan [has] become an enduring feature of post-September 11 international terrorism."[85]

Lower-tech attacks are still possible and can be quite deadly. As the seemingly unending spate of shootings at US schools suggests, a single person with a gun can wreak horrors. A member of Al Qaeda sent to the United States to perpetrate such an attack, or simply a twisted chucklehead who found inspiration in a sermon by Zawahiri or a new leader like Baghdadi, can still kill people. Some terrorism along the lines of the Boston Marathon bombing is perhaps inevitable in the years to come. But we need to distinguish between the limited damage such attacks can do and the massive effects of 9/11-type attacks or a sustained terrorism campaign that could undermine faith in government.

A key question, however, goes beyond the US homeland and even beyond the lives of Americans: how does Al Qaeda-linked terrorism affect US interests overseas? Here the record is more disturbing. Al Qaeda did not cause the civil wars in Iraq, Libya, Syria, and Yemen, but its affiliated or like-minded fighters made them bloodier and made negotiations far harder: tens if not hundreds of thousands more Muslims have died as a result. Al Qaeda's ideology also influences terrorists in Egypt, Gaza, Saudi Arabia, Tunisia, and other more stable areas, distorting politics in these countries as well as contributing to the deaths of Muslims there. Many of these organizations are not "Al Qaeda" in any traditional sense of the term: the killers are not under Zawahiri's command, funded by the core organization, or otherwise linked. Nevertheless, part of Bin Laden's and now Zawahiri's goal is to spawn like-minded groups to carry out their agenda in the Muslim world and beyond. To the extent that US interests include promoting good governance and stability in a critical part of the world, the operations of Al Qaeda and especially its affiliate organizations pose a danger. And to the extent that the wanton killing of innocents is an affront to basic human decency, Al Qaeda and those it inspires are a threat to us all, regardless of where we live.

Can We Defeat Al Qaeda, the Islamic State, and the Broader Jihadist Movement?

Defeating Al Qaeda depends on understanding what victory means. If we define victory as the death or arrest of every Al Qaeda member and a complete cessation of all attacks from the core, affiliates, and like-minded or inspired individuals and groups, then we are a long way off—and will remain so for the foreseeable future. Parts of Al Qaeda's ideology remain appealing, and an array of groups throughout the Muslim world champion parts of Zawahiri's agenda, with weak and illegitimate regional regimes often unable to repress them. And even if the core is hurt, new groups like the Islamic State are attracting many young Muslims, convincing them to join the jihad and often to act brutally. Individuals in Europe and the United States, though small in number, are also prone to radicalization and violence, often as Lone Wolves or as part of small cells that are difficult to identify and disrupt. So unrest and civil wars in the Muslim world, and occasional terrorist attacks at home, are likely to continue.

A "snapshot" of the state of jihad today done by British scholar Peter Neumann paints a disturbing picture. In November 2014—just one month—jihadists of various stripes carried out almost 700 attacks and killed over 5,000 people: more than the number of people killed on 9/11. Syria and Iraq suffered the most, but so too did Nigeria, Afghanistan, Yemen, Somalia, and Pakistan. Neumann finds that "the vast majority" of the jihadists' victims were their fellow Muslims. Most of the violence was done by groups that had little or no formal relationship with the Al Qaeda core. The Islamic State was the bloodiest, but the Nigerian group Boko Haram killed almost 1,000 people too. And the Taliban, which seemed defeated in 2002, killed almost 800 people as the United States prepared to withdraw the bulk of its forces from Afghanistan.[86]

Yet Al Qaeda is far from achieving its own goals—even farther than it was on 9/11, in fact. The core organization has been hit hard, with many of its leaders killed, arrested, or constantly on the run. The United States is not on its knees, and it remains active in the Middle

East. For most Americans and Westerners in general, the threat of terrorism does not shape their daily lives, as it seemed to in the immediate aftermath of 9/11. In the Middle East, Al Qaeda-linked organizations are carving out swaths of territory, but they control no governments. Many local affiliates also champion more local and regional agendas or espouse sectarianism, priorities that Al Qaeda sought to move jihadists away from when it was first created in 1988. Most Muslims reject the organization and others like it, believing—correctly—that it is responsible for the deaths of many innocent Muslims as well as Westerners and that its ideology, in the end, will lead to ruin. Indeed, the Islamic State, in its own sick way, has achieved far more than Al Qaeda ever did. But even though the Islamic State may call itself a state and try to act like a legitimate government, few accept it as such, and it is unlikely that we will ever see the Islamic State get a seat at the UN General Assembly or send athletes to compete for a gold medal at the Olympics.

The United States cannot end attacks by appeasing Al Qaeda or the Islamic State. Zawahiri's organization is simply too ambitious: the United States would have to cease its political influence in the Middle East, ending support for allies there, severing ties to Israel, and so on—none of which would be politically acceptable at home or sensible as a policy goal. Small shifts in policy on all these issues may occur, but none would satisfy Zawahiri. Because he and his followers see the United States as evil as well as mistaken in its policies, they will always assume the worst about any US move. At best, the United States may find itself lower on the priority list as other countries commit actions that Al Qaeda deems more worthy of attention. This might involve attacks on local Muslims, controversial free speech decisions like publishing cartoons mocking the Prophet Muhammad, or other provocations. But because of America's cultural and political prominence, it is likely that the United States will remain at or near the center of Al Qaeda's sights. The Islamic State is less interested in America for now, but it seeks control over large swaths of territory, and should it succeed, it would want even more—again, not in America's interest.

A broader hope is that the ideology espoused by the likes of Al Qaeda and the Islamic State becomes passé or even laughable. At the turn of the last century, anarchism inspired a spate of terrorist attacks that killed several European prime ministers and US

President William McKinley. The ideology inspired millions but today is confined to a few fringe actors who wield no real influence and goofy teenagers who think buying a shirt with an anarchy symbol on it at the mall makes them "edgy." Even more potently, communists took power in the Soviet Union, China, and elsewhere. They killed their own citizens by the millions and engaged in both civil and regional wars, as well as engaging in a standoff with the United States that risked the use of nuclear weapons. Today, communist true believers are few and far between. (Teenagers also like to buy Che Guevara shirts at the mall.) These ideological declines required the United States to remain steadfast in its own beliefs, to support its allies, and at times to act on its own while its adversaries' own divisions, violence, failures, and absurdities tore them apart.

How Is Fighting the Islamic State Different from Fighting Al Qaeda?

Al Qaeda is primarily a counterterrorism challenge, but the Islamic State is also a military one. The Al Qaeda core has a global presence, but it is a small organization. In much of the world the United States is working with allies to find and disrupt any Al Qaeda presence, while in Pakistan there is reportedly an aggressive drone campaign to hunt the leadership and force them to hide. The United States also tries to bolster the counterterrorism and internal defense capacity of allies facing Al Qaeda affiliate-linked insurgencies, working with the Yemeni, Somali, and other governments to improve their militaries and intelligence services.

The Islamic State, in contrast, is massive—over 30,000 fighters as of October 2014—and its primary form of aggression involves conquering territory. So here the US and allied role is more straightforward. On the one hand, US airstrikes are being used to degrade Islamic State forces and make it harder for them to conquer territory and smuggle oil. Air strikes weaken the Islamic State, but by themselves, they do not retake territory: someone must push the Islamic State back on the ground. So at the same time, the United States has sent trainers to build up some (though not all) of the Islamic State's enemies, notably the Iraqi army, Iraqi Kurds, western Iraqi tribes, and select elements of the Syrian opposition. In addition, by taking on the trappings of a state, the group has linked its cause to governance; as such, if the United States and its allies can hinder the Islamic State's ability to provide services, its popularity will decline.

To fight the Islamic State, the Obama administration has constructed a large coalition: over 60 countries as of October 2014. These include long-standing European allies like the United Kingdom and France, but also important regional states like Jordan, Saudi Arabia, and the United Arab Emirates. Some allies are bombing the Islamic State directly. Others are helping train local forces or are providing weapons and supplies. Although the United States is doing the bulk of the air strikes, the allies are politically vital. Their contributions help the United States justify intervention at home and bolster the perception that the fight against the Islamic State is not US imperialism in disguise.

Making the problem harder, the Islamic State has two theaters of operation—Iraq and Syria—but the United States and its allies face different challenges in each. In Iraq, the United States is coming in at the request of an allied government: a legally straightforward matter. However, the Iraqi government under Maliki was weak and corrupt and discriminated against the Sunni population—creating opportunities for the Islamic State to exploit by posing as the champion of the Sunnis against an oppressive Shi'ite regime. Maliki also politicized Iraq's armed forces, making it hard for them to gain the loyalty of Iraq's Sunnis or to fight well. It remains to be seen whether the new Iraqi prime minister, Haider al-Abadi, will try to correct these mistakes and begin to turn the country around or whether he will continue the disastrous policies of his predecessor. Because it needs competent ground power *now,* the United States has supported Iraqi Kurdish militias and is reaching out to Sunni tribal groups. These groups are vital to pushing back the Islamic State given the weak condition of the Iraqi army, but by strengthening them, the central government's control over the country weakens even more. The challenge for the United States is to build up both local and central capacity so that Iraqi forces can retake territory from the Islamic State and govern effectively to prevent its return. The Obama administration has sent in advisors to improve the Iraqi military, but progress is likely to be slow and uneven. Much of the challenge is political, and the United States is pressing the Abadi government to become more inclusive of Sunnis and otherwise pry them away from the Islamic State.

The Iraqi challenge looks simple when compared to Syria. Not only is Syria in the throes of a civil war, but its government is hostile to the United States: indeed, Washington's policy is that Asad must leave power. So the legality of the US intervention is unclear, as it is neither aiding a friendly government nor going after a terrorist group that was linked to 9/11 or is an immediate threat to the United States. Legal issues aside, it is also unclear exactly who the United States' allies in Syria are. As in Iraq, air strikes in isolation will not do much to change the situation on the ground in Syria. The United States needs forces that can help it oust the Islamic State from the territory it holds and fill the void. The Syrian opposition is fragmented and weak, and many of the most important groups are linked to jihadists. In Syria, the lines separating the "good" opposition (secular, pro-democracy groups) and the "bad" opposition (Islamic jihadists) are frequently blurred, as the various groups often work together or share intelligence and equipment by necessity—after all, they are all ostensibly fighting on the same side against Asad. This causes major problems for the US effort to arm and equip the Syrian opposition, as there is no guarantee that weapons given to a vetted opposition group will not end up being used by a decidedly less savory group. Perhaps even more difficult is the fact that, at the end of the day, most Syrian opposition groups are more focused on bringing down the Asad regime than fighting the Islamic State, and thus, US efforts to bolster the Syrian opposition may not end up having much effect on the Islamic State. Moreover, because the United States is also bombing Al Qaeda-linked groups like Jabhat al-Nusra—which many Syrians see as a dedicated foe of the Asad regime and not abusive in its treatment of civilians—in addition to bombing the Islamic State, Syrians are skeptical of US intentions. Some believe that Washington secretly wants to aid Asad. So Washington is stepping up support for the Syrian opposition and asking its allies to do so as well, but this remains at best a long-term project.

In the fight against both Al Qaeda and the Islamic State, local allies are the key. The Obama administration does not want to deploy US ground forces to fight the Islamic State, and the American people support this caution. Where allies are strong, the United States can rely on them to police their borders, hinder jihadist financing, and disrupt any jihadist presence. Where they are weak, the United States is trying to build them up and at times may even use its own forces to strike directly (usually from the air). Particularly tricky are allies like Pakistan, which has allowed jihadists to flourish; Iraq, whose policies make groups like the Islamic State more appealing; and Kuwait, which tolerates jihadist fundraising.

The US strategy for fighting the Islamic State is evolving. The Obama administration steadily upped US involvement after August 2014, increasing its diplomatic and military efforts. Military leaders have even floated the idea of US forces again playing a limited combat role to bolster Iraqi forces and to make US airpower more effective. Should current efforts fail to push back the Islamic State, these and other increases in US involvement are likely to gain more and more support.

10

SUGGESTIONS FOR FURTHER READING

Al Qaeda is over 25 years old, and the broader jihadist movement is older still. Especially after 9/11, the appetite for books that could explain this group and the overall jihadist phenomenon was voracious, and many notable works appeared. Work is scant on the Islamic State, but its history is interwoven with that of its fellow jihadists.

Four books offer an excellent assessment of the pre-9/11 period, explaining the evolution of Al Qaeda, the trajectory of the broader jihadist movement, and the US counterterrorism response. They have the additional virtue of being wonderfully written: two even won Pulitzer prizes. Steve Coll's *Ghost Wars: The Secret History of the CIA, Afghanistan, and bin Laden, from the Soviet Invasion to September 10, 2001* (Penguin, 2004) is a stunning work that is notably strong on US policy toward Pakistan and Afghanistan as well as on Al Qaeda and US counterterrorism. Lawrence Wright's *The Looming Tower: Al Qaeda and the Road to 9/11* (Vintage, 2007) is another impressive work. Among its many strengths are its description of the role of Egyptians in Al Qaeda and its ability to get inside the politics of the jihadist movement. The report of the National Commission on Terrorist Attacks upon the United States (better known as "The 9/11 Commission Report") is also justly famous (note that I served as one of the staff on the Commission—though, alas, I cannot claim credit for its success). Unusual for a government document, it is accessible and stylish. It is particularly definitive on the details of the

9/11 plot and the US government response: what did we know and when did we know it? I would also single out the Commission's less-read but important monographs on terrorist travel and terrorist financing, both of which are in-depth looks at subjects hard to understand in the unclassified realm. The last of the four, Peter Bergen's *The Osama bin Laden I Know: An Oral History of al Qaeda's Leader* (Free Press, 2006), is quite different in its approach and value. It is a compendium of Bergen's interviews with Al Qaeda-related figures, along with important internal documents and other primary-source information that has become available on the group. The result is a history that reveals the complexity of this movement in its own terms.

There are other important books that discuss the pre-9/11 period. I am a fan of Michael Scheuer's *Through Our Enemies' Eyes* (Potomac Books, 2002). Although much of Scheuer's writing is polemical, this and several other works of his on Al Qaeda are clearheaded and surprisingly sympathetic to Al Qaeda, from a man who was responsible for targeting its leadership when he was at the Central Intelligence Agency. A host of smaller works, more academic in tone, also offer many insights, and I stole from them liberally when writing this book. R. Kim Cragin's "Early History of Al-Qa'ida" in *The Historical Journal* is a strong work about the formative period of Al Qaeda, and Steven Brooke's "Jihadist Strategic Debates before 9/11" in *Studies in Conflict & Terrorism* offers many insights about the different approaches Al Qaeda considered.

Jihadists themselves also write, of course. There are many collections of Bin Laden's own words available, and I find Ayman al-Zawahiri's *Knights Under the Prophet's Banner* particularly insightful. For a different look at Zawahiri's real thoughts, Alan Cullison's "Inside Al Qaeda's Hard Drive" in *The Atlantic* (2004) is based on his chance recovery of a computer that belonged to Ayman al-Zawahiri. It offers a fascinating look at Al Qaeda as an organization, complete with infighting, bickering, and other pettiness.

Islam, Salafism, and jihadist variants are discussed by many authors now, but a straightforward and informed work is Quintan Wiktorowicz's "Anatomy of the Salafi Movement" in *Studies in Conflict & Terrorism*. I draw on Wiktorowicz's other works as well to explain the internal theological debates within the jihadist movement. I am particularly fond of his co-authored piece with John

Kaltner, "Killing in the Name of Islam: Al-Qaeda's Justification for September 11" in *Middle East Policy*.

The post-9/11 era is also rich but far more diffuse. Probably the best book on Al Qaeda's post-9/11 activities as a terrorist group is the volume edited by Bruce Hoffman and Fernando Reinares, *The Evolution of the Global Terrorist Threat: From 9/11 to Osama bin Laden's Death* (Columbia University Press, 2014), which systematically goes through a wide range of attacks and assesses the role of the Al Qaeda core. The list of more focused works is long, but I would single out Thomas Hegghammer, whose work on Saudi Arabia and foreign fighters is superb and draws on a range of new sources to illuminate some of the most important but most opaque questions about Al Qaeda. C. Christine Fair is usually the first person I turn to when I want to understand the bewildering dynamics of jihadist groups in Pakistan. Gregory D. Johnsen has emerged as an impressive scholar of Yemen and its militant groups. A notable post-9/11 creation is the Combating Terrorism Center (CTC) at West Point. Many impressive scholars work there or have gone through their doors, and their publications typically draw on captured documents, exposing the inner workings of Al Qaeda; the CTC has also made many of these documents available in a searchable online database. As one example, the work by Nelly Lahoud and her colleagues on the documents discovered in Abbottabad during the Bin Laden raid, *Letters from Abbottabad: Bin Laden Sidelined?* (Combating Terrorism Center at West Point, May 3, 2012), is another look at how Al Qaeda views the world, but this time drawing on what its leaders were privately saying to one another. If you are looking for a skeptic—and one who is well informed and writes well—you cannot do better than John Mueller, whose collective works question how serious the terrorism threat to the US homeland is today.

Because the Islamic State is a relatively new organization (at least compared to Al Qaeda), literature on the group is more limited, but several scholars I know and admire have recently produced fantastic works that provide remarkable insight into the group. *ISIS: The State of Terror* by Jessica Stern and J.M. Berger (HarperCollins, 2015) looks at how the group has used propaganda and social media to recruit thousands of fighters, including many from the West. Charles Lister's *Profiling the Islamic State* (Brookings Institution, 2014) traces the group's origins and evolution and provides detailed information on its leadership, tactics, and capabilities. Finally, there is William McCants's *The ISIS Apocalypse: The History, Strategy, and Doomsday Vision of the Islamic State* (Palgrave Macmillan, forthcoming 2015). Based almost entirely on primary-source documents in Arabic, McCants's book is a fascinating examination of the religious apocalyptic prophecies fueling the Islamic State's rise and driving its bloody mission.

There are a host of books that look at the US counterterrorism response, or at least some aspects of it. These range from Peter Bergen's gripping *Manhunt* (Crown Publishers, 2012), which tells the story of the long effort to locate and kill Bin Laden, to works like Jane Mayer's *The Dark Side* (Anchor Books, 2009) that reveal the world of renditions and secret prisons. Jack Goldsmith's *The Terror Presidency* (W. W. Norton, 2007) offers excellent insights into the Bush administration's legal approach to counterterrorism and the associated controversies. Hank Crumpton's *The Art of Intelligence* (Penguin, 2012) offers a practitioner's view of how intelligence can, and should, be done when fighting terrorists. Finally, Mark Mazzetti's *The Way of the Knife* (Penguin, 2013) explains the world of drones and secret warriors in riveting detail.

Those interested in Al Qaeda and the Islamic State might be interested in terrorism in general. Bruce Hoffman's *Inside Terrorism* (Columbia University Press, 2006) remains the strongest overall book on the logic of terrorism, its history, and its dynamics. A more scholarly but excellent recent addition is Jacob Shapiro's *The Terrorist's Dilemma: Managing Violent Covert Organizations* (Princeton University Press, 2013), which delves into the organizational problems that terrorist groups face. Audrey Kurth Cronin's *How Terrorism Ends: Understanding the Decline and Demise of Terrorist Campaigns* (Princeton University Press, 2011) looks at counterterrorism from a different perspective, evaluating the different reasons that groups collapse or stop fighting and drawing valuable lessons.

The above is only a sample. Although my work centers on counterterrorism, there is now so much out there that I cannot possibly read it all, and I do not expect others to do so. But if you draw from the authors above, you will understand Al Qaeda, the jihadist movement, and the Islamic State far better and have informed opinions on the best way to fight them.

NOTES

CHAPTER 1

1. Quoted in S. Coll, *Ghost Wars: The Secret History of the CIA, Afghanistan, and bin Laden, from the Soviet Invasion to September 10, 2001*, New York, Penguin Press, 2004, p. 97.
2. T. Hegghammer, "The Rise of Muslim Foreign Fighters: Islam and the Globalization of Jihad," *International Security*, vol. 35, no. 3, Winter 2010–2011, p. 62, http://www.mitpressjournals.org.proxy.library.georgetown.edu/doi/pdf/10.1162/ISEC_a_00023.
3. P. Bergen, *The Osama bin Laden I Know: An Oral History of al Qaeda's Leader*, New York, Free Press, 2006, p. 41; Hegghammer, "The Rise of Muslim Foreign Fighters," p. 61.
4. "The 9/11 Commission Report," National Commission on Terrorist Attacks upon the United States, July 22, 2004, p. 56, http://www.9-11commission.gov/report/911Report.pdf.
5. R. Cook, "The struggle against terrorism cannot be won by military means," *The Guardian*, July 8, 2005, http://www.theguardian.com/uk/2005/jul/08/july7.development.
6. A. Anas, *Wiladat "al-Afghan al-'Arab": Sirat Abdullah Anas bayn Mas'ud wa 'Abdullah 'Azzam* [The Birth of the Arab Afghans: The Autobiography of Abdullah Anas between Masoud and Abdullah Azzam] (Arabic), London, Dar Al Saqi, 2002.
7. Hegghammer, "The Rise of Muslim Foreign Fighters," p. 62.
8. P. Bergen, "Bergen: Bin Laden, CIA Links Hogwash," *CNN*, September 6, 2006, http://www.cnn.com/2006/WORLD/asiapcf/08/15/bergen.answers/index.html?section=cnn_latest.
9. Quoted in Bergen, *The Osama bin Laden I Know*, p. 83.
10. A. Strick Van Linschoten and F. Kuehn, *An Enemy We Created: The Myth of the Taliban-Al Qaeda Merger in Afghanistan*, New York, Oxford University Press, 2012, p. 51.
11. Bergen, *The Osama bin Laden I Know*, p. 95.

12. M. Al-Zayyat et al., *The Road to Al Qaeda: The Story of Bin Laden's Right-Hand Man*, London, Pluto Press, 2004, p. 70; R. K. Cragin, "Early History of Al-Qa'ida," *The Historical Journal*, vol. 51, no. 4, 2008, p. 1055.
13. Bergen, *The Osama bin Laden I Know*, p. 105.
14. Bergen, *The Osama bin Laden I Know*, p. 82.
15. "The 9/11 Commission Report," p. 59.
16. L. Wright, *The Looming Tower: Al-Qaeda and the Road to 9/11*, New York, Alfred A. Knopf, 2006, p. 163.
17. J. M. Barr and R. O. Collins, *Revolutionary Sudan: Hasan al-Turabi and the Islamist State, 1989–2000*, Leiden, Netherlands, Koninklijke Brill, 2003, p. 121.
18. "The 9/11 Commission Report," p. 58.
19. A. M. Lesch, "Osama bin Laden's 'Business' in Sudan," *Current History*, vol. 101, no. 655, 2002, p. 203.
20. M. Taylor and M. E. Elbushra, "Research Note: Hassan al-Turabi, Osama bin Laden, and Al Qaeda in Sudan," *Terrorism and Political Violence*, vol. 3, no. 18, September 2006, pp. 449–464.
21. "Al Qa'ida's Structure and Bylaws [English translation]," internal Al Qaeda document, Harmony Project document #AFGP-2002-600048, Combating Terrorism Center at West Point, n.d., https://www.ctc.usma.edu/posts/al-qaida-bylaws-english-translation-2.
22. Wright, *The Looming Tower*, p. 154; Coll, *Ghost Wars*, pp. 221–222; Cragin, "Early History," p. 1057.
23. Cragin, "Early History," p. 1059; Wright, *The Looming Tower*, pp. 167–169.
24. "The 9/11 Commission Report," p. 59.
25. See the testimony of Jamal al-Fadl in *United States of America v. Usama bin Laden et al.*, Indictment S(9) 98 Cr. 1023 LBS, pp. 267–269.
26. Full text available at "Bin Laden's Fatwa," *PBS Newshour*, August 23, 1996, http://www.pbs.org/newshour/updates/military-july-dec96-fatwa_1996/.
27. "Interview: Osama Bin Laden," *PBS Frontline*, May 1998, http://www.pbs.org/wgbh/pages/frontline/shows/binladen/who/interview.html.
28. S. Brooke, "Jihadist Strategic Debates before 9/11," *Studies in Conflict & Terrorism*, vol. 31, no. 3, 2008, p. 216.
29. F. Gerges, *The Far Enemy: Why Jihad Went Global*, New York, Cambridge University Press, 2005, p. 87.
30. J. R. Williams, interview with the author, September 26, 2014. See also: A. Keats, "In The Spotlight: Al-Jihad (Egyptian Islamic Jihad)," Center for Defense Information, Terrorism Project, 2002, Part 6, http://www.cdi.org/terrorism/aljihad.cfm.
31. M. Gray, "Economic Reform, Privatization, and Tourism in Egypt," *Middle Eastern Studies*, vol. 34, no. 2, April 1998, p. 109.
32. A. Higgins and C. Cooper, "Cloak and Dagger: A CIA-Backed Team Used Brutal Means to Crack Terror Cell," *Wall Street Journal*, November 20, 2001, http://online.wsj.com/articles/SB1006205820963585440.
33. L. Wright, "The Man Behind Bin Laden: How an Egyptian Doctor Became a Master of Terror," *The New Yorker*, September 16, 2002, http://www.newyorker.com/archive/2002/09/16/020916fa_fact2.
34. Gerges, *The Far Enemy*, p. 140.

35. T. McKelvey, "U.S.-Funded Democracy Crushers?" *The Daily Beast*, October 13, 2011, http://www.thedailybeast.com/articles/2011/10/13/egyptian-military-u-s-funded-democracy-crushers.html.

36. J. Burke, *Al Qaeda: The True Story of Radical Islam*, New York, I. B. Tauris, 2006, p. 171.

37. T. Hegghammer, *Jihad in Saudi Arabia: Violence and Pan-Islamism Since 1979*, New York, Cambridge University Press, 2010, p. 109.

38. "The 9/11 Commission Report," p. 67.

39. C. J. Chivers and D. Rohde, "Afghan Camps Turn Out Holy War Guerrillas and Terrorists," *New York Times*, March 18, 2002, http://www.nytimes.com/2002/03/18/world/turning-out-guerrillas-and-terrorists-to-wage-a-holy-war.html.

CHAPTER 2

1. As quoted in Wright, *The Looming Tower*, p. 198.

2. "The 9/11 Commission Report," p. 68.

3. "Bombings of the US Embassies in Nairobi, Kenya and Dar es Salaam, Tanzania on August 7, 1998," Report of the Accountability Review Board, US State Department, January 1999, http://www.fas.org/irp/threat/arb/board_nairobi.html.

4. P. Bushnell, "Prudence Bushnell on the U.S. Embassy Nairobi Bombings," *Association for Diplomatic Studies and Training*, August 2012, http://adst.org/2012/08/prudence-bushnell-on-the-us-embassy-nairobi-bombings/.

5. "The 9/11 Commission Report," p. 68.

6. "The 9/11 Commission Report," p. 69.

7. Full text of the *fatwa* available at Federation of American Scientists, http://fas.org/irp/world/para/docs/980223-fatwa.htm.

8. Bushnell, "Prudence Bushnell on the U.S. Embassy Nairobi Bombings."

9. T. R. Eldridge et al., *9/11 and Terrorist Travel*, Washington, DC, National Commission on Terrorist Attacks upon the United States, 2004, p. 52.

10. *United States of America v. Usama bin Laden et al.*, pp. 36–43.

11. S. Berger quoted in "Joint Inquiry into Intelligence Community Activities before and after the Terrorist Attacks of September 11, 2001," House Permanent Select Committee on Intelligence and Senate Select Committee on Intelligence, December 2002, http://fas.org/irp/congress/2002_rpt/911rept.pdf.

12. Quoted in E. Hill, "Joint Inquiry Staff Statement, Part I," Joint Investigation into September 11th: First Public Hearing—Joint House/Senate Intelligence Committee Hearing, September 18, 2002, http://fas.org/irp/congress/2002_hr/091802hill.html.

13. J. Astill, "Strike one," *The Guardian*, October 2, 2001, http://www.theguardian.com/world/2001/oct/02/afghanistan.terrorism3.

14. "The 9/11 Commission Report," pp. 59–60.

15. "The 9/11 Commission Report," pp. 59–61.

16. D. Kohn, "60 Minutes: The Man Who Got Away," *60 Minutes*, CBS, May 31, 2002, http://www.cbsnews.com/news/60-minutes-the-man-who-got-away/.

17. C. Whitlock, "Zarqawi building his own terror network," *Philadelphia Post-Gazette*, October 3, 2004, http://old.post-gazette.com/pg/04277/388966.stm.

18. D. Heath, "Ahmed Ressam, mastermind of foiled LAX plot, gave up valuable details about al-Qaida without harsh interrogation," *The Center for Public Integrity*, June 3, 2011, http://www.publicintegrity.org/2011/06/03/4802/ahmed-ressam-mastermind-foiled-lax-plot-gave-valuable-details-about-al-qaida-without.

19. T. Joscelyn, "From Al Qaeda in Italy to Ansar al Sharia Tunisia," *The Long War Journal*, November 21, 2012, http://www.longwarjournal.org/archives/2012/11/from_al_qaeda_in_ita.php; D. Muriel, "Thwarting Terror Cells in Europe," *CNN*, January 23, 2002, http://edition.cnn.com/2001/WORLD/europe/10/26/inv.thwarting.cells/index.html.

20. B. M. Jenkins, "International Terrorism: A New Mode of Conflict," in D. Carlton and C. Schaerf, eds., *International Terrorism and World Security*, London, Croom Helm, 1975, p. 15.

21. "The 9/11 Commission Report," p. 145.

22. "The 9/11 Commission Report," p. 169.

23. "The 9/11 Commission Report," p. 154.

24. T. McDermott, *Perfect Soldiers: The Hijackers: Who They Were, Why They Did It*, New York, HarperCollins, 2005, p. 229.

25. "The 9/11 Commission Report," p. 157.

26. "The 9/11 Commission Report," p. 270.

27. "The 9/11 Commission Report," p. 226.

28. McDermott, *Perfect Soldiers*, p. 221.

29. "The 9/11 Commission Report," pp. 254–277, 355–356.

30. Coll, *Ghost Wars*, p. 435.

31. M. Scheuer / "Anonymous," *Imperial Hubris: Why the West is Losing the War on Terror*, Dulles, VA, Potomac Books, 2004, p. ix.

32. R. Posner, "The 9/11 Report: A Dissent," *New York Times*, August 29, 2004, http://www.nytimes.com/2004/08/29/books/the-9-11-report-a-dissent.html.

33. "The 9/11 Commission Report," p. 368.

34. Quoted in R. Burns, "CIA Chief Calls bin Laden Biggest Threat to US Security," *Associated Press*, February 7, 2001.

35. "The 9/11 Commission Report," p. 340.

36. As quoted in Q. Wiktorowicz and J. Kaltner, "Killing in the Name of Islam: Al-Qaeda's Justification for September 11," *Middle East Policy*, vol. 10, no. 2, June 2003, p. 77.

37. "Attacks on US Are Un-Islamic, Say Clerics," *IOL News*, September 14, 2001, http://www.iol.co.za/news/world/attacks-on-us-are-un-islamic-say-clerics-1.69136.

38. As quoted in Wiktorowicz and Kaltner, "Al-Qaeda's Justification for September 11," p. 82.

39. As quoted in Wiktorowicz and Kaltner, "Al-Qaeda's Justification for September 11," p. 96.

40. As quoted in Wiktorowicz and Kaltner, "Al-Qaeda's Justification for September 11," p. 86.

41. Wiktorowicz and Kaltner, "Al-Qaeda's Justification for September 11," p. 90.

42. For a list, see "The Global War on Terrorism: The First 100 Days," *The Coalition Information Centers*, US Department of State Archives, 2001, http://2001-2009. state.gov/s/ct/rls/wh/6947.htm.

43. L. Wright, "The Rebellion Within," *The New Yorker*, June 2, 2008, http://www.newyorker.com/reporting/2008/06/02/080602fa_fact_wright?currentPage=all.

44. P. L. Bergen, *The Longest War: The Enduring Conflict Between America and al-Qaeda*, New York, Free Press, 2011, p. 91.

45. G. W. Bush, "President Bush Addresses the Nation," *Washington Post*, September 20, 2001, http://www.washingtonpost.com/wp-srv/nation/specials/attacked/transcripts/bushaddress_092001.html.

46. Quoted in J. Burke, *The 9/11 Wars*, Kindle Edition, New York, Penguin Books, 2011, p. 156.

47. D. Benjamin and S. Simon, *The Age of Sacred Terror*, New York, Random House, 2002, p. 113.

CHAPTER 3

1. "Jihad Against Jews and Crusaders," World Islamic Front Statement, February 23, 1998, available at Federation of American Scientists, http://fas.org/irp/world/para/docs/980223-fatwa.htm; V. Brown, *Cracks in the Foundation: Leadership Schisms in Al Qaeda from 1989–2006*, Combating Terrorism Center at West Point, September 2007, https://www.ctc.usma.edu/posts/cracks-in-the-foundation-leadership-schisms-in-al-qaida-from-1989-2006; see also the August 2001 Al Qaeda videotape that addresses what bin Laden and others describe as the evil influence of Jews, as described in Bergen, *The Osama bin Laden I Know*, p. 291.

2. "Jihad Against Jews and Crusaders."

3. Hegghammer, *Jihad in Saudi Arabia*, p. 135.

4. N. Lahoud, "Metamorphosis," in N. Lahoud et al., *The Group That Calls Itself a State: Understanding the Evolution and Challenges of the Islamic State*, Combating Terrorism Center at West Point, December 2014, p. 15, https://www.ctc.usma.edu/v2/wp-content/uploads/2014/12/CTC-The-Group-That-Calls-Itself-A-State-December20141.pdf.

5. "Zawahiri Urges Hamas to Fight On," *BBC News*, March 5, 2006, http://news.bbc.co.uk/2/hi/middle_east/4775222.stm.

6. Wright, *The Looming Tower*, pp. 370–371.

7. A. Al-Zawahiri, *Knights Under the Prophet's Banner* [English translation], n.d., available at *Jihadology*, https://azelin.files.wordpress.com/2010/11/6759609-knights-under-the-prophet-banner.pdf. According to Aaron Y. Zelin, the book was completed sometime around 9/11 and was originally published in serial form by the Arabic-language Saudi newspaper *Ash-Sharq al-'Awsat* in October 2001. A second edition (also in Arabic) was published by *As-Sahab Media Production* (Al Qaeda's media arm) in November 2010. Both the first and second editions are available at *Jihadology*, http://jihadology.net/2010/11/27/as-sa%E1%B8%A5ab-media-production-releases-second-edition-of-dr-ayman-a%E1%BA%93-%E1%BA%93awahiris-knights-under-the-prophets-banner/.

8. As quoted in Brown, *Cracks in the Foundation*, p. 10.
9. "Interview: Osama Bin Laden."
10. Hegghammer, *Jihad in Saudi Arabia*, p. 102.
11. "Full Transcript of Bin Laden's Speech," *Al Jazeera*, November 1, 2004, http://www.aljazeera.com/archive/2004/11/200849163336457223.html; for a review of al-Suri's decentralized approach, see B. Lia, *Architect of Global Jihad: The Life of Al-Qaeda Strategist Abu Mus'ab al-Suri*, New York, Columbia University Press, 2008.
12. "Full Transcript of Bin Laden's Speech."
13. A. B. Naji, "The Management of Savagery: The Most Critical Stage Through Which the Umma Will Pass," translated by W. McCants, John M. Olin Institute for Strategic Studies at Harvard University, May 23, 2006, http://azelin.files.wordpress.com/2010/08/abu-bakr-naji-the-management-of-savagery-the-most-critical-stage-through-which-the-umma-will-pass.pdf.
14. Qur'an 4:29–30, Sahih International translation, http://quran.com/4/29-30.
15. "Suicide Attack Database," Chicago Project on Security and Terrorism (CPOST), July 18, 2014, http://cpostdata.uchicago.edu/.
16. "The Qaradawi Fatwas," *Middle East Quarterly*, Summer 2004, pp. 78–80, http://www.meforum.org/646/the-qaradawi-fatwas#_ftn3.
17. Gerges, *The Far Enemy*, pp. 142–143.
18. "The 9/11 Commission Report," pp. 67–68, 470–471.
19. "Suicide Attack Database"; A. Moghadam, "Motives for Martyrdom: Al-Qaida, Salafi Jihad, and the Spread of Suicide Attacks," *International Security*, vol. 33, no. 3, Winter 2008–2009, p. 46.
20. Moghadam, "Motives for Martyrdom," p. 62.
21. B. Hoffman, "The Logic of Suicide Terrorism," *The Atlantic Monthly*, June 2003, http://www.theatlantic.com/magazine/archive/2003/06/the-logic-of-suicide-terrorism/302739/; see also A. Gilli and M. Gilli, "The Spread of Military Innovations: Adoption Capacity Theory, Tactical Incentives, and the Case of Suicide Terrorism," *Security Studies*, vol. 23, 2014, pp. 513–547.
22. M. Bloom, *Dying to Kill: The Allure of Suicide Terror*, New York, Columbia University Press, 2005, pp. 78–79.
23. "The Hijacked Caravan: Refuting Suicide Bombings as Martyrdom Operations in Contemporary Jihad Strategy," *Ihsanic Intelligence*, n.d., http://www.ihsanic-intelligence.com/dox/The_Hijacked_Caravan.pdf.
24. "Muslim Views on Suicide Bombing," Pew Research Global Attitudes Project, June 30, 2014, http://www.pewglobal.org/2014/07/01/concerns-about-islamic-extremism-on-the-rise-in-middle-east/pg-2014-07-01-islamic-extremism-10/.
25. Moghadam, "Motives for Martyrdom," p. 78.
26. S. Laville et al., "Woolwich Attack: Horror on John Wilson Street," *The Guardian*, May 25, 2013, http://www.theguardian.com/uk/2013/may/22/woolwich-attack-horror-soldier.
27. The Associated Press, "Obama Says 'Lone Wolf' Terror Attack More Likely Than Major Coordinated Effort," *Huffington Post*, August 16, 2011, http://www.huffingtonpost.com/2011/08/16/obama-lone-wolf-terror_n_928880.html.
28. J. D. Simon, *Lone Wolf Terrorism: Understanding the Growing Threat*, Amherst, NY, Prometheus Books, 2013.

29. B. Lia, "Al-Suri's Doctrines for Decentralized Jihadi Training—Part 1," *Terrorism Monitor*, vol. 5, no. 1, February 21, 2007, http://www.jamestown. org/single/?no_cache=1&tx_ttnews%5Btt_news%5D=1001#.

30. B. Roggio, "Abu Musab Al-Suri Released from Syrian Custody: Report," *The Long War Journal*, February 6, 2012, http://www.longwarjournal.org/ archives/2012/02/abu_musab_al_suri_re.php#.

31. For a list of violent plots in Europe involving Syrian returnees, see A. Zammit, "List of Alleged Violent Plots in Europe Involving Syria Returnees," *The Murphy Raid*, June 29, 2014, http://andrewzammit.org/2014/06/29/list-of-alleged-violent-plots-in-europe-involving-syria-returnees/. The Brussels Jewish Museum is the only one of the plots that came to fruition.

32. A. Y. Zelin, "Free Radical," *Foreign Policy*, February 4, 2012, http://www.foreignpolicy.com/articles/2012/02/03/free_radical.

33. "EDL Terror Attack Plot: Six Men Plead Guilty," *Sky News*, April 30, 2013, http://news.sky.com/story/1084922/edl-terror-attack-plot-six-men-plead-guilty.

34. Quoted in P. Cruickshank and T. Lister, "The 'Lone Wolf'—The Unknowable Face of Terror," *CNN*, February 18, 2012, http://www.cnn.com/2012/02/18/ opinion/lone-wolf-terror/.

35. N. Lahoud et al., *Letters from Abbottabad: Bin Laden Sidelined?* Combating Terrorism Center at West Point, May 3, 2012, p. 15, https://www.ctc.usma. edu/posts/letters-from-abbottabad-bin-ladin-sidelined.

36. Quoted in G. Corera, "Al-Qaeda chief Zawahiri urges 'lone-wolf' attacks on US," *BBC News*, September 13, 2013, http://www.bbc.com/news/ world-middle-east-24083314.

37. "Camp Acceptance Requirements [English translation]," internal Al Qaeda document, Harmony Project document #AFGP-2002-6000849, Combating Terrorism Center at West Point, n.d., https://www.ctc.usma.edu/posts/ camp-acceptance-requirements-english-translation-2.

38. D. Rohde and C. J. Chivers, "A NATION CHALLENGED: Qaeda's Grocery Lists and Manuals of Killing," *New York Times*, March 17, 2002, http:// www.nytimes.com/2002/03/17/world/a-nation-challenged-qaedas-grocery-lists-and-manuals-of-killing.html.

39. Rohde and Chivers, "A NATION CHALLENGED."

40. "Al Qa'ida Staff Count Public Appointments [English translation]," internal Al Qaeda document, Harmony Project document #AFGP-2002-000112, Combating Terrorism Center at West Point, n.d., p. 2, https://www.ctc.usma. edu/posts/al-qaida-staff-count-public-appointments-original-language-2.

41. "Trail of a Terrorist," Testimony of Ahmed Ressam, *PBS Frontline*, October 2001, pp. 8–11, http://www.pbs.org/wgbh/pages/frontline/shows/trail/.

42. "Al Qa'ida Staff Count Public Appointments [English translation]."

43. Rohde and Chivers, "A NATION CHALLENGED."

44. As quoted in J. Burke, "Omar was a normal British teenager who loved his little brother and Man Utd. So why at 24 did he plan to blow up a nightclub in central London?" part 2, *The Guardian / The Observer*, January 19, 2008, http:// www.theguardian.com/ theobserver/2008/jan/20/features.magazine117.

45. As quoted in Burke, "Omar was a normal British teenager."

46. M. Purdy and L. Bergman, "Unclear Danger: Inside the Lackawanna Terror Case," *New York Times*, October 12, 2003, http://www.nytimes. com/2003/10/12/nyregion/12LACK.html?src=pm&pagewanted=6.

47. A. M. Al-Amriiki, "The Story of An American Jihaadi—Part One," May 16, 2012, p. 54, available at *Jihadology*, https://azelin.files.wordpress. com/2012/05/omar-hammami-abc5ab-mane1b9a3c5abr-al-amrc4abkc4ab-22the-story-of-an-american-jihc481dc4ab-part-122.pdf.

48. S. Rotella, "Al Qaeda Recruits Back in Europe, But Why?" *Los Angeles Times*, May 29, 2009, http://articles.latimes.com/2009/may/24/world/ fg-junior-jihadis24.

49. "The Al Qaeda Manual [English translation]," internal Al Qaeda document, n.d., available at US Department of Justice, http://www.justice.gov/ag/man-ualpart1_1.pdf.

50. B. Obama, "President Obama's Remarks in Prague on Nuclear Materials, April 2009," Council on Foreign Relations, April 5, 2009, http://www.cfr. org/nuclear-energy/president-obamas-remarks-prague-nuclear-materials-april-2009/p32649.

51. The best evidence for this is the testimony of former Al Qaeda member Jamal al-Fadl. See testimony of Jamal al-Fadl in *United States v. Usama bin Laden et al.*, February 6, 2001, pp. 35–41. Lawrence Wright reports, however, that several of those allegedly involved in the plot claim that this particular episode is fictional; see Wright, *The Looming Tower*, pp. 411–412.

52. Quoted in "Wrath of God," *Time*, January 11, 1999, http://content.time.com/ time/world/article/0,8599,2054517,00.html.

53. R. Mowatt-Larssen, "Al Qaeda Weapons of Mass Destruction Threat: Hype or Reality?" Belfer Center for Science and International Affairs, John F. Kennedy School of Government, January 2010, p. 26, http://belfercenter. ksg.harvard.edu/publication/19852/al_qaeda_weapons_of_mass_destruc-tion_threat.html.

54. D. Campell, "The ricin ring that never was," *The Guardian*, April 14, 2005, http://www.theguardian.com/world/2005/apr/14/alqaida.terrorism.

55. Q. Wiktorowicz, "Anatomy of the Salafi Movement," *Studies in Conflict & Terrorism*, vol. 29, 2006, p. 216.

56. N. Al-Fahd, "A Treatise on the Legal Status of Using Weapons of Mass Destruction Against Infidels," May 2003, http://ahlussunnahpublicaties. files.wordpress.com/2013/04/42288104-nasir-al-fahd-the-ruling-on-using-weapons-of-mass-destruction-against-the-infidels.pdf. Also available on Scribd here: http://www.scribd.com/doc/53962350/A-Treatise-on-the-Legal-Status-of-Using-Weapons-of-Mass-Destruction-Against-Infidels-May-2003, just in case the other link disappears (as sometimes happens with this kind of material).

57. Quoted in J. Mueller, "The Atomic Terrorist: Assessing the Likelihood," Presentation Paper, Program for International Security Policy, University of Chicago, January 15, 2008, p. 6, http://politicalscience.osu.edu/faculty/ jmueller//APSACHGO.PDF.

58. As noted in Mueller, "The Atomic Terrorist," p. 4.

59. D. Linzer, "Nuclear Capabilities May Elude Terrorists," *Washington Post*, December 29, 2004, p. A1.

60. Mueller, "The Atomic Terrorist," p. 11. Michael Levi points out that Aum Shinrikyo, a wealthy group with considerable scientific expertise and one that was not being hunted at the time, did not expand its nuclear program because it feared detection if it did so. See M. Levi, "Stopping Nuclear

Terrorism: The Dangerous Allure of Perfect Defense," *Foreign Affairs*, vol. 87, no. 1, January–February 2008, http://www.foreignaffairs.com/articles/63055/michael-levi/stopping-nuclear-terrorism.

61. Mueller, "The Atomic Terrorist," p. 10.
62. Linzer, "Nuclear Capabilities May Elude Terrorists," p. A1.
63. Mueller, "The Atomic Terrorist," p. 24.
64. "Summary of Jose Padilla's Activities with Al Qaeda," US Department of Justice, 2004, http://fas.org/irp/news/2004/06/padilla060104.pdf.
65. M. A. Weaver, "The Short, Violent Life of Abu Musab al-Zarqawi," *The Atlantic*, July 1, 2006, http://www.theatlantic.com/magazine/archive/2006/07/the-short-violent-life-of-abu-musab-al-zarqawi/304983/2/.
66. "10 Truly Ridiculous Criminal Acts," *Listverse*, July 16, 2010, http://listverse.com/2010/07/16/10-truly-ridiculous-criminal-acts/. Some of the more salacious details of this story are not confirmed.
67. Mueller, "The Atomic Terrorist," pp. 5–6.
68. "1919 Bombings," The Federal Bureau of Investigation, Philadelphia Division, http://www.fbi.gov/philadelphia/about-us/history/famous-cases/famous-cases-1919-bombings.

CHAPTER 4

1. F. Rahman, *Islam and Modernity: Transformation of an Intellectual Tradition*, Chicago, University of Chicago Press, 1982, p. 41.
2. Wiktorowicz, "Anatomy of the Salafi Movement," p. 214.
3. Wiktorowicz, "Anatomy of the Salafi Movement," p. 210.
4. Brooke, "Jihadist Strategic Debates before 9/11," p. 207.
5. Hegghammer, "The Rise of Muslim Foreign Fighters," p. 79.
6. C. Bunzel, "Toward an Islamic Spring: Abu Muhammad al-Maqdisi's Prison Production," *Jihadica*, June 11, 2013, http://www.jihadica.com/toward-an-islamic-spring-abu-muhammad-al-maqdisi%E2%80%99s-prison-production/.
7. J. Wagemakers, *A Quietist Jihadi: The Ideology and Influence of Abu Muhammad al-Maqdisi*, New York, Cambridge University Press, 2012.
8. Bunzel, "Toward an Islamic Spring: Abu Muhammad al-Maqdisi's Prison Production."
9. P. Bergen and P. Cruickshank, "The Unraveling," *The New Republic*, June 11, 2008, http://www.newrepublic.com/article/the-unraveling.
10. See "The Open Meeting with Shaykh Ayman al-Zawahiri—Part One," *As-Sahab Media Production*, 2008, available at the *Washington Post*, http://www.washingtonpost.com/wp-srv/world/OpenMeetingZawahiri_Part1.pdf.
11. Wright, "The Rebellion Within."
12. D. Blair, "Al-Qaeda founder launches fierce attack on Osama bin Laden," *The Telegraph*, February 20, 2009, http://www.telegraph.co.uk/news/worldnews/africaandindianocean/egypt/4736358/Al-Qaeda-founder-launches-fierce-attack-on-Osama-bin-Laden.html.
13. See "Major Jihadi Cleric and Author of Al-Qaeda's Shari'a Guide to Jihad: 9/11 Was a Sin," Middle East Media Research Institute (MEMRI), Special Dispatch No. 1785, December 14, 2007, http://www.memri.org/report/en/0/0/0/0/0/0/2636.htm.

14. As quoted in Wright, "The Rebellion Within."
15. As quoted in Wright, "The Rebellion Within."
16. Quoted in I. Black, "Violence won't work: how author of 'jihadists' bible' stirred up a storm," *The Guardian*, July 27, 2007, http://www.theguardian. com/world/2007/jul/27/alqaida.egypt.
17. Bergen, *The Osama bin Laden I Know*, p. 119.
18. Full text of the 1998 statement available at Federation of American Scientists, http://fas.org/irp/world/para/docs/980223-fatwa.htm.
19. O. B. Laden, "Letter to the American People," *The Guardian*, November 24, 2002, http://www.theguardian.com/world/2002/nov/24/theobserver.
20. Laden, "Letter to the American People."
21. "Interview: Osama Bin Laden."
22. Wiktorowicz and Kaltner, "Al-Qaeda's Justification for September 11," pp. 76–92.
23. Wiktorowicz and Kaltner, "Al-Qaeda's Justification for September 11," p. 90.
24. Wiktorowicz and Kaltner, "Al-Qaeda's Justification for September 11," p. 90.
25. A. Al-Zawahiri, "Zawahiri's Letter to Zarqawi [English translation]," personal correspondence from Ayman al-Zawahiri to Abu Musab al-Zarqawi, Harmony Project, Combating Terrorism Center at West Point, n.d., https://www.ctc.usma.edu/posts/zawahiris-letter-to-zarqawi-english-translation-2.
26. Wright, *The Looming Tower*, p. 264.
27. All 12 issues of *Inspire* are available at *Jihadology*, http://jihadology. net/2014/03/14/al-qaidah-in-the-arabian-peninsulas-al-mala%E1%B8% A5im-media-releases-inspire-magazine-issue-12/.
28. Al-Zawahiri, *Knights Under the Prophet's Banner*.

CHAPTER 5

1. Quoted in Bergen, *The Osama bin Laden I Know*, p. 215.
2. P. Bergen, "Five Myths about Osama Bin Laden," *Washington Post*, May 6, 2011, http://www.washingtonpost.com/opinions/five-myths-about-osama-bin-laden/2011/05/05/AFkG1rAG_story.html.
3. B. Hoffman, "Rethinking Terrorism and Counterterrorism Since 9/11," *Studies in Conflict & Terrorism*, vol. 25, no. 5, 2002, p. 304. Martha Crenshaw argues that, in general, "Terrorists are impatient for action." See M. Crenshaw, "The Logic of Terrorism: Terrorist Behavior as a Product of Choice," *Terrorism and Counterterrorism*, vol. 2, no. 1, 1998, p. 58.
4. Wright, "The Man Behind Bin Laden," p. 59.
5. As quoted in Brooke, "Jihadist Strategic Debates before 9/11," p. 210.
6. As quoted in Brooke, "Jihadist Strategic Debates before 9/11," p. 211.
7. L. Wright, "Zawahiri at the Helm," *The New Yorker*, June 16, 2011, http:// www.newyorker.com/online/blogs/newsdesk/2011/06/zawahiri-at-the-helm.html.
8. Wright, "The Man Behind Bin Laden," p. 58.
9. As quoted in Brooke, "Jihadist Strategic Debates before 9/11," p. 210.
10. As quoted in Wright, *The Looming Tower*, p. 217.
11. "Al Qa'ida's Structure and Bylaws [English translation]."

12. B. Hoffman and F. Reinares, "Conclusion," in B. Hoffman and F. Reinares, *The Evolution of the Global Terrorist Threat: From 9/11 to Osama bin Laden's Death*, New York, Columbia University Press, 2014, pp. 618–640, p. 618.

13. L. Farrall, "How al Qaeda Works," *Foreign Affairs*, vol. 90, no. 2, March–April 2011, pp. 128–138.

14. See *United States of America v. Usama bin Laden et al.*, pp. 8–10; A. Cullison and A. Higgins, "Files Found: A Computer in Kabul Yields a Chilling Array of al Qaeda Memos," *Wall Street Journal*, December 31, 2001; and "Egypt: Egyptian Paper Details Fugitives' Aliases, Passports," U.S. Foreign Broadcast Information Service Daily Reports, June 18, 1998.

15. "The Al Qaeda Manual [English translation]," pp. BM-26 and 29.

16. As quoted in P. Bergen, *Holy War, Inc.: Inside the Secret World of Osama bin Laden*, New York, Free Press, 2001, p. 32.

17. "Osama Bin Laden Video Tape," *PBS Newshour*, December 13, 2001, http://www.pbs.org/newshour/bb/terrorism-july-dec01-video_12-13a/.

18. T. Noah, "Al-Qaida's Rule of Threes," *Slate*, December 5, 2005, http://www.slate.com/articles/news_and_politics/chatterbox/2005/12/alqaidas_rule_of_threes.html.

19. Quoted in R. Mackey, "Eliminating Al Qaeda's No. 3, Again," *New York Times*, June 1, 2010, http://thelede.blogs.nytimes.com/2010/06/01/eliminating-al-qaedas-no-3-again/.

20. M. Townsend, "Mass rape, amputations and killings—why families are fleeing terror in Mali," *The Guardian*, December 15, 2012, http://www.theguardian.com/world/2012/dec/15/rape-killings-terror-mali.

21. "Mali-Al-Qaida's Sahara Playbook," internal Al Qaeda documents, n.d., provided by the Associated Press, http://hosted.ap.org/specials/interactives/_international/_pdfs/al-qaida-manifesto.pdf.

22. As quoted in Brooke, "Jihadist Strategic Debates before 9/11," p. 204.

23. As quoted in Wiktorowicz, "Anatomy of the Salafi Movement," p. 230.

24. D. Shinn, "Al Shabaab's Foreign Threat to Somalia," in M. P. Noonan, ed., *The Foreign Fighters Problem, Recent Trends and Case Studies: Selected Essays*, Philadelphia, Foreign Policy Research Institute, April 2011, p. 36.

25. A. Cullison, "Inside Al-Qaeda's Hard Drive," *The Atlantic*, September 1, 2004, http://www.theatlantic.com/magazine/archive/2004/09/inside-al-qaeda-s-hard-drive/303428/.

26. M. Silber and A. Bhatt, "Radicalization in the West: The Homegrown Threat," New York City Police Department, 2007, p. 2.

27. V. Nasr, interview for "Saudi Time Bomb?" *PBS Frontline*, October 25, 2001, http://www.pbs.org/wgbh/pages/frontline/shows/saudi/interviews/nasr.html.

28. See, for instance, C. C. Fair, "Militant Recruitment in Pakistan: Implications for Al Qaeda and Other Organizations," *Studies in Conflict & Terrorism*, vol. 27, 2004, pp. 489–504.

29. P. Bergen and S. Pandey, "The Madrassa Scapegoat," *The Washington Quarterly*, vol. 29, no. 2, Spring 2006, pp. 117–125.

30. O. B. Laden, "Letter to Mullah Muhammed 'Umar from Bin Laden [English translation]," internal Al Qaeda document, Harmony Project document #AFGP 2002-600321, Combating Terrorism Center at West Point, n.d., https://

www.ctc.usma.edu/posts/letter-to-mullah-muhammed-umar-from-bin-laden-english-translation-2.

31. M. Sageman, *Leaderless Jihad: Terror Networks in the Twenty-First Century*, Philadelphia, University of Pennsylvania Press, 2008, pp. 66–67.

32. Hegghammer, "The Rise of Muslim Foreign Fighters," p. 53.

33. For an overview of this model, see C. Watts, "Countering Terrorism from the Second Foreign Fighters Glut," *Small Wars Journal*, 2009, http://smallwarsjournal.com/blog/journal/docs-temp/247-watts.pdf?q=mag/docs-temp/247-watts.pdf.

34. T. Hegghammer, "Should I Stay or Should I Go? Explaining Variation in Western Jihadists' Choice between Domestic and Foreign Fighting," *American Political Science Review*, vol. 107, no. 1, February 2013, pp. 1–15, 11.

35. Silber and Bhatt, "Radicalization in the West: The Homegrown Threat," p. 44.

36. "The 9/11 Commission Report," p. 164.

37. B. M. Jenkins, "Is Al Qaeda's Internet Strategy Working?" Testimony before the House Committee on Homeland Security Subcommittee on Counterterrorism and Intelligence, December 6, 2011, pp. 1–3, http://homeland.house.gov/sites/homeland.house.gov/files/Testimony%20Jenkins%20.pdf.

38. Fourth Report of the United Nations 1267 Monitoring Team, March 2006, http://www.un.org/ga/search/view_doc.asp?symbol=S/2006/154.

39. Sageman, *Leaderless Jihad*, p. 121.

40. R. Katz and J. Devon, "Jihad on YouTube," SITE Intelligence Group, January 15, 2014, https://news.siteintelgroup.com/Featured-Article/jihad-on-youtube.html.

41. B. M. Jenkins, "Is Al Qaeda's Internet Strategy Working?"

42. M. Jacobson, "Terrorist Financing and the Internet," *Studies in Conflict & Terrorism*, vol. 33, 2010, pp. 353–363, 357.

43. Sageman, *Leaderless Jihad*, p. 114.

44. Bergen, *The Longest War*, pp. 212–213.

45. Jacobson, "Terrorist Financing and the Internet," p. 358.

46. J. Burns, "Where Bin Laden Has Roots, His Mystique Grows," *New York Times*, December 31, 2000, http://www.nytimes.com/2000/12/31/world/where-bin-laden-has-roots-his-mystique-grows.html.

47. "The 9/11 Commission Report," p. 170.

48. "The 9/11 Commission Report," p. 171.

49. S. E. Eckert, "Statement for the Record—Terrorist Financing since 9/11: Assessing an Evolving Al-Qa'ida and State Sponsors of Terrorism," House Committee on Homeland Security Subcommittee on Counterterrorism and Intelligence, May 18, 2012, pp. 1–9.

50. J. Roth et al., "Al Qaeda's Means and Methods to Raise, Move, and Use Money," in *National Commission on Terrorist Attacks upon the United States: Monograph on Terrorist Financing*, 2003, pp. 120–122, http://govinfo.library.unt.edu/911/staff_statements/911_TerrFin_Ch2.pdf; "The Consolidated List established and maintained by the 1267 Committee with respect to Al-Qaida, Usama bin Laden, and the Taliban and other individuals, groups, undertakings and entities associated with them," United Nations, January 25, 2010, http://www.un.org/sc/committees/1267/aq_sanctions_list.shtml.

51. S. Bell, *Cold Terror: How Canada Nurtures and Exports Terrorism Around the World*, Etobicoke, ON, Wiley Press, 2004, p. 141.

52. Z. Abuza, "Funding Terrorism in Southeast Asia: The Financial Network of Al-Qa'ida and Jemaah Islamiya," *Contemporary Southeast Asia: A Journal of International & Strategic Affairs*, vol. 25, no. 2, 2003, pp. 169–199.
53. Roth et al., *Monograph on Terrorist Financing*, p. 8.
54. "The 9/11 Commission Report," p. 171.
55. R. Callimachi, "Paying Ransoms, Europe Bankrolls Qaeda Terror," *New York Times*, July 29, 2014, http://www.nytimes/com/2014/07/30/world/africa/ransoming-citizens-europe-becomes-al-qaedas-patron.html?_r=1.
56. I. Katz and J. Walcott, "Al-Qaeda Members Gripe over Cash Crunch as U.S. Goes after Terror Funding," *Bloomberg*, January 9, 2012, http://www.bloomberg.com/news/2012-01-09/al-qaeda-members-gripe-over-cash-crunch-as-u-s-goes-after-terror-funding.html.
57. "Al Qa'ida's Structure and Bylaws [English translation]"; "Abu Hafs Report on Operations in Somalia [English translation]," internal Al Qaeda document, Harmony Project document #AFGP-2002-800597, Combating Terrorism Center at West Point, n.d., https://www.ctc.usma.edu/posts/abu-hafs-report-on-operations-in-somalia-english-translation-2.
58. "The 9/11 Commission Report," p. 62.
59. Katz and Walcott, "Al-Qaeda Members Gripe over Cash Crunch."
60. Rotella, "Al Qaeda Recruits Back in Europe, But Why?"

CHAPTER 6

1. "The 9/11 Commission Report," p. 66.
2. Al-Zawahiri, "Zawahiri's letter to Zarqawi [English translation]."
3. R. Leung, "Bin Laden Expert Steps Forward," *CBS News*, February 11, 2009, http://www.cbsnews.com/8301-18560_162-655407.htm.
4. N. Lahoud, "Metamorphosis," p. 10.
5. S. McChrystal, *My Share of the Task: A Memoir*, New York, Penguin, 2013, p. 107.
6. B. Fishman, *Dysfunction and Decline: Lessons Learned from Inside al-Qa'ida in Iraq*, Combating Terrorism Center at West Point, 2009, p. 2, http://www.dtic.mil/dtic/tr/fulltext/u2/a502816.pdf.
7. C. Lister, "Profiling the Islamic State," The Brookings Institution, December 1, 2014, http://www.brookings.edu/research/reports2/2014/12/profiling-islamic-state-lister.
8. M. Levitt, "Declaring an Islamic State, Running a Criminal Enterprise," *The Hill*, July 7, 2014, http://thehill.com/blogs/pundits-blog/211298-declaring-an-islamic-state-running-a-criminal-enterprise.
9. Lister, "Profiling the Islamic State."
10. Lister, "Profiling the Islamic State."
11. McChrystal, *My Share of the Task*, p. 121.
12. As quoted in Burke, *The 9/11 Wars*, p. 252.
13. As quoted in O. Ashour, "Post-Jihadism: Libya and the Global Transformations of Armed Islamist Movements," *Terrorism and Political Violence*, vol. 23, no. 3, 2011, p. 379.
14. M. Chulov, "Isis: the inside story," *The Guardian*, December 11, 2014, http://www.theguardian.com/world/2014/dec/11/-sp-isis-the-inside-story.
15. "US Says 80% of al-Qaeda leaders in Iraq removed," *BBC News*, June 8, 2010, http://www.bbc.co.uk/news/10243585.

16. "CIA Director Michael Hayden Says Al Qaeda Is on 'Verge' of Defeat in Iraq," *Fox News*, May 30, 2008, http://www.foxnews.com/story/2008/05/30/cia-director-michael-hayden-says-al-qaeda-is-on-verge-defeat-in-iraq/; Bergen and Cruickshank, "The Unraveling."

17. J. D. Clapper, "Unclassified Statement for the Record on the Worldwide Threat Assessment of the US Intelligence Community for the Senate Committee on Armed Services," US Office of the Director of National Intelligence, February 16, 2012, http://www.dni.gov/files/documents/Newsroom/Testimonies/20120216_SASC%20Final%20Unclassified%20-%202012%20ATA%20SFR.pdf.

18. "The 9/11 Commission Report," p. 61.

19. "Al-Zawahiri in Two Recent Messages: 'Iran Stabbed a Knife into the Back of the Islamic Nation;' Urges Hamas to Declare Commitment to Restoring the Caliphate," Middle East Media Research Institute (MEMRI), Special Dispatch No. 1787, December 18, 2007, http://www.memri.org/report/en/0/0/0/0/0/0/2481.htm.

20. As quoted in T. Joscelyn, "Analysis: Al Qaeda's interim emir and Iran," *The Long War Journal*, May 18, 2011, http://www.longwarjournal.org/archives/2011/05/analysis_al_qaedas_i.php.

21. V. Brown, "Abu Ghaith and Al Qaeda's Dissident Faction in Iran," *Jihadica*, March 11, 2013, http://www.jihadica.com/abu-ghaith-and-al-qaidas-dissident-faction-in-iran/.

22. T. Joscelyn, "Treasury Department Identifies another Iran-based Facilitator for Al Qaeda," *The Long War Journal*, February 6, 2014, http://www.longwarjournal.org/archives/2014/02/treasury_department.php.

23. Al-Zawahiri, "Zawahiri's letter to Zarqawi [English translation]."

24. Brown, "Abu Ghaith and Al Qaeda's Dissident Faction in Iran."

25. "Al-Zawahiri: 'Iran Stabbed a Knife into the Back of the Islamic Nation;' Urges Hamas to Declare Co," *LiveLeak*, December 18, 2007, http://www.liveleak.com/view?i=9a5_1198012243.

26. Lahoud et al., *Letters from Abbottabad.*

27. As quoted (derisively) in R. Baer, *Sleeping with the Devil: How Washington Sold Our Soul for Saudi Crude*, New York, Three Rivers Press, 2004, p. 202.

28. L. Beyer, "After 9: SAUDI ARABIA: Inside the Kingdom," *Time*, September 15, 2003, http://content.time.com/time/magazine/article/0,9171,1005663-6,00.html.

29. Hegghammer, *Jihad in Saudi Arabia*, p. 142.

30. "Overview of the Enemy," National Commission on Terrorist Attacks upon the United States, June 16, 2004, p. 10, http://www.9-11commission.gov/archive/hearing12/9-11Commission_Hearing_2004-06-16.htm.

31. Quoted by S. M. Collins in opening statement, "An Assessment of Current Efforts to Combat Terrorism Financing," US Senate Committee on Governmental Affairs, June 15, 2004, http://www.gpo.gov/fdsys/pkg/CHRG-108shrg95189/html/CHRG-108shrg95189.htm.

32. C. C. Fair, "Time for Sober Realism: Renegotiating U.S. Relations with Pakistan," *The Washington Quarterly*, vol. 32, no. 2, April 2009, p. 160.

33. For a review of the nuclear risk, especially as it relates to terrorism, see B. Riedel, *Avoiding Armageddon: America, India, and Pakistan to the Brink and Back*, Washington, DC, Brookings Institution Press, 2013.

34. B. Riedel, "Tensions Rising Dangerously in South Asia," *The Daily Beast*, October 19, 2014, http://www.brookings.edu/research/opinions/2014/10/ 19-tensions-rising-dangerously-south-asia-riedel.

35. A. J. Tellis, *Pakistan and the War on Terror: Conflicted Goals, Compromised Performance*, Washington, DC, Carnegie Endowment for International Peace, 2008, p. 18, http://carnegieendowment.org/files/tellis_pakistan_ final.pdf.

36. C. C. Fair and S. G. Jones, "Pakistan's War Within," *Survival: Global Politics and Strategy*, vol. 51, no. 6, 2009, p. 162.

37. "Afghanistan: Crisis of Impunity: The Role of Pakistan, Russia, and Iran in Fueling the Civil War," *Human Rights Watch*, vol. 13, no. 3, July 2001, http:// www.hrw.org/reports/2001/afghan2/Afghan0701.pdf.

38. S. Shah, "Pakistan Moves to End Policy on 'Good Taliban'," *Wall Street Journal*, December 21, 2014, http://www.wsj.com/articles/pakistan-moves-to-end-policy-on-good-taliban-1419013453.

39. J. Kaleem, "Religious Minorities in Islamic Pakistan Struggle But Survive Amid Increasing Persecution," *Huffington Post*, February 10, 2014, http://www.huff-ingtonpost.com/2014/02/10/religious-minorities-pakistan_n_4734016.html.

40. Fair and Jones, "Pakistan's War Within," pp. 174, 177.

41. D. Walsh, "Pakistan army officer held over suspected Hizb ut-Tahrir links," *The Guardian*, June 21, 2011, http://www.theguardian.com/world/2011/ jun/21/pakistan-army-officer-hizb-ut-tahrir; K. Brulliard, "Pakistani military worried about collaborators," *Washington Post*, May 27, 2011, http:// www.washingtonpost.com/world/pakistani-military-worried-about-collaborators-in-its-ranks-officials-say-2011/05/27/AGgN1oCH_story. html?hpid=z1; S. Rotella, "Terror Group Recruits From Pakistan's 'Best and Brightest'," *ProPublica*, April 4, 2013, http://www.propublica.org/article/ terror-group-recruits-from-pakistans-best-and-brightest.

42. Riedel, "Tensions Rising in South Asia."

43. Y. Trofimov, "In Its Own War on Terror, Pakistan Piles Up Heavy Losses," *Wall Street Journal*, March 10, 2014, http://online.wsj.com/news/articles/SB1 0001424052702304691904579348820227129270; M. Raja, "Pakistani Victims: War on Terror Total Put at 49,000," *The Express Tribune* with the *International New York Times*, March 27, 2013, http://tribune.com.pk/story/527016/ pakistani-victims-war-on-terror-toll-put-at-49000/.

44. Bergen, *Holy War, Inc.*, p. 66.

45. "The 9/11 Commission Report," p. 64.

46. C. C. Fair, "Militant Recruitment in Pakistan: Implications for Al Qaeda and Other Organizations," *Studies in Conflict & Terrorism*, vol. 27, 2004, p. 489.

47. Z. Hussain, *Frontline Pakistan: The Struggle with Militant Islam*, New York, Columbia University Press, 2007, p. 122.

48. Hoffman and Reinares, "Conclusion," p. 618.

49. C. Gall, "What Pakistan Knew about Bin Laden," *New York Times*, March 19, 2014, http://www.nytimes.com/2014/03/23/magazine/what-pakistan-knew-about-bin-laden.html?_r=0.

50. Fair, "Time for Sober Realism," p. 154.

51. Figures from "Direct Overt U.S. Aid Appropriations for and Military Reimbursements to Pakistan, FY 2002–FY 2015," *Congressional Research Service*, http://www.fas.org/sgp/crs/row/pakaid.pdf.

52. G. Miller, "CIA Pays for Support in Pakistan," *Los Angeles Times,* November 15, 2009, http://articles.latimes.com/2009/nov/15/world/fg-cia-pakistan15.
53. Fair, "Time for Sober Realism," p. 149.
54. "Interview: Osama Bin Laden."
55. Al-Zawahiri, *Knights Under the Prophet's Banner.*
56. G. Kahn, "Al Qaeda Says No Recognition for 'Alleged' Israel," *Israel National News,* June 16, 2011, http://www.israelnationalnews.com/News/News. aspx/144994#.U6MeYPldUeA; "Interview: Osama Bin Laden."
57. Al-Zawahiri, *Knights Under the Prophet's Banner.*
58. "Evidence Links al-Qaeda to Kenya Attacks," *ABC News,* December 3, 2002, http://abcnews.go.com/GMA/story?id=125556.
59. "Osama bin Laden Largely Discredited Among Muslim Publics in Recent Years," Pew Research Global Attitudes Project, May 2, 2011, http://www.pewglobal.org/2011/05/02/osama-bin-laden-largely-discredited-among-muslim-publics-in-recent-years/; I. Tharoor, "Study: Muslims Hate Terrorism Too," *Washington Post,* July 1, 2014, http://www.washingtonpost.com/blogs/worldviews/wp/2014/07/01/study-muslims-hate-terrorism-too/.
60. Gerges, *The Rise and Fall of Al-Qaeda,* p. 113 (see pp. 113–117 for an in-depth look).
61. "Osama bin Laden Largely Discredited Among Muslim Publics in Recent Years."
62. For example, see M. Burns, "Fox Isn't Paying Attention: Muslims Across The World Have Condemned Kenya Attack," *Media Matters,* September 24, 2013, http://mediamatters.org/research/2013/09/24/fox-isnt-paying-attention-muslims-across-the-wo/196058.
63. For a valuable list, see the collection by Charles Kurzman at http://kurzman.unc.edu/bio-contact/.
64. "Osama bin Laden Largely Discredited Among Muslim Publics in Recent Years"; I. Tharoor, "Study: Muslims Hate Terrorism Too."
65. "Muslims Poll," ICM Research, February 2006, http://www.icmresearch.com/pdfs/2006_february_sunday_telegraph_muslims_poll.pdf.
66. A. Al-Zawahiri, "Advice to Reject the Fatwa of Bin Baz," reprinted in G. Kepel and J. P. Milelli, eds., *Al Qaeda in Its Own Words,* Cambridge, MA, Belknap Press, 2008, p. 184.
67. M. Fick, "Insight: Ex-Qaeda allies ready to fight for Mursi in Luxor," *Reuters,* June 23, 2013, http://in.reuters.com/article/2013/06/23/egypt-protests-gamaa-idINDEE95M04U20130623.

CHAPTER 7

1. B. Obama, "Speech at the National Defense University," *Washington Post,* May 23, 2013, http://articles.washingtonpost.com/2013-05-23/politics/39467399_1_war-and-peace-cold-war-civil-war.
2. US Department of State, "Annex of Statistical Information," *Country Reports on Terrorism 2013,* April 2014, p. 8, "Table 3: Ten perpetrator groups with the most attacks worldwide, 2013," http://www.state.gov/documents/organization/225043.pdf.
3. T. Hegghammer, "Terrorist Recruitment and Radicalization in Saudi Arabia," *Middle East Policy,* vol. XIII, no. 4, Winter 2006, pp. 41–46.

4. Lahoud et al., *Letters from Abbottabad*, p. 29.
5. "Al-Qaeda 'issues France threat'," *BBC News*, September 14, 2006, http://news.bbc.co.uk/2/hi/europe/5345202.stm.
6. L. Panetta and M. Dempsey, "Press Briefing by Secretary Panetta and General Dempsey from the Pentagon," US Department of Defense, January 24, 2013, http://www.defense.gov/transcripts/transcript.aspx?transcriptid=5183.
7. See N. Lahoud, "The Merger of Al-Shabab and Qa'idat-al-Jihad," *CTC Sentinel*, February 16, 2012, http://www.ctc.usma.edu/posts/the-merger-of-al-shabab-and-qaidat-al-jihad.
8. C. Watts et al., *Al Qaeda's (Mis)Adventures in the Horn of Africa*, Combating Terrorism Center at West Point, July 2, 2007, pp. 14–43.
9. Shinn, "Al Shabaab's Foreign Threat to Somalia"; A. Kahan, "Al Shabaab's Rise in the Al Qaeda Network," *Critical Threats*, American Enterprise Institute, August 9, 2011, http://www.criticalthreats.org/somalia/kahan-shabaab-rise-qaeda-network-august-9-2011; "Al-Shabaab joining al Qaeda, monitor group says," *CNN*, February 10, 2012, http://articles.cnn.com/2012-02-09/africa/world_africa_somalia-shabaab-qaeda_1_al-zawahiri-qaeda-somali-americans?_s=PM:AFRICA.
10. "Al Qaeda in Yemen and Somalia: A Ticking Time Bomb," Report to the United States Senate Committee on Foreign Relations, January 21, 2010, p. 15, http://www.foreign.senate.gov/imo/media/doc/Yemen.pdf.
11. Shinn, "Al Shabaab's Foreign Threat to Somalia."
12. N. Benotman and R. Blake, "Jabhat al-Nusra: A Strategic Briefing," *Quilliam Foundation*, January 8, 2013, p. 2.
13. B. M. Jenkins, "Brothers Killing Brothers: The Current Infighting Will Test al Qaeda's Brand," *Perspective*, RAND Corporation, 2014, p. 3, http://www.rand.org/content/dam/rand/pubs/perspectives/PE100/PE123/RAND_PE123.pdf.
14. "Letter to Azmarai [English translation]," internal Al Qaeda correspondence, Harmony Project document #SOCOM-2012-0000006, Combating Terrorism Center at West Point, n.d., https://www.ctc.usma.edu/posts/letter-to-azmarai-english-translation-2. An easier to read copy is available at *National Journal*, http://assets.nationaljournal.com/pdf/OBL4.pdf.
15. F. Gerges, *The Far Enemy: Why Jihad Went Global* (New York: Cambridge University Press, 2005), p. 58; Hegghammer, *Jihad in Saudi Arabia*.
16. J. P. Filiu, "Al-Qaeda in the Islamic Maghreb: Algerian Challenge or Global Threat?" *Carnegie Papers*, vol. 104, October 2009, p. 14.
17. N. Robertson and P. Cruickshank, "Al Qaeda's Training Adapts to Drone Attacks," *CNN*, July 31, 2009, http://www.cnn.com/2009/CRIME/07/30/robertson.al.qaeda.training/index.html?iref=topnews.
18. C. Harnisch, "The Terror Threat from Somalia: The Internationalization of Al Shabaab," *Critical Threats*, American Enterprise Institute, February 12 2010, p. 29, http://www.criticalthreats.org/sites/default/files%20/pdf_upload/analysis/CTP_Terror_Threat_From_Somalia%20_Shabaab_Internationalization.pdf.
19. A. Moghadam, *The Globalization of Martyrdom*, Baltimore, MD, Johns Hopkins University Press, 2011.

20. K. Menkhaus, quoted in T. Helfont, "The Foreign Fighters Problem: Recent Trends and Case Studies," in M. P. Noonan, ed., *The Foreign Fighter Problem, Recent Trends and Case Studies: Selected Essays*, p. 5.
21. Lahoud et. al, *Letters from Abbottabad*, pp. 33–35.
22. T. Hegghammer, "The Failure of Jihad in Saudi Arabia," Combating Terrorism Center at West Point Occasional Paper, February 25, 2010, pp. 22–25.
23. Lahoud et al., *Letters from Abbottabad*, p. 12.
24. Burke, *The 9/11 Wars*, p. 417.
25. J. P. Filiu, "Al-Qaeda in the Islamic Maghreb: Algerian Challenge or Global Threat?" p. 14.
26. L. K. Boudali, "The GSPC: Newest Franchise in Al Qa'ida's Global Jihad," Combating Terrorism Center at West Point, April 2007, p. 1, http://www.dtic.mil/dtic/tr/fulltext/u2/a466539.pdf.
27. As quoted in Lahoud et al., *Letters from Abbottabad*, p. 13.
28. As quoted in Burke, *The 9/11 Wars*, p. 156. For a broader look at al-Suri, see Lia, *Architect of Global Jihad*.
29. Rotella, "Al Qaeda Recruits Back in Europe, but Why?"
30. C. Whitlock, "Al-Qaeda's Far Reaching New Partner," *Washington Post*, October 5, 2006, p. A1, http://www.washingtonpost.com/wp-dyn/content/article/2006/10/04/AR2006100402006.html.
31. "The 9/11 Commission Report," p. 67.
32. P. Bergen and B. Hoffman, "Assessing the Terrorist Threat: A Report of the Bipartisan Policy Center's National Security Preparedness Group," Bipartisan Policy Center, September 10, 2010, http://bipartisanpolicy.org/library/report/assessing-terrorist-threat.
33. D. Milbank, "With al-Qaeda, What's in a Name?" *Washington Post*, January 14, 2014, http://www.washingtonpost.com/opinions/dana-milbank-with-al-qaeda-whats-in-a-name/2014/01/14/15dfa354-7d5b-11e3-93c1-0e8881 70b723_story.html. For a superb explanation of the complexity of the Benghazi attack, see D. Kirkpatrick, "A Deadly Mix in Benghazi," *New York Times*, December 13, 2013, http://www.nytimes.com/projects/2013/benghazi/#/?chapt=0.
34. S. Kull et al., "Public Opinion in the Islamic World on Terrorism, al Qaeda, and US Policies," WorldPublicOpinion.org, February 25, 2009, http://www.worldpublicopinion.org/pipa/pdf/feb09/STARTII_Feb09_rpt.pdf.

CHAPTER 8

1. R. Sherlock, "How a talented footballer became the world's most wanted man, Abu Bakr al-Baghdadi," *The Telegraph*, July 5, 2014, http://www.telegraph.co.uk/news/worldnews/middleeast/iraq/10948846/How-a-talented-footballer-became-worlds-most-wanted-man-Abu-Bakr-al-Baghdadi.html.
2. Chulov, "Isis: the inside story."
3. C. Freeman, "Meet al-Qaeda's new poster boy for the Middle East," *The Telegraph*, January 11, 2014, http://www.telegraph.co.uk/news/worldnews/middleeast/iraq/10566001/Meet-al-Qaedas-new-poster-boy-for-the-Middle-East.html.

4. Al-Zawahiri, "Zawahiri letter to Zarqawi [English translation]."
5. "Report on the Protection of Civilians in Armed Conflict in Iraq: 6 July–10 September 2014," Human Rights Office of the High Commissioner for Human Rights and the United Nations Assistance Mission for Iraq (UNAMI) Human Rights Office, September 10, 2014, p. i, http://www.ohchr.org/Documents/Countries/IQ/UNAMI_OHCHR_POC_Report_FINAL_6July_10September2014.pdf.
6. L. Sly, "Al-Qaeda Disavows Any Ties with Radical Islamist ISIS Group in Syria, Iraq," Washington Post, February 3, 2014, http://www.washingtonpost.com/world/middle_east/al-qaeda-disavows-any-ties-with-radical-islamist-isis-group-in-syria-iraq/2014/02/03/2c9afc3a-8cef-11e3-98ab-fe5228217bd1_story.html.
7. Al-Zawahiri, "Zawahiri letter to Zarqawi [English translation]."
8. A. Y. Zelin, "The War Between ISIS and al-Qaeda for Supremacy of the Global Jihadist Movement," Research Notes, Number 20, The Washington Institute for Near East Policy, June 2014, p. 3, http://www.washingtoninstitute.org/uploads/Documents/pubs/ResearchNote_20_Zelin.pdf.
9. Zelin, "The War Between ISIS and al-Qaeda for Supremacy of the Global Jihadist Movement," p. 4.
10. Lister, "Profiling the Islamic State."
11. J. D. Lewis, "The Islamic State: A Counter-Strategy for a Counter-State," Institute for the Study of War, July 2014, http://www.understandingwar.org/report/islamic-state-counter-strategy-counter-state.
12. As quoted in C. Bunzel, "Islamic State of Disobedience: al-Baghdadi Triumphant," Jihadica, October 5, 2013, http://www.jihadica.com/the-islamic-state-of-disobedience-al-baghdadis-defiance/.
13. See W. McCants, "Black Flag [Slide Show]," Foreign Policy, November 7, 2011, http://www.foreignpolicy.com/articles/2011/11/07/black_flag_al_qaeda.
14. D. Kirkpatrick, "ISIS' Harsh Brand of Islam Is Rooted in Austere Saudi Creed," New York Times, September 24, 2014. http://www.nytimes.com/2014/09/25/world/middleeast/isis-abu-bakr-baghdadi-caliph-wahhabi.html?_r=0; "The other beheaders," Economist, September 20, 2014, http://www.economist.com/news/middle-east-and-africa/21618918-possible-reasons-mysterious-surge-executions-other-beheaders.
15. "Umayyad dynasty," Encyclopaedia Britannica, 2014, http://www.britannica.com/EBchecked/topic/613719/Umayyad-dynasty.
16. W. McCants, interview with the author, April 7, 2014.
17. M. Keneally, "Garland Shooting: Inside the Group Hosting the 'Draw the Prophet' Event," ABC News, May 4, 2015, http://abcnews.go.com/US/garland-shooting-inside-group-hosting-draw-prophet-event/story?id=30779738; H. Yan, "ISIS claims responsibility for Texas shooting but offers no proof," CNN, May 5, 2015, http://www.cnn.com/2015/05/05/us/garland-texas-prophet-mohammed-contest-shooting/.
18. N. Lahoud et al., The Group That Calls Itself a State, p. 4.
19. "Islamic State fighter estimate triples—CIA," BBC News, September 12, 2014, http://www.bbc.com/news/world-middle-east-29169914.
20. N. Rasmussen, "Countering Violent Extremism: The Urgent Threat of Foreign Fighters and Homegrown Terror," prepared statement before the

House Committee on Homeland Security, February 11, 2015, p. 1, http://docs.house.gov/meetings/HM/HM00/20150211/102901/HHRG-114-HM00-Wstate-RasmussenN-20150211.pdf.

21. N. A. Youssef, "Is ISIS Building A Drone Army," *The Daily Beast*, March 18, 2015, http://www.thedailybeast.com/articles/2015/03/18/is-isis-building-a-drone-army.html.

22. E. Dickinson, "Playing with Fire: Why Private Gulf Financing for Syria's Extremist Rebels Risks Igniting Sectarian Conflict at Home," The Brookings Project on U.S. Relations with the Islamic World, Analysis Paper Number 16, The Saban Center at Brookings, December 2013, http://www.brookings.edu/~/media/research/files/papers/2013/12/06%20private%20gulf%20financing%20syria%20extremist%20rebels%20sectarian%20conflict%20dickinson/private%20gulf%20financing%20syria%20extremist%20rebels%20sectarian%20conflict%20dickinson.pdf.

23. L. Al-Khateeb, "The UN Strikes Back at ISIL's Black Economy," *Huffington Post*, August 23, 2014, http://www.huffingtonpost.com/luay-al-khatteeb/the-un-strikes-back-at-isil_b_5702240.html.

24. R. Noack, "Here's How the Islamic State Compares with Real States," *Washington Post*, September 12, 2014, http://www.washingtonpost.com/blogs/worldviews/wp/2014/09/12/heres-how-the-islamic-state-compares-to-real-states/.

25. N. Thompson and S. Attika, "The Anatomy of ISIS," *CNN*, September 18, 2014, http://www.cnn.com/2014/09/18/world/meast/isis-syria-iraq-hierarchy/.

26. H. Al-Hashimi and Telegraph Interactive Team, "Revealed: the Islamic State 'cabinet', from finance minister to suicide bomb deployer," *The Telegraph*, July 9, 2014, http://www.telegraph.co.uk/news/worldnews/middleeast/iraq/10956193/Revealed-the-Islamic-State-cabinet-from-finance-minister-to-suicide-bomb-deployer.html.

27. C. Lister, "Profiling the Islamic State."

28. C. Lister, "Profiling the Islamic State."

29. A. Zelin, "The Islamic State of Iraq and Syria Has a Consumer Protection Office," *The Atlantic*, June 13, 2014, http://www.theatlantic.com/international/archive/2014/06/the-isis-guide-to-building-an-islamic-state/372769/.

30. D. Milton, "The Islamic State: An Adaptive Organization Facing Increasing Challenges," in Lahoud et al., *The Group That Calls Itself a State*, p. 75.

31. "UN: ISIS wants to build 'house of blood,'" *Al Arabiya*, September 8, 2014, http://english.alarabiya.net/en/News/middle-east/2014/09/08/U-N-ISIS-wants-to-build-house-of-blood-.html.

32. L. Markoe, "Muslim Scholars Release Open Letter to Islamic State Meticulously Blasting Its Ideology," *Huffington Post*, September 24, 2014, http://www.huffingtonpost.com/2014/09/24/muslim-scholars-islamic-state_n_5878038.html.

33. D. Balz and P. M. Craighill, "Poll: Public supports strikes in Iraq, Syria; Obama's ratings hover near his all-time lows," *Washington Post*, September 9, 2014, http://www.washingtonpost.com/politics/poll-public-supports-strikes-in-iraq-syria-obamas-ratings-hover-near-his-all-time-lows/2014/09/08/69c164d8-3789-11e4-8601-97ba88884ffd_story.html?hpid=z1; M. Murray, "Poll: Americans feel unsafe, support action against ISIS," *MSNBC*, September 9, 2014, http://www.msnbc.com/msnbc/poll-americans-support-action-against-isis.

34. Al-Zawahiri, "Zawahiri letter to Zarqawi [English translation]."
35. M. Abi-Habib, "Assad Policies Aided Rise of Islamic State Militant Group," *Wall Street Journal*, August 22, 2014, http://online.wsj.com/articles/assad-policies-aided-rise-of-islamic-state-militant-group-1408739733#.
36. Not to be confused with "ISIL in Khorasan," which is a "formal province" of the Islamic State (that is, they have pledged allegiance to Abu Bakr al-Baghdadi and their pledge has been formally accepted by the Islamic State) in the Afghanistan-Pakistan region that includes former members of Tehrik-e Taliban Pakistan (TTP) and the Afghan Taliban.
37. A. Taylor, "The Strange Story behind the Khorasan Group's Name," *Washington Post*, September 25, 2014, http://www.washingtonpost.com/blogs/worldviews/wp/2014/09/25/the-strange-story-behind-the-khorasan-groups-name/.
38. A. Taylor, "The Strange Story behind the Khorasan Group's Name."
39. R. Katz, "The 'Khurasan Group': A Misleading Name in the Politics of War," *INSITE Blog on Terrorism & Extremism*, SITE Intelligence Group, n.d., accessed on October 26, 2014, http://news.siteintelgroup.com/blog/index.php/about-us/21-jihad/4432-the-khurasan-group-a-misleading-name-in-the-politics-of-war.
40. M. Levitt, "The Khorasan Group Should Scare Us," *Politico*, September 25, 2014, http://www.politico.com/magazine/story/2014/09/why-the-khorasan-group-should-scare-us-111307.html#.VC610CldVZE.
41. "What is the Khorasan Group?" *BBC News*, September 24, 2014, http://www.bbc.com/news/world-middle-east-29350271.
42. M. Mazzetti et al., "Struggle to Gauge ISIS Threat, Even as U.S. Prepares to Act," *New York Times*, September 10, 2014, http://www.nytimes.com/2014/09/11/world/middleeast/struggling-to-gauge-isis-threat-even-as-us-prepares-to-act.html.
43. Quoted in C. Johnson, "FBI Director: Radicalization of Westerners in Syria Is of Great Concern," *The Two-Way*, NPR, May 2, 2014, http://www.npr.org/blogs/thetwo-way/2014/05/02/309045229/fbi-director-radicalization-of-westerners-in-syria-is-of-great-concern.
44. P. Steinhauser and J. Helton, "CNN Poll: Public Against Syria Strike Resolution," *CNN*, September 9, 2013, http://www.cnn.com/2013/09/09/politics/syria-poll-main/; A. Dugan, "U.S. Support for Action in Syria Is Low vs. Past Conflicts," Gallup, September 6, 2013, http://www.gallup.com/poll/164282/support-syria-action-lower-past-conflicts.aspx.
45. D. Pletka, "Think Again: The Republican Party," *Foreign Policy*, January 2, 2013, http://www.foreignpolicy.com/articles/2013/01/02/think_again_the_republican_party?wp_login_redirect=0; "Fox News Exit Poll Summary: Obama's Key Groups Made the Difference," *Fox News*, November 7, 2012, http://www.foxnews.com/politics/2012/11/07/fox-news-exit-poll-summary/.
46. J. Stewart, "Whose Line Is It Anyway?" *The Daily Show*, April 30, 2013, http://thedailyshow.cc.com/videos/8py17l/whose-line-is-it-anyway-.
47. E. Swanson, "Syria Poll Finds Low Approval for Barack Obama, John Kerry," *Huffington Post*, September 20, 2013, http://www.huffingtonpost.com/2013/09/20/syria-poll-obama_n_3957259.html.
48. B. Obama, "Statement by the President," Office of the Press Secretary, The White House, August 7, 2014, http://www.whitehouse.gov/the-press-office/2014/08/07/statement-president.

49. B. Obama, "Statement by the President on ISIL," Office of the Press Secretary, The White House, September 10, 2014, http://www.whitehouse.gov/the-press-office/2014/09/10/statement-president-isil-1.
50. Obama, "Statement by the President on ISIL."

CHAPTER 9

1. P. Pillar, *Terrorism and U.S. Foreign Policy*, Washington, DC, Brookings Institution Press, 2003, p. 73.
2. J. F. Harris et al., "Cheney Warns of New Attacks," *Politico*, February 4, 2009, http://www.politico.com/news/stories/0209/18390.html.
3. "Trying Terrorist Suspects in Federal Court," Human Rights First, June 18, 2014, http://www.humanrightsfirst.org/resource/trying-terrorist-suspects-federal-court.
4. Pillar, *Terrorism and U.S. Foreign Policy*, pp. 84–85.
5. "Abu Hamza legal fight - timeline," *The Guardian*, September 24, 2012, http://www.theguardian.com/world/2012/sep/24/abu-hamza-timeline.
6. O. Bowcott and V. Dodd, "Human rights court blocks extradition of UK-based terror suspect to US," *The Guardian*, April 16, 2013, http://www.theguardian.com/law/2013/apr/16/human-rights-extradition-terror-suspect.
7. B. Stokes, "Which countries don't like America and which do?" *Fact Tank*, Pew Research Center, July 15, 2014, /http://www.pewresearch.org/fact-tank/2014/07/15/which-countries-don't-like-america-and-which-do.
8. "President Issues Military Order," Office of the Press Secretary, The White House, November 13, 2001, http://georgewbush-whitehouse.archives.gov/news/releases/2001/11/20011113-27.html.
9. G. Urza, "Why Khalid Sheikh Mohammed's Lawyer Is Leaving the Defense Team—and the Army," *Slate*, August 26, 2014, http://www.slate.com/articles/news_and_politics/jurisprudence/2014/08/khalid_sheikh_mohammed_s_guantanamo_defense_lawyer_jason_wright_is_departing.html.
10. D. Bennett, "Civilian Courts Are Way Better Than Military Courts at Convicting Terrorists," *The Wire*, April 23, 2013, http://www.thewire/com/politics/2013/04/civilians-courts-vs-military-courts-terrorism/64489/.
11. "Q&A: Guantanamo detentions," *BBC News*, April 30, 2013, http://www.bbc.com/news/world-us-canada-12966676.
12. G. Tenet, testimony before the National Commission on Terrorist Attacks upon the United States, March 24, 2004, http://www.9-11commission.gov/archive/hearing8/9-11Commission_Hearing_2004-03-24.htm; "U.S. Rendition Practice since 9/11," Human Rights Watch, n.d., http://www.hrw.org/legacy/backgrounder/eca/canada/arar/3.htm.
13. "Extraordinary Rendition in U.S. Counterterrorism Policy: The Impact on Transatlantic Relations," Joint Hearing before the Subcommittee on International Organizations, Human Rights, and Oversight and the Subcommittee on Europe of the Committee on Foreign Affairs, US House of Representatives, US Government Printing Office, Washington, DC, April 17, 2007, http://www.fas.org/irp/congress/2007_hr/rendition.pdf.
14. *U.S. v. Yousef, et al.*, United States Court of Appeals for the Second Circuit, August Term, 2001, argued May 3, 2002, decided April 4, 2003, Docket Nos. 98-1041 L, 98-1197, 98-1355, 99-1544, 99-1554, pp. 15–16, available at

FindLaw,   http://fl1.findlaw.com/news.findlaw.com/cnn/docs/terrorism/usyousef40403opn.pdf.

15. S. Grey, "Five Facts and Five Fictions about CIA Rendition," *PBS Frontline,* November 4, 2007, http://www.pbs.org/frontlineworld/stories/rendition701/updates/updates.html.

16. M. Scheuer, testimony in "Extraordinary Rendition in U.S. Counterterrorism Policy: The Impact on Transatlantic Relations."

17. "Globalizing Torture: CIA Secret Detention and Extraordinary Rendition," Open Society Justice Initiative, Open Society Foundations, February 2013, http://www.opensocietyfoundations.org/reports/globalizing-torture-cia-secret-detention-and-extraordinary-rendition.

18. A. Davidson, "Torturing the Wrong Man," *The New Yorker,* December 13, 2012, http://www.newyorker.com/news/amy-davidson/torturing-the-wrong-man.

19. For a review, see J. Zarate, *Treasury's War: The Unleashing of a New Era of Financial Warfare,* New York, Public Affairs, 2013.

20. Full text of the resolution available at http://www.un.org/en/sc/ctc/specialmeetings/2012/docs/United%20Nations%20Security%20Council%20Resolution%201373%20(2001).pdf.

21. Zarate, *Treasury's War,* p. 48.

22. "Economic and Social Consequences of Drug Abuse and Illicit Trafficking," United Nations Office on Drugs and Crime (UNODC), Technical Series Number 6, January 1, 1998, p. 3, https://www.unodc.org/pdf/technical_series_1998-01-01_1.pdf.

23. Zarate, *Treasury's War,* p. 43.

24. A. Belasco, "Troop Levels in the Afghan and Iraq Wars, FY2001–FY2012: Cost and Other Potential Issues," *Congressional Research Service,* p. 54, http://fas.org/sgp/crs/natsec/R40682.pdf.

25. E. Schmitt and M. Mazzetti, "Secret Order Lets U.S. Raid Al Qaeda," *New York Times,* November 9, 2008, http://www.nytimes.com/2008/11/10/washington/10military.html?pagewanted=all.

26. J. Masters, "Targeted Killings," *CFR Backgrounders,* Council on Foreign Relations, May 23, 2013, http://www.cfr.org/counterterrorism/targeted-killings/p9627.

27. "Drone Wars Pakistan: Analysis," International Security Data Site, New America Foundation, accessed on September 9, 2014, http://securitydata.newamerica.net/drones/pakistan/analysis.

28. "Drone Wars Pakistan: Analysis."

29. O. B. Laden, "Letter from UBL to 'Atiyatullah Al-Libi 3 [English translation]," internal Al Qaeda correspondence between Osama bin Laden and Abu Abd al- Rahman Atiyyat Allah (a/k/a "Atiyya"), Harmony Project document # SOCOM-2012-0000015, Combating Terrorism Center at West Point, October 21, 2010 (date on original letter), p. 3, https://www.ctc.usma.edu/posts/letter-from-ubl-to-atiyatullah-al-libi-3-english-translation-2. An easier to read copy is available at *National Journal,* http://assets.nationaljournal.com/pdf/OBL13.pdf. On the death of Atiyya in a drone strike, see W. McCants, "Al Qaeda After Atiyya," Foreign Affairs Report: After Bin Laden, *Foreign Affairs,* August 30, 2011, http://www.foreignaffairs.com/articles/68236/william-mccants/al-qaeda-after-atiyya.

30. Incidents and fatalities can be accessed at the START database at http://www.start.umd.edu/gtd/search/Results.aspx?chart=overtime&casualties_type=&casualties_max=&perpetrator=20029.
31. B. C. Price, "Targeting Top Terrorists: How Leadership Decapitation Contributes to Counterterrorism," *International Security*, vol. 36, no. 4, Spring 2012, pp. 9–46.
32. "The Al Qaida Papers-Drones," internal Al Qaeda documents, n.d., provided by the Associated Press, http://hosted.ap.org/specials/interactives/_international/_pdfs/al-qaida-papers-drones.pdf.
33. Pillar, *Terrorism and U.S. Foreign Policy*, p. 103.
34. S. Shane, "C.I.A. Claim of No Civilian Deaths from Drones is Disputed," *New York Times*, August 11, 2011, http://www.nytimes.com/2011/08/12/world/asia/12drones.html?pagewanted=all&_r=0.
35. "Get the Data: Drone Wars," The Bureau of Investigative Journalism, accessed January 7, 2015, http://www.thebureauinvestigates.com/category/projects/drones/drones-graphs/.
36. E. Voeten, "The Problems with Studying Civilian Casualties from Drone Usage in Pakistan: What We Can't Know," *The Monkey Cage*, August 17, 2011, http://themonkeycage.org/2011/08/17/the-problems-with-studying-civilian-casualties-from-drone-usage-in-pakistan-what-we-can%E2%80%99t-know/.
37. P. Z. Shah, "My Drone War," *Foreign Policy*, February 27, 2012, http://www.foreignpolicy.com/articles/2012/02/27/my_drone_war.
38. Shah, "My Drone War."
39. C. C. Fair et al., "Pakistani Opposition to American Drone Strikes," *Political Science Quarterly*, vol. 129, no. 1, 2014, pp. 3–4, http://onlinelibrary.wiley.com/doi/10.1002/polq.12145/pdf.
40. A. K. Cronin, "Why Drones Fail: When Tactics Drive Strategy," *Foreign Affairs*, July/August 2013.
41. Quoted in M. Mazzetti and S. Shane, "As New Drone Policy Is Weighed, Few Practical Effects Are Seen," *New York Times*, March 21, 2013, http://www.nytimes.com/2013/03/22/us/influential-ex-aide-to-obama-voices-concern-on-drone-strikes.html?ref=us&_r=1&.
42. P. D. Shinkman, "Blowback Likely from Latest U.S. High Profile Drone Strike," *U.S. News & World Report*, November 1, 2013, http://www.usnews.com/news/articles/2013/11/01/blowback-likely-from-latest-us-high-profile-drone-strike.
43. C. Friedersdorf, "The Wedding That a U.S. Drone Strike Turned into a Funeral," *The Atlantic*, January 9, 2014, http://www.theatlantic.com/international/archive/2014/01/the-wedding-that-a-us-drone-strike-turned-into-a-funeral/282936/.
44. J. Carter, "A Cruel and Unusual Record," *New York Times*, June 24, 2012, http://www.nytimes.com/2012/06/25/opinion/americas-shameful-human-rights-record.html.
45. "Muslim-Western Tensions Persist," Pew Research Global Attitudes Project, July 21, 2011, http://www.pewglobal.org/2011/07/21/muslim-western-tensions-persist/.
46. D. Soni, "Survey: 'government hasn't told truth about 7/7'," *Channel 4 News*, June 4, 2007, http://www.channel4.com/news/articles/society/

religion/survey+government+hasnt+told+truth+about+77/545847.html;
R. Tait, "Mahmoud Ahmadinejad accuses the West of destroying Iran's rain
clouds," *The Telegraph*, September 10, 2012, http://www.telegraph.co.uk/
news/worldnews/middleeast/iran/9533842/Mahmoud-Ahmadinejad-
accuses-the-West-of-destroying-Irans-rain-clouds.html.

47. K. Dozier, "Total U.S. intelligence bill tops $80 billion," *Seattle Times*, October
28, 2010, http://seattletimes.com/html/politics/2013281602_apusintelli-
gencebudget.html; see also D. Priest and W. Arkin, *Top Secret America: The
Rise of the New American Security State*, New York, Hachette Book Group, 2011.

48. In the Bible (Joshua 2: 1–2), Joshua sent two spies to Jericho. They stayed with
a prostitute, who practiced the oldest profession.

49. A. Goldman and M. Apuzzo, "CIA Turned Some Guantanamo Bay Prisoners
into Double Agents Against al-Qaeda," *Washington Post*, November 26, 2013,
http://www.washingtonpost.com/world/national-security/cia-turned-s
ome-guantanamo-bay-prisoners-into-double-agents-against-al-qaeda-
ap-reports/2013/11/26/e98163b2-56ac-11e3-8304-caf30787c0a9_story.html.

50. M. Aid, "All Glory is Fleeting: Sigint and the Fight Against International
Terrorism," *Intelligence and National Security*, vol. 18, no. 4, 2003, pp. 75–105.

51. G. Miller et al., "Documents Reveal NSA's Extensive Involvement in
Targeted Killing Program," *Washington Post*, October 16, 2013, http://www.
washingtonpost.com/world/national-security/documents-reveal-n
sas-extensive-involvement-in-targeted-killing-program/2013/10/16/
29775278-3674-11e3-8a0e-4e2cf80831fc_story.html.

52. "Measuring the Impact of the Snowden Leaks on the Use of Encryption by
Online Jihadists," Flashpoint Partners, September 16, 2014, https://fpjintel.
com/public-reports/measuring-the-impact-of-the-snowden-leaks-on-
the-use-of-encryption-by-online-jihadists/.

53. J. Risen and S. Engelberg, "Failure to Heed Signs of Change in Terror
Goals," *New York Times*, October 14, 2001, p. A1, http://www.nytimes.
com/2001/10/14/international/14INQU.html.

54. T. Aaronson, "The Informants," *Mother Jones*, September/October 2011,
http://www.motherjones.com/print/125137.

55. A. Goldman and M. Apuzzo, "NYPD: Muslim Spying Led to No Leads,
Terror Cases," *Associated Press*, August 21, 2012.

56. US Senate Permanent Subcommittee on Investigations, "Federal Support
for and Involvement in State and Local Fusion Centers—Majority and
Minority Staff Report," US Senate Committee on Homeland Security and
Governmental Affairs, October 3, 2012, p. 1, http://www.hsgac.senate.
gov/download/report_federal-support-for-and-involvement-in-state-
and-local-fusions-centers.

57. J. Brennan, "Open Hearing on the Nomination of John O. Brennan to be
Director of the Central Intelligence Agency," US Senate Select Committee on
Intelligence, February 7, 2013, http://www.intelligence.senate.gov/130207/
transcript.pdf.

58. M. Potok, "FBI: Anti-Muslim Hate Crimes Still Up," *Salon*, December 10, 2012,
http:/www.salon.com/2012/12/10/fbi_anti-Mulsim_hate_crimes_still_up/;
C. Friedersdorf, "Was There Really a Post-9/11 Backlash against Muslims," *The
Atlantic*, May 4, 2012, http://www.theatlantic.com/politics/archive/2012/05/
was-there-really-a-post-9-11-backlash-against-muslims/256725/.

59. N. Wing, "Newt Gingrich Calls 'Ground Zero Mosque' Organizations 'Radical Islamists' Seeking 'Supremacy,' Compares Them to Nazis," *Huffington Post*, August 16, 2010, http://www.huffingtonpost.com/2010/08/16/newt-gingrich-calls-groun_n_683548.html.

60. See, for example, "Most Muslims Want Democracy, Personal Freedoms, and Islam in Political Life," Pew Research Global Attitudes Project, July 10, 2012, http://www.pewglobal.org/2012/07/10/most-muslims-want-democracy-personal-freedoms-and-islam-in-political-life/.

61. A. Bauer quoted in Silber and Bhatt, "Radicalization in the West: The Homegrown Threat," p. 13.

62. "Annual Report on Assistance Related to International Terrorism: Fiscal Year 2013," US Department of State, February 11, 2014.

63. D. Priest, "Foreign Network at Front of CIA's Terror Fight," *Washington Post*, November 18, 2005, http://www.washingtonpost.com/wp-dyn/content/article/2005/11/17/AR2005111702070.html.

64. For the problem with insufficient linguists, see "Joint Inquiry into Intelligence Community Activities before and after the Terrorist Attacks of September 11, 2001," House Permanent Select Committee on Intelligence and Senate Select Committee on Intelligence, p. 382.

65. M. R. Gordon and M. Mazzetti, "U.S. Used Base in Ethiopia to Hunt Al Qaeda," *New York Times*, February 23, 2007, http://www.nytimes.com/2007/02/23/world/africa/23somalia.html?pagewanted=all; S. D. Naylor, "The Secret War: Tense Ties Plagued Africa Ops," *Army Times*, November 28, 2011, http://www.armytimes.com/news/2011/11/army-tense-ties-plagued-africa-ops-112811w/.

66. E. Knickmeyer and S. Gorman, "Behind Foiled Jet Plot, Stronger Saudi Ties," *Wall Street Journal*, May 9, 2012, http://www.wsj.com/articles/SB10001424052702304543904577394373945627482.

67. "Counter-Terrorism in Somalia: Losing Hearts and Minds?" International Crisis Group, Africa Report No. 95, July 11, 2005, pp. 8–11, http://www.crisisgroup.org/~/media/Files/africa/horn-of-africa/somalia/Counter-Terrorism%20in%20Somalia%20Losing%20Hearts%20and%20Minds.pdf.

68. M. Rudner, "Hunters and Gatherers: The Intelligence Coalition Against Islamic Terrorism," *International Journal of Intelligence and Counterintelligence*, vol. 17, no. 2, 2004, p. 217.

69. A. Gendron, "Confronting Terrorism in Saudi Arabia," *International Journal of Intelligence and Counterintelligence*, vol. 23, 2010, pp. 491–492; "The 9/11 Commission Report," p. 373.

70. Rudner, "Hunters and Gatherers," p. 219.

71. Priest, "Foreign Network at Front of CIA's Terror Fight."

72. Priest, "Foreign Network at Front of CIA's Terror Fight."

73. S. Shane, "C.I.A. Role in Visit of Sudan Intelligence Chief Causes Dispute within Administration," *New York Times*, June 18, 2005, http://www.nytimes.com/2005/06/18/politics/18sudan.html?_r=0.

74. Hoffman and Reinares, "Conclusion," p. 636.

75. See "Full text: bin Laden's 'letter to America'," *The Guardian*, November 24, 2002, http:/www.theguardian.com/world/2002/nov/24/theobserver; Agence

France-Presse (AFP)/Reuters, "Al Qaeda tape urges boycotts over cartoons," *Australian Broadcasting Corporation (ABC) News*, March 4, 2006, http://www.abc. net.au/news/2006-03-05/al-qaeda-tape-urges-boycotts-over-cartoons/811522; "Bin Laden: Goal Is to bankrupt U.S.," *CNN*, November 1, 2004, http://www. cnn.com/2004/WORLD/meast/11/01/binladen.tape/.

76. D. Benjamin, "U.S. Government Efforts to Counter Violent Extremism," testimony before the Emerging Threats and Capabilities Subcommittee of the Senate Armed Services Committee, March 10, 2010, http://www.state. gov/j/ct/rls/rm/2010/138175.htm.

77. W. McCants and C. Watts, "U.S. Strategy for Countering Violent Extremism: An Assessment," *E-Notes*, Foreign Policy Research Institute, December 2012, http:// www.fpri.org/articles/2012/12/us-strategy-countering-violent-extre mism-assessment.

78. McCants and Watts, "U.S. Strategy for Countering Violent Extremism: An Assessment."

79. O. Ashour, "Online De-Radicalization? Countering Violent Extremist Narratives: Message, Messenger and Media Strategy," *Perspectives on Terrorism*, vol. 4, no. 6, 2010, http://www.terrorismanalysts.com/pt/index. php/pot/article/view/128.

80. Bergen and Cruickshank, "The Unraveling."

81. F. Vermeulen, "Suspect Communities: Targeting Violent Extremism at the Local Level," *Terrorism and Political Violence*, vol. 26, 2014, pp. 286–306.

82. Hoffman and Reinares, "Conclusion," p. 637.

83. For a discussion, see J. Mueller and M. G. Stewart, "The Terrorism Delusion: America's Overwrought Response to September 11," *International Security*, vol. 37, no. 1, Summer 2012, pp. 81–110.

84. B. M. Jenkins, *Would-Be Warriors: Incidents of Jihadist Terrorist Radicalization in the United States Since September 11, 2001*, Santa Monica, CA, RAND, 2010, pp. 8–9.

85. Hoffman and Reinares, "Conclusion," p. 628.

86. P. R. Neumann, "The New Jihadism: A Global Snapshot," The International Centre for the Study of Radicalisation and Political Violence, December 2014, http://icsr.info/wp-content/uploads/2014/12/ICSR-REPORT-The-New-Jihadism-A-Global-Snapshot.pdf.

INDEX